THE RABBIS' BIBLE

Volume Three: The Later Prophets

THE RABBIS' BIBLE

VOLUME THREE: THE LATER PROPHETS

Isaiah, Jeremiah, Ezekiel, Hosea,
Joel, Amos, Obadiah, Jonah, Micah,
Nahum, Habakkuk, Zephaniah, Haggai,
Zechariah, Malachi

by Solomon Simon and Abraham Rothberg
illustrations by Devorah Taub and Rachel Hacohen

BEHRMAN HOUSE, Inc.
Publishers   New York

To the memory of Solomon Simon,
whose passion for learning was
in the tradition, and a
continuation of it.

2   3   4   5   82   81   80

© *Copyright 1974, by Behrman House, Inc., 1261 Broadway, New York, N.Y. 10001*

Library of Congress Catalog Card Number: 66-20409

Standard Book Number: 87441-026-6

MANUFACTURED IN THE UNITED STATES OF AMERICA

PREFACE

Turn it, turn it again and again, for everything is in it.
Contemplate it, grow gray and old over it, for there is
no greater good.

PIRKE AVOT 5:25

THE BIBLE is a world in itself and the books of the great prophets its peaks. In the history of civilizations no voices have spoken more profoundly and passionately of the problems that puzzle men's minds and pain their hearts. In words that scald and solace, stir and soar, the prophets have defended justice, righteousness and mercy against evil, injustice and oppression. They call on men and society to reform, to create and abide by a moral order, to assume the special responsibilities that an ethical life requires; in short, to transcend themselves. If ever men were radical, the prophets are radicals, refusing to countenance war, the oppression of the poor, selfishness, luxury, hypocrisy, cant, and depravity; if ever men were conservative, the prophets are conservatives, for they refuse to surrender freedom and individuality, restraint and responsibility, mercy and compassion, righteous conduct and obedience to law.

Patriots all, theirs was not a blind patriotism. They spoke not only to and for Israel, but to and for all nations. Wherever men and societies have calcified into valleys of dry bones, the prophetic vision breathes life into them, calling on them to live up to that simple, yet most difficult injunction of Micah's:

What does the Lord require of you,
But to do justly, to love mercy,
And to walk humbly with your God.

In this volume, an abridged version of the prophetic books is arranged as a continuous text across the tops of pages, with a continuing keyed commentary below. The commentary is meant to illuminate the text from the vast literature of biblical interpretation, including the two Talmudim, the Midrashim, medieval and modern Jewish scholarship, as well as legends and folklore. Text and commentary, each reinforcing and interpreting the other, weave three thousand years of Jewish wisdom into a single strand.

Sometimes the order of verses has been rearranged in the text, to provide a more continuous flow of narrative or argument; and sections of non-prophetic biblical books have been interpolated where they help clarify the historical circumstances in which the prophet spoke. The translation has tried to avoid both archaism and colloquialism in order to maintain the dignity yet convey the clear meaning of the biblical text.

A Teacher's Resource Book is also available to make the complexities and historical setting of the prophetic texts more accessible.

CONTENTS

10. JEREMIAH

11. EZEKIEL

15. JOEL

16. AMOS

1. ISAIAH [1–10]

THE VISION OF ISAIAH the son of Amoz, which he saw concerning Judah and Jerusalem in the days of Uzziah, Jotham, Ahaz and Hezekiah, kings of Judah.

Hear, O heavens, and give ear, O earth, for the Lord has spoken: "I have raised and brought up children, [1] but they rebelled against Me. Even an ox

---

[1] AND BROUGHT UP CHILDREN: Rabbi Yehudah and Rabbi Meir disputed about these verses. Yehudah said that if children are loyal and respectful and obedient, then they deserve to be called children. If they are not, then they should not be called children. Meir declared that even if children are full of fault, rebel and do not conduct themselves as they should, they still remain children to their parents.

When should a man disown his own children? Ever? When should children disown their parents? Ever? What constitutes loyalty and love, obedience and responsibility?

and they rebeled

בָּנִים גִּדַּלְתִּי וְרוֹמַמְתִּי וְהֵם פָּשְׁעוּ בִי.

knows its owner and a donkey its master's stall; but Israel refuses to know its Lord."

Hear the word of the Lord, you rulers of Sodom; and give ear to the teaching of our God, you people of Gomorrah. Of what value to me is the multitude of your sacrifices? [2] I am glutted with burnt offerings of rams and the fat of fattened beasts, and I do not delight in the blood of bullocks or lambs or he-goats. When you come to see My face, who has asked you to trample My courts? Bring Me no more vain offerings, their smoke is an abomination to Me. Your new moon, your Sabbath and your calling of assemblies—I cannot endure injustice with solemn assemblies.

My soul hates your celebration of the new moon and the festivals; they are a burden to Me. When you spread your hands [in prayer], I will hide Mine eyes from you. Even when you will offer many prayers, I will not hear because your hands are full of blood. Wash yourself, make yourself clean, put away the evil of your deeds from before Mine eyes. Cease to do evil; learn to do good, [3] seek justice, succor the oppressed, uphold the rights of the orphan and defend the cause of the widow. Then, said the Lord, though your sins be as scarlet, they shall become white as snow; though they be red as crimson, they shall become as wool.

JERUSALEM'S MORAL DECAY

HOW HAS the once faithful city become a harlot! She that was full of justice, righteousness lodged in her, but now murderers. Your silver has become dross, your wine mixed with water, your rulers are unruly men and companions of thieves. Every one loves bribes [4] and runs after gifts. They nei-

---

⋙ [2] THE MULTITUDE OF YOUR SACRIFICES: *The Lord does not concern Himself with formalities of worship; He hates hypocrisy and insincerity, but loves humility and honesty, justice and mercy.*

⋙ [3] LEARN TO DO GOOD: *Man must not merely eschew evil; he must seek out the good and perform acts of righteousness.*

[4] EVERY ONE LOVES BRIBES: *Bribery and corruption undermine the city's righteousness. Worship of wealth is idolatry. Both debase man.*

לִמְדוּ הֵיטֵב, דִּרְשׁוּ מִשְׁפָּט, אַשְּׁרוּ חָמוֹץ, שִׁפְטוּ יָתוֹם, רִיבוּ אַלְמָנָה.

ther uphold the rights of the orphan nor does the cause of the widow come before them.

Therefore, said the Lord, I will take vengeance of My foes. I will turn My hand against you, and I will purge away your dross in the furnace, and take away all your alloy. I will restore your judges as at first and your counselors as in the beginning; afterward you shall again be called the city of righteousness, the faithful city. Zion shall be redeemed by justice and her inhabitants by righteousness.

Thou hast forsaken your people, the house of Jacob, because they are full of diviners from the east and soothsayers like the Philistines, and they indulge themselves in alien customs. Their land is filled with silver and gold and there is no end to their treasures; their land is also full of horses and there is no end to their chariots, [5] so that the land has be-

come full of idols. They worship the work of their hands, that which their fingers have made. Man has sunk low, man has abased himself; and Thou canst not forgive them.

THE LORD'S DAY

THE LORD OF HOSTS has a day set against all that is arrogant and haughty, and all that is lifted up shall be brought low, against all the cedars of Lebanon and against all the oaks of Bashan; against the high mountains and all the towering hills, against every high tower and fortified wall; against all the ships of Tarshish and all the gallant barks. The loftiness of man shall be brought low and the haughtiness of man shall be humbled; and the Lord alone shall be exalted [6] on that day. The idols one and all shall utterly pass away.

On that day man shall cast away to the

❧ [5] TO THEIR CHARIOTS: *Horses and chariots were the means of war. In worshiping military and material might, man commits idolatry and abases himself.*

❧ [6] THE LORD SHALL BE EXALTED: Rabbi Shimon, the son of Jecho, asks; "When is the Lord's name exalted?" Only when the evildoer is punished by law is the name of the Lord exalted; only when the Lord applies His law through justice is His name exalted.

The Lord and His law are inseparable; to worship is to obey the commandments and to perform deeds of goodness.

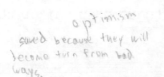

צִיּוֹן בְּמִשְׁפָּט תִּפָּדֶה וְשָׁבֶיהָ בִּצְדָקָה.

moles and bats his idols of silver and gold which he made for himself to worship; and he shall go into the clefts of the rocks and into the crevices of the crags from the dread presence of the Lord, and from the glory of His majesty when He arises to shake the earth with His might. Stop living in fear of man, [7] in whose nostrils is only breath, for how little is he to be accounted.

God is more imp.
Fear God

WARNING TO RULERS

THE LORD RISES to strive against and judge His people. He will bring an indictment against the elders and princes [8] of His people: "It is you that have eaten up the vineyard; the plunder of the poor is in your houses. Why do you crush My people and grind the faces of the poor?"

Therefore, behold, the Lord of hosts will remove from Jerusalem and from Judah every prop and stay: the mighty man, the man of war, the judge and the prophet, the diviner and his elder, the captain of fifty and the counselors. Children I will give them for princes and babes shall rule over them. The people shall oppress one another, every man his fellow and every man his neighbor. The young will behave insolently against the aged and the base man against the honorable.

Per: m'yam
they will not good/m leaders
rebel

THE HAUGHTY DAUGHTERS OF ZION

THE LORD SAID: Because the daughters

⋲§ [7] STOP LIVING IN FEAR OF MAN: *The words that men speak are only wind; fear only the word of the Lord which is the law.*

⋲§ [8] THE ELDERS AND PRINCES: If the princes sinned, our Sages ask, how did the elders sin? The Rabbis reply that the Lord brings punishment on the elders because they did not protest the sins of the princes. Even if the elders protested that the princes would have paid them no heed, the Lord says: "Was it revealed to them in advance that their protest would not affect the princes in power?" The duty of the elders was to protest, in the determined hope that their innocence might sway those who exercised power.

When the poor are plundered and the weak abused, all must protest or society and man will become evil and chaotic.

talking of unjust rulers why they are being mean

מַה־לָּכֶם תְּדַכְּאוּ עַמִּי וּפְנֵי עֲנִיִּים תִּטְחָנוּ!

of Zion are haughty, they walk with outstretched necks and wanton eyes, mincing as they go and jingling their anklets; therefore the Lord shall smite the daughters of Zion [9] with scabs on the crown of the head and will lay bare their secret parts.

On that day the Lord will take away the finery of their anklets and tiaras, their necklaces, their earrings and their bracelets and their veils; the headtires and the armlets, the sashes, the corselets and the amulets; the rings and the nose-jewels; the aprons, the shawls and the purses; the gauze robes and the fine linen; the turbans and the mantles. And it shall come to pass that instead of sweet scent there shall be stench; instead of a girdle rags and instead of curled hair baldness; and instead of a silk sash sackcloth and instead of beauty the mark of slavery.

Your men shall fall by the sword and your warriors in battle. The gates of Zion shall lament and mourn; and Zion shall sit despoiled upon the earth.

THE SONG OF THE VINEYARD [10]

⇜ [9] DAUGHTERS OF ZION : *Concentration on luxury, display and decoration are vanity and arrogance. They turn women's heads from righteousness and morality to superficial and sinful concerns.*

⇜ [10] THE SONG OF THE VINEYARD : Isaiah tells the simple story of the love of a man for a woman, and her betrayal. But the story is a parable : the wife, the vineyard, which is Judah; the husband, the owner of the vineyard, the Lord. Because Judah betrayed Him, the Lord will take his protection and support away. Because Judah and Israel have betrayed the Lord; because all He found in them when He looked for justice was violence, He will finally abandon them.

Our Sages note that the song opens cheerfully and joyfully, and ends with grief and impending doom in seven short thundering prophecies of woe for this disloyal nation.

The vineyard of Israel shall be left to the savagery and invasion of its enemies, its land shall be ridden by drought and aridity, because violence has smitten righteousness and the oppressed are denied justice.

וַתֵּלַכְנָה נְטוּיוֹת גָּרוֹן וּמְשַׂקְּרוֹת עֵינָיִם, הָלוֹךְ וְטָפֹף תֵּלַכְנָה וּבְרַגְלֵיהֶם תְּעַכַּסְנָה.

Let me sing for my well-beloved *God*
The song of my well-beloved about
  his vineyard. *Israel–God*
My well-beloved had a vineyard
On a fertile hill.
He enclosed it with a hedge,
And built a fence around it.
He cleared it of stones,
Planted it with choicest vines, [11]
Built a watchtower in the midst of it
And also hewed out a vat therein.
He hoped that it would yield good
  grapes
But it yielded sour grapes.
Now, inhabitants of Jerusalem and
  men of Judah,
Judge, I pray, between me and my
  vineyard.
What more could I have done to my
  vineyard
Than I have done for it?
Why then when I expected it to
  yield good grapes
Did it yield sour grapes?

threat
Now let me tell you
What I will do to my vineyard:
I will take away its hedge,
And leave it for the teeth of animals;
I will take away its fence,
And it will be trampled down.
I will not prune it or hoe it,
And it will be overgrown with
  briers and thorns.
I will also command the clouds
That they rain no rain on it.
Now, the vineyard of the Lord is
  the house of Israel,
And the men of Judah are His cher-
  ished plantation.
He looked for Justice, but behold–
  violence;
For righteousness, but behold—a
  cry [of the oppressed].

God's disappointment

WOE TO THE UNRIGHTEOUS

WOE TO THOSE who join house to house
and add field to field [12] till there is no

⋙ [11] THE CHOICEST VINES : Rabbi Simeon ben Lakish said : Israel is like
a vine. Its branches are the aristocracy, its clusters the scholars, its leaves
the common people, and its brambles those who are devoid of learning.
Let the clusters pray for the leaves, for were it not for the leaves, the
clusters could not survive.

⋙ [12] FIELD TO FIELD : The prophet was reproving those who foreclosed

וַיְקַו לְמִשְׁפָּט – וְהִנֵּה מִשְׂפָּח, לִצְדָקָה – וְהִנֵּה צְעָקָה.

room [for the poor] in all the land.

Woe to those who rise up early in the morning to run after strong drink, who sit late into the night till wine inflames them. They feast and play the guitar, the tambourine and the flute, but they heed not the work of the Lord and the doings of His hands they see not. Man is brought low but God, the Holy One, is sanctified through righteousness.

Woe to those who draw iniquity upon themselves with slender cords, then they pull sin with cart ropes. [13]

Woe to those who call evil good and good evil; who change darkness to light and light to darkness; who make bitter sweet and sweet bitter.

Woe to those who are wise in their own eyes and shrewd in their own sight. *think they know all they need to*

Woe to those who are heroes in drinking wine and warriors in mixing strong drink; who acquit the guilty for a bribe and take away the right of the righteous from him. *people who are drink + bribes*

Woe to those who decree unrighteous decrees and to those who record the decisions of iniquity, who turn aside the needy from judgment, and take away the rights of the poor of My people so that the widow may be their spoil and the orphaned their prey. What will you do in the day of judgment and in the face of the storm which will come from far? To whom will you flee for help? And where will you hide your wealth? [14]

rich shouldn't be bad + take advantage of poor it is the rich fault not the poors fault

Isaih is warning what will happen. blaming these people

mortgages to take land and houses from those in debt. To these cruel creditors the Lord declared: "Do you think you will become heirs to the land and not My people? You should know that without farmers the land and the houses shall become desolate and the entire country will be ruined."

Greed and the lust for power in their excesses destroy societies, people and land alike.

ৎ [13] SIN WITH CART ROPES: *Small transgressions attract and lead to greater sins.*

ৎ [14] HIDE YOUR WEALTH: *In times of great stress and danger, neither the reed of wealth nor of other men can be leaned upon; only reliance on the Lord sustains.*

הוֹי הָאוֹמְרִים לָרַע טוֹב וְלַטּוֹב רָע.

ISAIAH'S VISION

IN THE YEAR that king Uzziah died I saw the Lord sitting upon a high and lofty throne and His trailing robes filled the Temple. Seraphim stood around Him, each one had six wings: with two he covered his face, with two he covered his feet, and with two did he fly. They called one to the other:

> Holy, holy, holy, [15] is the Lord of the host;
> The whole earth is full of His glory.

The threshold under the posts shook at the sound of those who called and the house was filled with smoke. Then I said: "Woe is me! For I am lost because I am a man of unclean lips and I dwell among people of unclean lips and my eyes have seen the King, the Lord of hosts."

Then one of the seraphim flew to me with a glowing coal [16] in his hand which he had taken with tongs from the altar; and he touched my mouth with it and said: "This has touched your lips so guilt is removed and your sin forgiven." [17] *angel cleaned him*

Then I heard the voice of the Lord,

ᥫ᭡ [15] HOLY, HOLY, HOLY : *Holiness lies in living uprightly every day. It is more important than religious devotion or prayer, for in righteous life men exalt God more than any angelic choir.*

ᥫ᭡ [16] A GLOWING COAL : The Hebrew word for a glowing or live coal is *ritzpah*. Our Sages declare that the term also means to smash, break or slap (like *ratzetz*). When Isaiah told the Lord that he was a man of unclean lips and living among people of unclean lips, the Lord grew angry and said: "I hate those who slander My children. You may call yourself 'a man of unclean lips,' but how dare you say this of My people! I offered My Torah to all seventy nations of the world and none was willing to accept it; but when I offered it to Israel, all the people cried out in unison (Exodus 19 :8) : 'All that the Lord has spoken, we will do and obey.' When I made My covenant with them, they also willingly declared (Exodus 24 :7) : 'All that the Lord has spoken we will do and obey.' And you call them a people of unclean lips?" Then the Lord commanded an angel to slap Isaiah's mouth.

ᥫ᭡ [17] YOUR SIN FORGIVEN : *How do confession and repentance remove guilt*

קָדוֹשׁ קָדוֹשׁ קָדוֹשׁ יְיָ צְבָאוֹת.

saying, "Whom shall I send? [18] Who will go for us?" I answered: "Here am I; send me."

Then He said: "Go and say to this people: Indeed you hear but you do not understand. You see but you do not have insight. The heart of the people is fat, [19] their ears are heavy and their eyes are turned away lest they, seeing with their eyes and hearing with their ears, and understanding with their heart, repent and be healed."

Then I said: "Lord, how long?" And He answered: "Until cities lie waste without inhabitants and houses without men, the land left desolate, and the Lord has exiled men far away and the forsaken places be many in the land. Even if a tenth remain in it, it shall be burned up again.

But as a terebinth and an oak when they cast their leaves yet their trunk remains so shall the holy seed be the stock which will be the remnant. [20]

---

and forgive sin? The burning coal of the Lord burns away the dross of loose speech, leaving mouth and spirit purified.

[18] WHOM SHALL I SEND: After Isaiah was punished for slandering Israel, he heard the voice of God asking who would go to preach to Israel. Quickly, Isaiah said that he would go, but the Lord cautioned: "Beware! Consider! I sent Moses to this people and they vexed and troubled him; and he was afraid they might stone him (Exodus 17:4). I sent them the prophet Amos amd they mocked him by calling him 'the stammerer.' This rebellious people will insult, despise and persecute you. Before you accept, know and consider the fate of the prophet's mission." Isaiah answered: "I accept." Then the Lord declared: "Because you love justice and righteousness so much that you are willing to suffer for it, I anoint you My prophet."

[19] THE PEOPLE IS FAT: *Prosperity and comfort had made the people callous, without feeling or compassion.*

[20] THE REMNANT: *Men will not see their own soulless splendor or heartless oppression until they have brought destruction down upon themselves and thus opened their eyes and hearts. Only then shall a remnant be saved.*

אֶת מִי אֶשְׁלַח וּמִי יֵלֶךְ לָנוּ? וָאֹמַר: הִנְנִי שְׁלָחֵנִי.

2. ISAIAH   [7–30] II KINGS [16] II CHRONICLES [28]

WAR AGAINST JUDAH

IN THE DAYS OF AHAZ, king of Judah, Rezin, king of Aram and Pekah, king of Israel, went up to Jerusalem to make war against it. When the house of David was told: "Aram is allied with Israel," his heart and the hearts of his people shook as the trees of the forest shake before a wind.

Then the Lord said to Isaiah: "Go out with your son Shear-jashub [1] to the end of the aqueduct of the upper pool on the laundrymen's field and say to Ahaz: Keep calm and be quiet; fear not, neither let your heart be faint because of these two smoking stumps of firebrands, the fierce anger of Rezin, king of Aram and Pekah, king of Israel. They plotted mischief against you, saying: Let us march against Judah, throw it into a panic, break in and seize it, then set up as a king the son of Tabeel." [2] Thus said the

---

[1] SHEAR-JASHUB: *The name means "a remnant shall return."*

[2] TABEEL: Our Sages say that they examined all Scripture and could

וַיָּנַע לְבָבוֹ וּלְבַב עַמּוֹ כְּנוֹעַ עֲצֵי יַעַר מִפְּנֵי רוּחַ.

Lord: "It shall not come to pass. If you do not have faith, you will surely not succeed." [3]

The Lord spoke again [to Isaiah], saying: ["Speak again to Ahaz, saying:] 'Ask a sign of the Lord your God, ask it either from the depth of the underworld or from the high heavens.'" But Ahaz said: "I will not ask, neither will I test the Lord." [4] Isaiah said: "Hear now, house of David, is it not enough for you to weary men that you must weary my God? Therefore, the Lord Himself shall give you an omen. Behold, a young woman shall conceive and bear a son, and shall call him Immanuel. [5] Before the child shall discern between good and evil, the land of the two kings of whom you are in terror will be forsaken. But the Lord will bring upon you and upon your people and your father's house such days as have never been since Ephraim broke away from Judah. He will bring against you the king of Assyria." *conquer Israel & Aram*

It shall come to pass on that day that the Lord shall hiss for the fly that is in the uttermost part of the rivers of Egypt, and for the bee that is in the land of Assyria. They shall come and swarm, all of them, in the steep ravines and in the clefts of the crags, upon all the thorns and upon all the brambles. And it shall

they would be redeemed & brought back

trying to tell people not to worry about syria

find no place called Tabeel. Truly, they believed, the name is made of two words—*tov el*—meaning good to people. The kings of Samaria and Aram sent to the people of Jerusalem, saying: "We came to abolish the word of the Lord and to teach ways of idolatry. Now you are under the yoke of the Torah which gives you laws and restricts your life. We will establish paganism, which abolishes all restrictions on the people, so that you may indulge to your heart's desire.

ﻼ [3] SURELY NOT SUCCEED: *Why doesn't the Lord declare: "If you have faith, you will surely succeed"?*

ﻼ [4] TEST THE LORD: *So obstinate is Ahaz in his unbelief that he refuses to give credence to the divine origin of Isaiah's prophecy.*

ﻼ [5] IMMANUEL: *In Hebrew, composed of* immanu *which means "with us," and* el *which means "God"; God is with us.*

אִם לֹא תַאֲמִינוּ, כִּי לֹא תֵאָמֵנוּ.

come to pass on that day that every place where there were a thousand vines worth a thousand silver shekels shall be all thorns and thistles. All the [slopes of the] hills that were hoed you shall not be able to go there for fear of briers and thorns. They shall become a place for sending oxen and where sheep may trample. [6]

SAMARIA'S DOOM FORETOLD

YET THE PEOPLE turned not to Him who punished them, nor did they seek the Lord of hosts; so the Lord has cut off from Israel head and tail, palm-branch and reed, in a single day. The elders and the men of rank are the head, and the prophet who teaches lies is the tail. The leaders of the people became misleaders and those who were led by them were destroyed. Therefore the Lord will not spare their young men, for every one of them is godless and an evildoer and every mouth speaks wantonness. [7] For all this His anger has not turned away and His hand is still outstretched to punish them.

Because wickedness burned like fire, it devoured briers and thorns, then kindled the thickets of the forest and they rolled up in columns of smoke. The people were food for the fire. They carved on the right hand but were hungry still; they devoured on the left hand but were not satisfied. Each one devoured his neighbor's flesh, Manasseh Ephraim, and Ephraim Manasseh, while together they fell upon Judah. For all this His anger has not turned away and His hand is still stretched out [8] to punish them.

They have rejected the law of the Lord of hosts, and have spurned the word of the Holy One of Israel. Therefore, the

---

⊱ [6] WHERE SHEEP MAY TRAMPLE: *Assyria (the bee) and Egypt (the fly) will come down from the north and south and devastate Judah between them.*

⊱ [7] EVERY MOUTH SPEAKS WANTONNESS: Our Sages emphasized that speaking obscenely or lewdly was punished severely, not by law but by decree of heaven. Rabbi Hannan said: "All know for what purpose the bride enters the bridal chamber, but he who speaks obscenely of it is severely punished."

⊱ [8] HIS HAND IS STILL STRETCHED OUT: *Because the people have not turned away from their transgressions, the Lord's anger shall not be turned away.*

זָקֵן וּנְשׂוּא־פָנִים הוּא הָרֹאשׁ, וְנָבִיא מוֹרֶה שֶׁקֶר הוּא הַזָּנָב.

anger of the Lord blazed against the people and He stretched forth His hand against them, that the mountains quaked and corpses were like refuse in the midst of the street. In spite of all this, His anger is not turned away and His hand is still stretched out to punish them.

THE INSCRIBED TABLET

THE LORD SAID TO ME: "Take a great tablet and write upon it in ordinary script: 'Speeding is the spoil; hastening is the prey. *Maher-shalal-hash-baz*.' And have it attested by two reliable witnesses, Uriah the priest and Zechariah the son of Jeberechiah."

Then my wife conceived and gave birth to a son. The Lord said to me: "Call him 'Speeding is the spoil; hastening is the prey—*Maher-shalal-hash-baz*.' For before the child shall know how to say 'My father' and 'My mother,' the wealth of Damascus and the spoil of Samaria shall be carried away before the king of Assyria."

The Lord spoke to me again, saying: "Because this people has rejected the waters of Shiloah [9] that flow softly, therefore the Lord will bring upon them the

---

ঙ্গ [9] THE WATERS OF SHILOAH: Rabbi Joshua asked: "How could Sennacherib claim to have God's command to destroy Jerusalem when he said (Isaiah 36:10): 'Did I come up without the permission of the Lord against this land to destroy it?'" Sennacherib took Isaiah's prophecy, "Because this people has rejected the waters of Shiloah, that flow softly, therefore the Lord will bring upon them the waters of the Euphrates, mighty and many, the king of Assyria and all his host," to be the Lord's sanction to invade Judah.

But the prophet was speaking to the people of Judah who, discontented with the house of David, which ruled gently, like the waters of Shiloah, wanted a stronger ruler. Then the Lord said: "Because you want a strong ruler I shall satisfy your foolish longing by bringing the king of Assyria down upon you. Then you shall have a taste of a truly strong and ruthless tyrant." Why, then, was Sennacherib punished? Because he took the prophet's words, which referred to the Kingdom of Ephraim, as his sanction to destroy Jerusalem.

וּכְתֹב עָלָיו בְּחֶרֶט אֱנוֹשׁ: לְמַהֵר שָׁלָל חָשׁ בַּז.

waters of the Euphrates, mighty and many, the king of Assyria and all his host. And he shall fill all the channels and overflow his banks. He shall sweep through Judah, overflowing as he passes through. He shall reach up to the neck, and the stretching of his wings shall fill the breadth of your land, O Immanuel."

Woe to the crown of pride of the drunkards of Ephraim and the fading flower of his glorious beauty which rests on the heads of those overcome with wine. The Lord has a foe who is mighty and strong, as a storm of hail, a tempest of destruction, like a storm of mighty overwhelming water that beats down on the earth with violence. The proud crown of the drunkards of Ephraim will be trampled under foot. The fading flower of his glorious beauty which rests on the head of the fertile valley will be like the first ripe fig before the summer, which as soon as a man sees it he swallows it while it is still in his hand. But on that day the Lord of hosts shall be a beautiful crown and a diadem of beauty to the remnant of His people.

THE FATE OF SAMARIA AND DAMASCUS

HE WILL RAISE AN ENSIGN to a nation from afar: He will whistle for them from the end of earth, and they will come swiftly and speedily. None shall be weary nor stumble among them; none shall sleep or slumber. No loin-girdle shall be loosed nor sandal-thong snapped. His arrows are sharp, his bows all bent; their horses' hoofs are like flint, his wheels like a whirlwind. His roar is like that of a lioness. Like young lions will he growl and roar. He will seize his prey and will carry it off, none to rescue.

Behold, Damascus will cease to be a city and will become a heap of ruins; the cities of Aroer shall be forsaken and given over to flocks which shall lie down there and none to make them afraid. The fortresses of Ephraim shall be destroyed and the kingdom of Damascus and the remnant of Aram [10] will perish like the glory of the children of Israel, says the Lord of hosts.

It shall come to pass on that day that the glory of Jacob shall be humbled and

---

❧ [10] THE REMNANT OF ARAM: *The young lions of Assyria will not only seize Judah as their prey but also the surrounding nations who are arrayed against them.*

הוֹי עֲטֶרֶת גֵּאוּת שִׁכּוֹרֵי אֶפְרַיִם, וְצִיץ נֹבֵל צְבִי תִפְאַרְתּוֹ.

the fat of his flesh grow lean. It shall be as a reaper harvests, collects the reaped corn and cuts down the ears left [so that hardly any are left] standing; so you will be as when one gleans ears in the valley of Rephaim. Or [you will become] as an olive tree shaken so that two or three berries are left on the uppermost branches, four or five on all the boughs, says the Lord, the God of Israel.

In that day shall your fortified cities be deserted like the deserted cities of the Amorites and Hivites which they deserted before the children of Israel. It shall be a desolation, because you have forgotten the God of your salvation and you have not heeded the Rock of your refuge.

Then Ahaz, [11] king of Judah, sent messengers to Tiglath-Pileser, king of Assyria, saying: "I am your servant and your son; come save me from the hand of the king of Aram and from the hand of the king of Israel who rise up against me." And Ahaz took the silver and gold that was found in the house of the Lord and in the treasures of the king's house and sent it as tribute to the king of Assyria.

The king of Assyria listened to him

⋖ [11] AHAZ: *In Hebrew, Ahaz means to seize, clutch, get hold of.* After his treaty with Assyria, Ahaz wanted the people of Israel to forget the Torah and its commands for justice and righteousness to follow in the way of the Assyrians. Ahaz knew that if he issued such a decree, the people would not only disobey but revolt, so he seized all the schools and academies and forbade teaching and learning Torah. If there were no children to study, he thought, there would be no students in the academies and no Sages; if there were no Sages, there would be no prophets and then no Divine Presence in Israel; and thus would the Israelites become like the Assyrians.

Isaiah thwarted his scheme by gathering around him a group of disciples to whom he taught Torah. They kept the knowledge and teaching of the Law alive until Ahaz died.

Ahaz's assimilationism was not the first time such a policy was adopted by a ruler, nor the first time it failed. Why do the schools and education become the first and usually most important focus of such efforts?

עַבְדְּךָ וּבִנְךָ אָנִי, עֲלֵה וְהוֹשִׁיעֵנִי.

and went up against Damascus and captured it, and carried its inhabitants away captive to Kir, and slew Rezin.

And in the time of his distress this king Ahaz acted still more treacherously against the Lord, for he sacrificed to the gods of Assyria who were victorious over him, and he said: "Because the gods of the kings of Assyria helped them, therefore will I sacrifice [12] to them that they may help me."

A CLOSED BOOK

ALL THE PROPHECIES are to you as the words of a letter that is sealed [13] and which is delivered to one who is learned, saying: "Pray, read this." He will answer: "I cannot read."

[Thus said the Lord:] "Bind the testimony, seal the teaching among My disciples." And I will wait for the Lord that hides His face from the house of Jacob and I will look for Him. Here I am, and the children whom the Lord has given to me for signs and portents in Israel, from the Lord of hosts who dwells in Mount Zion.

A REMNANT SHALL REMAIN

IT SHALL COME TO PASS on that day that the remnant of Israel and the survivors of the house of Jacob shall lean no more for support on the enemy that smote them but shall rely on the Holy One of Israel.

A remnant shall return to God the Mighty. Destruction is decided upon, an act of destruction complete and decisive. The Lord God of hosts is about to execute it in the midst of all the earth. But a remnant of Israel shall be saved because the force of righteousness is overwhelming.

---

even though exiled a few will survive

[12] THEREFORE WILL I SACRIFICE: Not only does Ahaz seek to sacrifice Israel's God and faith to Assyria, but its freedom and independence as well. How does one necessarily follow the other?

[13] A LETTER THAT IS SEALED: Every prophet has his own peculiar speech through which he communicates his vision. Its real meaning is often given in figurative and oratorical language, in allegory and parable. Often ordinary readers cannot comprehend such a language, and

the name of Yahweh

שְׁאָר יָשׁוּב, שְׁאָר יַעֲקֹב, אֵל אֵל גִּבּוֹר.

shall return remnant

It shall come to pass on that day that the Lord shall raise His hand the second time to redeem the remnant of His people that shall remain from Assyria and from Egypt, from Pathros and from Cush, from Elam and from Shinar, from Hamath and the islands of the sea. He will raise an ensign for all the nations and will assemble the dispersed of Israel and gather together the scattered of Judah from the four corners of the earth. Then all envy against Ephraim will cease and the adversaries of Judah shall be cut off. Ephraim will not envy Judah and Judah shall not be hostile to Ephraim. There shall be a highway [from Assyria] for the remnant of His people that shall remain in Assyria, as there was for Israel on that day when it came up out of the land of Egypt.

THE GREAT REDEMPTION

GO, MY PEOPLE, enter your chambers and shut the door behind you. Hide yourself for a little while until the wrath shall pass by. For, behold, the Lord is coming out of His place to punish the inhabitants of the earth for their sins, The earth shall uncover the blood shed [in her] and shall no longer cover the slain.

Now go and write it for them on a tablet and inscribe it in a book that it may be for the time to come, for ever and ever. For it is a rebellious people, lying children who refuse to hear the teaching of the Lord, that say to the seers: "See not," and to the prophets, "Prophesy not unto us righteous things. Speak to us of smooth things; prophesy delusions. Get out of the way, turn aside out of the path, and do not trouble us with the Holy One of Israel." Therefore, said the Lord, because you despised My word and have trusted in oppression and crookedness, and relied upon them, therefore this iniquity shall be to you as a breach in a high wall descending and widening. The crash comes suddenly. It breaks like a potter's vessel is broken in pieces so small that there cannot be found among them a shard to take fire from the hearth or to scoop water from the cistern.

It shall come to pass on that day that the Lord will punish the host of high heaven above and the kings of the earth below. They shall be gathered as pris-

---

Isaiah therefore complains: "The vision of all has become to you like the words of a letter that is sealed."

וְאָסַף נִדְחֵי יִשְׂרָאֵל, וּנְפֻצוֹת יְהוּדָה יְקַבֵּץ מֵאַרְבַּע כַּנְפוֹת הָאָרֶץ.

oners are gathered in a dungeon. They will be shut up in prison for many days and they will be punished. Then the moon will be confounded, and the sun ashamed; for the Lord of hosts will reign on Mount Zion and in Jerusalem, and before the Elders shall be revealed His glory.

DIALOGUE IN THE TEMPLE COURT

[THE PROPHET:] And these also reel with wine [14] and stagger with strong drink. They reel amid their visions and totter while giving judgment. All the tables are filthy with vomit and no place is clean.

[The elders:] To whom does he impart knowledge? To babes just weaned from milk? To those who have just been taken away from the breast? For it is rule by rule, rule by rule, line by line, line by line, a little here, a little there.

[The prophet replies:] Yes, with stammering lips and an alien tongue shall it be spoken to this people, to whom it was said: This is the rest you shall give to the weary [of war] and this is the refreshing

---

❦ [14] REEL WITH WINE: A good, pious man had a drunkard for a father. Often when the father was drunk, he fell in the street and was abused by the street urchins. They plucked his beard, called him names, pelted him with stones. When the son saw his father so disgraced and abused, he said: "Father, stay at home and I shall bring you all the best wines and brandies." The father agreed and the son kept his promise.

One rainy day the son was walking in the street and saw a drunkard rolling in the street. The filthy water of the streets had soaked him and jeering boys taunted and beat him. Each time they struck him with a stick or stone he grunted like an animal. The son thought it a good opportunity to show his father how drunkenness humiliated men, and went home and brought his father back to see what was happening. The father looked at the drunkard lying in the gutter, then bent down and whispered in his ear: "Eh, brother, tell me, where did you get such good whisky?"

Judaism has always blessed the fruit of the vine as a comfort to man's spirit, to be enjoyed, but not to be indulged in to excess and so abused.

כִּי צַו לָצָו צַו לָצָו, קַו לָקָו קַו לָקָו, זְעֵיר שָׁם זְעֵיר שָׁם.

rest. But you would not listen. So the word of the Lord will be to them rule by rule, rule by rule, line by line, line by line, a little here, a little there. They will be like one who walks backward; they shall fall, be broken, snared and captured.

Hear the word of the Lord, the scoffers, rulers of this people in Jerusalem. You said: "We have made a covenant with death [15] and with Sheol we have made an agreement, that when the scouring scourge shall pass through, it shall not reach us. For we have made lies our refuge and we have concealed ourselves under falsehood. Therefore said the Lord God: I will make justice the line and righteousness the plummet; [16] and hail shall shatter the refuge of lies and the waters shall flood the hiding place. Your covenant with death shall be annulled, your agreement with Sheol shall not stand. When the overwhelming scourge shall pass through, you will be trodden down by it. For the beḍ is too short for a man to stretch himself and the covering too narrow when he gathers himself up. Therefore scoff no more lest your hands be drawn tighter, for I have heard from the Lord God of hosts a sentence of doom, utter and decisive against the whole land.

Because the people draw near Me and honor Me with their mouths and with their lips, but their heart is far away from Me. Their reverence for Me is a tradition of men learned by rote; [17] therefore I will deal with this people in a marvellous way and a wonder: The wisdom of their wise men shall perish and the intelligence of their understanding men shall vanish.

---

    [15] COVENANT WITH DEATH: *Those who live lives of falsehood are condemned to living death. Because their lives are lies they have sealed a covenant with death.*

    [16] RIGHTEOUSNESS THE PLUMMET: *The Law shall show the straightness of truth, the crookedness of falsehood.*

    [17] LEARNED BY ROTE: *Reverence for God is not acquired by rote but personally, with joy and travail, each and every day.*

בְּפִיו וּבִשְׂפָתָיו כִּבְּדוּנִי וְלִבּוֹ רִחַק מִמֶּנִּי, וַתְּהִי יִרְאָתָם אוֹתִי מִצְוַת אֲנָשִׁים מְלֻמָּדָה.

3. ISAIAH [14–37]

THE FALL OF A TYRANT

HOW HUSHED is the tyrant! How still is the terror! The Lord has broken the staff of the wicked, the scepter of the rulers who smote the peoples in wrath with incessant strokes, that ruled the nations in anger with a persecution that none restrained. [1] The whole earth is at rest and is quiet. All the people of the earth break forth into song. The cypresses rejoice at your fate and the cedars of Lebanon [say]: "Since you were laid low, no woodsman comes to fell us."

Sheol was in turmoil to meet you at your coming; the shades were roused for you, all the chief ones of the earth, all the kings of nations, were raised up from their thrones. All of them cried out and said to you: "So you too have become weak as we are? Your pomp has been brought down to the grave, and the din

---

[1] A PERSECUTION THAT NONE RESTRAINED: *Tyranny, persecution, the rule of rage and terror shall forever cease.*

נָחָה שָׁקְטָה כָּל הָאָרֶץ, פָּצְחוּ רִנָּה.

of your harps. Beneath you maggots are spread and the worms cover you."

How you did fall from heaven, O shining star of the dawn! How you were cut down to the ground, you that cast lots over the nations! You said in your heart: "I will ascend unto heaven; I will exalt my throne above the stars of God; and I will sit on the mount of God in the uttermost part of the north. I will ascend above the heights of the clouds and will be like the Most High." [2] But you were brought down to the netherworld, to the bottom of the pit. Those who see you will gaze at you, look at you closely, and say: "Is this the man [3] that made the earth tremble, that did shake kingdoms, that made the world a wilderness, destroying its cities, that never opened the doors of his prisons?"

All the kings of the nations, all of them, sleep in glory, every one in his own house. But you are flung out of your sepulcher like an abhorred offshoot, in the garments in which you were slain, thrust through with the sword.

You shall not be joined with them [the kings] in burial because you have destroyed your land and slain your people. The descendants of the evildoers shall never be renowned.

My heart is bewildered, terror has overwhelmed me; the night of my pleasure He has turned into trembling. They prepared a table, lit the lamps, ate and drank, [when suddenly the outcry]: "Rise up, princes, and anoint the shields!" The watchman that was set was told: "What you see, call out." He saw a troop of horsemen in pairs, a troop of donkeys, a troop of camels, and he obeyed diligently. He called: "There comes a troop of men, horsemen in pairs." Then he cried out: "Fallen, fallen is Babylon; and all the images of her gods are shattered to the ground."

MOAB AND TYRE

IN A NIGHT Ar-Moab was laid waste; in a night Kir-Moab was brought to ruin. In their streets they have girded on sack-

---

&ᴈ [2] LIKE THE MOST HIGH: *Man is exalted but not deified. Overreaching can only bring man disaster, for despite his grandeur he is frail and fallible.*

&ᴈ [3] IS THIS THE MAN: *The tyrant is also a man and only a man; he can be brought down from the highest to the lowest estate in a night.*

אֵיךְ נָפַלְתָּ מִשָּׁמַיִם, הֵילֵל בֶּן שָׁחַר, נִגְדַּעְתָּ לָאָרֶץ – חוֹלֵשׁ עַל גּוֹיִם!

cloth; on their housetops and in their squares everyone wails and weeps profusely. My heart cries out for Moab; her fugitives reach to Zoar. Her cry of distress has gone round the borders of Moab and her howl reaches Eglaim, even as far as Beer-elim.

Howl, you ships of Tarshish, for your harbor is laid waste. On their way, in the land of Kittim, it was revealed to them. You are confounded. O Zidon; for the sea, the stronghold of the sea, has spoken: "I am as if I have not travailed, nor given birth to children, nor brought up maidens. When the report reaches Egypt, they shall writhe in pain at the news of Tyre. Is this the joyous city whose feet from ancient times carried her so far to sojourn? Who has devised this against Tyre, the crowning city, whose merchants were princes and whose traders the honored of the earth? The Lord of hosts devised it to abase the haughtiness of all glory, to bring into contempt all [those] honored of the earth.

And it shall come to pass in that day that Tyre shall be forgotten seventy years. At the end of seventy years, the Lord will remember Tyre and she will return to her strength and shall have commerce with all the kingdoms upon the face of the earth. But her gain from her commerce shall be dedicated to the Lord. It shall not be stored up nor hoarded, but will be given over to those who dwell in the presence of the Lord, for them to eat their fill and for stately clothing.

NAKED AND BAREFOOT

IN THE YEAR that Tartan came to Ashdod, when Sargon the king of Assyria sent him, and he fought against Ashdod and took it, the Lord spoke to Isaiah, saying: "Go and untie the sackcloth from your loins and put off the sandals from your feet." And he did so, walking naked and barefoot. Then the Lord said: "My servant Isaiah has walked naked and barefoot for three years as a sign and symbol upon Egypt and Ethiopia, that the king of Assyria shall lead the captives of Egypt and the exiles of Ethiopia, young and old, naked and barefoot to the shame of Egypt." And the inhabitants of this land shall say on that day: "Behold, this is the fate of those on whom we set our hope and to whom we fled for help to save us from the king of Assyria; how can we escape?"

Woe to them who bury their plans deeply from the Lord, and their work is done in the dark, and they say: "Who

כִּי לַיּוֹשְׁבִים לִפְנֵי יְיָ יִהְיֶה סַחְרָהּ לֶאֱכֹל לְשָׂבְעָה.

sees us? Who knows us?" [4] Woe to the rebellious children, says the Lord, who take counsel but not of Me; and that make alliances, but not according to My wish. They go down to Egypt without asking My counsel, to take refuge in the stronghold of Pharaoh, and to take shelter in the shadow of Egypt! Therefore shall the stronghold of Pharaoh turn to shame and the shelter in the shadow of Egypt to confusion. His princes are at Zoan and his ambassadors have come to Hanes. But they shall all be ashamed of a people that cannot benefit them, that bring no help, but are a shame and a disgrace.

Woe to those who go down to Egypt for help, and rely on horses and trust in chariots, because they are many, and in horsemen, because they are very mighty; but they look not to the Holy One of Israel, neither seek the Lord. Yet Egyptians are [mere] men and not God; and their horses flesh and not spirit, [5] so when the Lord shall stretch out His hand, both he who helps will stumble and he

who is helped will fall, and they shall perish together.

THE INVASION OF SENNACHERIB

NOW, IN THE FOURTEENTH YEAR of King Hezekiah, Sennacherib, king of Assyria, came up against the fortified cities of Judah and captured them. Then Hezekiah sent to the king of Assyria at Lachish, saying: "I have sinned. Withdraw from me and whatever you put on me, I will bear." The king of Assyria made Hezekiah pay three hundred talents of silver and thirty talents of gold.

Afterward the king of Assyria sent Tartan and Rab-saris and Rab-shakeh from Lachish to King Hezekiah with a great army to Jerusalem. They came and took up their position at the channel of the upper pool and they called out for the king. There came out to them Eliakim, who was the steward of the palace, Shebnah, the scribe, and Joah, the recorder.

Then Rab-shakeh said to them: "Say

⋐ [4] WHO KNOWS US: *Conspiracy of any kind—personal, religious, political— is to be abhorred; but the most dangerous conspiracy of all is between nations.*

⋐ [5] FLESH AND NOT SPIRIT: *Flesh must rely on spirit; reliance on military and material might must inevitably fail.*

וְהָיָה לָכֶם מָעוֹז פַּרְעֹה לְבֹשֶׁת וְהֶחָסוּת בְּצֵל מִצְרַיִם לִכְלִמָּה.

you now to Hezekiah: Thus says the great king, the king of Assyria: <u>What confidence is this in which you trust?</u> Do you think that a mere word of the lips is counsel and strength for war? Now in whom do you trust, that you have rebelled against Me? You have put your trust in Egypt, in the staff of this bruised reed, on which if a man leans, it will run into his hand and pierce it. But if you say to me, We trust in the Lord our God; is it not the Lord whose altars Hezekiah has taken away, and said to Judah: Worship at this altar in Jerusalem? Have I marched against this place to destroy it without God's sanction? For God said to me, Go up against this land and destroy it. So, make a wager with my master, the king of Assyria. I will give you two thousand horses if you have the riders to set upon them. So you can then repulse the attack of the least of my master's servants."

Then Eliakim, Shebnah, [6] and Joah said to Rab-shakeh: "Speak to us in Aramaic, for we understand it, but do not speak to us in Judean with the people listening on the wall."

Rab-shakeh answered them: "Did my master send me with this message to your master or to you? It was rather to the men who are sitting on the wall and die of hunger." Then he stood and cried with a loud voice in Judean, saying: "Here the words of the great king, the king of Assyria: Thus says the king: Do not let Hezekiah deceive you, for he will not be able to deliver you. Have any of the gods of the nations delivered his land from the hand of the king of Assyria? Was Samaria delivered out of my hand? Make peace with me and surrender to

---

    ✥ [6] SHEBNAH: Shebnah was an important nobleman and great scholar in Jerusalem. When Sennacherib besieged the city, Shebnah shot an arrow into the Assyrian camp with a note attached which read: "Shebnah and his followers are willing to conclude peace. Hezekiah and his followers are not." When he heard this, Hezekiah was afraid and said: "Perhaps the mind of the Holy One, blessed be He, is with the majority and since they would surrender we must do likewise." Whereupon Isaiah came to him and reassured him: "Shebnah's is a conspiracy of the wicked, and as such cannot be counted upon in making a just decision."

The decision of the majority is frequently neither ethical nor courageous.

מָה הַבִּטָּחוֹן הַזֶּה אֲשֶׁר בָּטָחְתָּ?

me. Then each man can eat from his own vine and from his own fig tree, and drink water from his own cistern, [7] until I come and take you away to a land like your own, that you may live and not die."

The people were silent and answered not a word, for the king commanded: "Do not answer him."

THE PROPHET'S REASSURANCE

THEN KING HEZEKIAH rent his clothes and covered himself with sackcloth, and sent Eliakim and Shebnah, and the elders of the priests covered with sackcloth, to the prophet Isaiah, the son of Amoz. They said to him: "Thus said Hezekiah: 'This is a day of trouble, rebuke, and disgrace. It may be that the Lord your God will hear the words of Rab-shakeh whose master, the king of Assyria, has sent him to insult the living God, and will rebuke the words which the Lord your God has heard.'"

Isaiah said to them: "Thus shall you say to your master: Thus said the Lord: Do not be afraid of the words of the servants of the king of Assyria who have blasphemed Me. He shall not enter the city, nor shoot an arrow there; neither shall he come before it with a shield, nor cast a mound against it. For I will defend and save the city for My own sake and for the sake of My servant David."

ASSYRIA ON THE MARCH

He has come to Ai,
He has passed through Migron;
At Michmas he left his baggage;
He has crossed the pass;
In Geba he has taken up his lodging;
Rama has trembled;
Gibeath-Shaul has fled.
Cry out with a shrill voice, O daughter of Gallim!
Hearken, O Laish, O you poor Anathoth!
Madmenah is in mad flight;
The inhabitants of Gebim fled to cover.
This very day he will halt at Nob,
Shaking his fist at the Mount of Zion,
The hill of Jerusalem.

ᴈᴦ [7] HIS OWN CISTERN: *Demagogues promise all things to all men, but cannot, nor can they expect to, fulfill their promises.*

לֹא יָבוֹא אֶל הָעִיר הַזֹּאת וְלֹא יוֹרֶה שָׁם חֵץ.

ASSYRIA'S ARROGANCE

O ASHUR, the rod of My anger, the staff of My fury, I sent him against an ungodly nation. I sent him against the people of My wrath. I charged him to spoil them and prey upon them and to trample them down like mud in the streets. But he does not think so, nor does his heart so devise; but destruction is in mind and to cut off nations, not a few. For he says: "Are not My princes all of them kings? Is it not Calno like Carchemish? Is not Hammoth like Arpad? Is not Samaria like Damascus? Shall I not do to Jerusalem and its images as I have done to Samaria and its idols?" He said: "By the strength of my hand I have done it and by my wisdom, for I have understanding. I have removed the boundaries of peoples and have plundered their treasures and have brought down the mighty. My hand has reached into the wealth of the people as into a nest, as one gathers eggs that are forsaken; I have gathered the whole earth and there was not one that fluttered a wing, nor opened the mouth, nor chirped.

Should the ax vaunt itself against him that cuts with it, or the saw magnify itself against him that moves it? It is as if a rod should swing him that lifts it up, or like the staff raising him that is not wood. Therefore, the light of Israel shall become a fire and the Holy One of Israel a flame; and it shall burn and devour his thorns and his briers and the glory of his forest, and of his fruitful field he will consume. And the remnant of the trees of his forest shall be so few that a child may write them down.

ASSYRIA'S PUNISHMENT

IT SHALL COME TO PASS that when the Lord has finished all His work on the Mount of Zion and Jerusalem, He will punish the arrogance of the king of Assyria and his vainglorious pride.

The Lord of hosts has sworn, saying: Surely as I have planned, so shall it come to pass; and as I have made it My purpose so shall it stand that I will break Ashur in My land, and trample him on My mountains. This is the plan I planned upon the whole earth; and this is the hand stretched out against all the nations. The Lord of hosts has made it His purpose, who shall annul it? And His hand is stretched out, who shall turn it back?

This is the word which the Lord has

הֲיִתְפָּאֵר הַגַּרְזֶן עַל הַחֹצֵב בּוֹ, אִם יִתְגַּדֵּל הַמַּשּׂוֹר עַל מְנִיפוֹ?

spoken against Sennacherib: The virgin daughter of Zion despises you and laughs you to scorn. The daughter of Jerusalem has shaken her head at you. <u>Whom have you insulted and blasphemed, against whom have you raised your voice</u> and lifted up your eyes on high? Against the Holy One of Israel! By your servants you have taunted the Lord and have said: With the multitude of my chariots have I ascended the height of the mountain, to the innermost parts of Lebanon; and I have cut down the tall cedars and the choicest cypresses. I have digged and drunk foreign waters, and with the soles of my feet I have dried up all the rivers of Egypt.

THE LORD'S DECREE

HAVE YOU NOT HEARD how I prepared it long ago, fashioned it in ancient times? Now have I brought it to pass that you should turn fortified cities into ruins. Therefore, their inhabitants were of little power and they were dismayed and confused; they became like grass in the field, like tender herbs and like grass on the housetops.

I know your sitting and rising, your going out and your coming in and your raging against Me. Because you have raged against Me and your arrogance has come up into My ears, therefore will I put My hook in your nose [8] and My bridle in your lips, and I will return you back by the way which you came.

The Angel of the Lord went forth and slew in the camp of the Assyrians a hundred and eighty-five thousand. When men arose early next morning, they saw all around them dead bodies. So Sennacherib, King of Assyria, departed and returned home and dwelt at Nineveh. It came to pass that as he was worshiping in the temple of Nisroch, his god, his sons killed him.

ISAIAH'S VISION OF THE END OF DAYS

IN THAT DAY there shall be a highway out of Egypt to Assyria, and the Assyrians shall come into Egypt and the Egyptians shall

---

୫§ [8] MY HOOK IN YOUR NOSE: *The Lord will take Assyria like an animal, hook in the nose and bridle in the mouth, and bring it to heel.*

אֶת מִי חֵרַפְתָּ וְגִדַּפְתָּ וְעַל מִי הֲרִימוֹתָה קּוֹל?

come into Assyria, and the Egyptians shall worship [the Lord] with the Assyrians. In that day Israel will be the third [member of the league] with Egypt and Assyria in the midst of the earth; for the Lord of hosts has blessed them: "Blessed be Egypt, My people, and Assyria, the work of My hands, and Israel, My inheritance."

On this mountain the Lord of hosts will make for all the people a feast of fat things and feast of wine on the lees. And He will destroy on this mountain the veil that covers all the nations. He will swallow up death [9] for ever; and the Lord God will wipe away tears from every face. And He will remove from all the earth the reproach of His people, for the Lord has spoken it.

The people that walked in the darkness have seen a great light. On them that dwelt in the land of the shadow of death has the light shone. For every boot worn by a warrior and every war cloak rolled in blood shall be burning fuel for fire. For a child has been born to us, a son has been given to us, and the government shall be on his shoulders and his name shall be called, "Wonderful in Counsel, God the Mighty, Everlasting Father, the Ruler of Peace." Great will be his dominion and endless the peace upon the throne of David and upon his kingdom,

---

&ε§ [9] HE WILL SWALLOW UP DEATH: In the happy days to come, Rabbi Joshua said, "Death will be abolished for all the world's people, Jews and Gentiles alike." The Lord will produce ten miracles: 1. The light of the moon shall equal the light of the sun. 2. A living spring in Jerusalem will cure all the sick who bathe in it. 3. Fruit trees will bear fresh fruit every month and their fruit will be healing medicines. 4. There will be no more abandoned or destroyed cities; even Sodom and Gomorrah will be rebuilt. 5. All nations will recognize the glory of the people of Israel. 6. The cow and bear shall feed together. 7. The Lord shall gather all the beasts, birds and creeping things and make a covenant with them not to hurt people or each other. 8. Weeping, wailing and sighing will be heard no more. 9. Death will be abolished. 10. All men will rejoice and be happy.

At the end of days all men will have health, peace, happiness and everlasting life.

הָעָם הַהֹלְכִים בַּחֹשֶׁךְ רָאוּ אוֹר גָּדוֹל.

to establish it and to uphold it, through justice and through righteousness from henceforth and for ever. The zeal of the Lord of hosts will do this.

Davids Father

THE MESSIANIC AGE

THE PROPHECY that Isaiah, the son of Amoz, saw concerning Judah and Jerusalem. And it shall come to pass in the end of days that the mountains of the Lord's house shall be established as the top of the exalted above the hills; and all nations shall flow unto it. And many people will go and say, "Come, you, let us go up to the mountains of the Lord, to the house of the God of Jacob; and He will teach us of His ways and we will walk in His paths. For out of Zion shall go forth the Torah, and the word of the Lord from Jerusalem. And He shall judge between nations and decide for many peoples. They shall beat their swords into plowshares and their spears into pruning

innocence

hooks. Nation shall not lift up sword against nation, neither shall they learn war any more.

A shoot will come forth from the stem of Jesse and a branch shall grow out of his roots. The spirit of the Lord shall rest upon him, the spirit of wisdom and understanding, the spirit of knowledge and of the fear of the Lord. He will not judge by that which his eyes see nor decide by that which his ears hear. But with righteousness shall he judge the poor and with fairness decide for the oppressed of the land. He shall smite the guilty of the land with the rod of his mouth and with the breath of his lips shall he slay the wicked. Righteousness shall be the girdle of his loins.

infinitely

Then a wolf shall dwell with the lamb [10] and the leopard shall lie down with the kid. The calf and the young lion will graze together, and a little child shall lead them. The cow and the bear shall be friends and their young ones shall lie

descendent

ᴗᚷ [10] DWELL WITH THE LAMB: Rabbi Simeon said: It is written: "And will cause evil beasts to cease out of the land" (Leviticus 26:6). The Lord will not destroy the beasts; instead he will change their natures so that they no longer hurt or destroy. Thus will the Lord's greatness be manifest.

At the end of days physical and human nature will be transformed so that pain and destruction will cease forever.

וְכִתְּתוּ חַרְבוֹתָם לְאִתִּים וַחֲנִיתוֹתֵיהֶם לְמַזְמֵרוֹת, לֹא יִשָּׂא גוֹי אֶל גוֹי חֶרֶב וְלֹא יִלְמְדוּ עוֹד מִלְחָמָה.

down together. The lion shall eat straw like the ox; and the infant shall play on the hole of the asp, and the baby shall put his hand into the viper's nest. They shall not hurt nor destroy [11] on all My holy mountain; for the earth shall be full of the knowledge of the Lord as waters cover the sea.

snake

peace — Eutopia

⋙ [11] THEY SHALL NOT HURT NOR DESTROY: Brigands in the neighborhood afflicted the community of Rabbi Meir so grievously that the rabbi finally prayed for their deaths. His wife, Beruria, rebuked him, saying: "How can you permit yourself such a prayer! Is it written, 'Let *hattaim* (sins) cease' or 'Let *hotim* (sinners) cease'? It is written *hattaim*, sins, not *hotim*, sinners. Psalms (105:35) says, 'And let the wicked be no more'; since the sins will cease, there will be no more wicked men. Therefore, instead of praying for the brigands to die, pray for them to repent!"

So rebuked, the rabbi did pray for the brigands, they repented, and ceased to afflict the community.

Punishment may destroy evil but repentance transforms it to good.

כִּי מָלְאָה הָאָרֶץ דֵּעָה אֶת יְיָ כַּמַּיִם לַיָּם מְכַסִּים.

4. ISAIAH [40–60]

COMFORT THE PEOPLE

COMFORT, O COMFORT [1] MY PEOPLE, says the Lord. Bid Jerusalem take heart and tell her that her time of suffering in exile is ended, that her guilt is paid in full, that she has received from the Lord's hand double for her sins.

---

[1] COMFORT, O COMFORT: The Lord said: "The time has come to redeem My children from the suffering of the exile in Babylonia. But first I shall send My prophets to comfort them." The prophets gathered and were sent to comfort the children of Israel and assure them of the prospect of a golden future. But the congregation of Israel *(keneset yisrael)* replied: "We have had our fill of your rebuke and chastisement. Your comforting words are empty and barren."

The prophets returned to the Lord and told Him that the people refused to be comforted, so the Lord said, "I Myself must comfort them." Then the Lord went to the congregation of Israel and asked why

נַחֲמוּ נַחֲמוּ עַמִּי, יֹאמַר אֱלֹהֵיכֶם.

Ascend a high mountain, Zion, herald of glad tidings; raise your voice loudly, Jerusalem, herald of good news; lift up, be not afraid. <u>Say to the cities of Judah</u>: "<u>Behold your God</u>!" The Lord God will come as a Mighty One, His arm will

---

they would not be comforted. They answered: "Are we not right to be angered? You exiled us, scattered us among the nations. You cursed us most vehemently. We have been oppressed, persecuted and humiliated by even the lowest of nations. Still we sanctified Your name even in exile. We did not reject You."

The Lord replied, saying: "You were not punished in vain. You transgressed My laws. Is it not written: 'Whoever sheds man's blood, his blood shall be shed, for in the image of God was man made'?"

The congregation of Israel replied: "When You exiled us among the nations, You broke the covenant. We are no longer Your sons. In exile we observed Your Sabbath and did not break any of Your commandments. We did not reject You; You rejected us."

Then the Lord said: "I will redeem you from among the nations and punish the nations who oppressed you. And I will be to you like a brother."

The congregation of Israel spoke to the Lord: "You may be a brother to us, but will it be as Cain was to Abel, Ishmael to Isaac and Esau to Jacob?"

"I will be to you as Joseph was to his brothers," the Lord said. "Despite what his brothers did to him, Joseph did not hate them, but showed them great consideration and compassion. As it is written (Genesis 50:21): 'Fear me not, I will feed and sustain you and your children, and he comforted them and spoke kindly to them." Such a brother will the Lord be to you. Be comforted, My people."

Then the congregation of Israel was comforted.

The people of Israel dare to enter a dialogue with the Lord, to question God about whether He has fulfilled His obligations to man and community.

אִמְרִי לְעָרֵי יְהוּדָה: הִנֵּה אֱלֹהֵיכֶם!

rule. His reward [to the righteous] lies with Him [2] and His recompense [for their good deeds] is from Him. Like a shepherd He will tend His flock, with His arm He will gather the lambs and carry them in His bosom, and gently lead the nursing ewes.

Zion said: "The Lord has forsaken me, [3] the Lord has forgotten me." Can a woman forget the child she nurses that she should not have compassion on the child she has born? Yes, even a mother may forget, but I will not forget you. I have graven you upon the palms of My

---

[2] HIS REWARD LIES WITH HIM: *Secharo*, reward, and *pe'ulato*, recompense, are different forms of repayment. Reward is often delayed; recompense is immediate payment. The righteous cannot expect to see the reward of their deeds immediately. Righteous deeds are intended to bring about change in the world, and their effects are slow and cumulative, and may not be evident for generations. The wrongdoer often succeeds in seeing the fruit of his work swiftly; he is recompensed, requited, paid in full. He sees immediate results because he intends to leave nothing useful for the generations to come.

[3] THE LORD HAS FORSAKEN ME: The Rabbis asked whether to be forsaken is not the same as to be forgotten, and Resh Lakish replied: The congregation of Israel said to the Holy One: "Sovereign of the Universe, when a man takes a second wife, he still remembers the love of his first wife, the companion of his youth. But You have both forsaken and forgotten us." The Holy One answered: "There is no forgetfulness before the Throne of My Glory. I remember your days in the desert, your great devotion and trust in Me."

Then the congregation of Israel said to Him: "Since there is no forgetfulness before You, perhaps You will not forget the time we made the golden calf and exclaimed: 'This is your God, O Israel.'"

The Lord promised: "That will be forgotten."

Israel said: "Since there is some forgetfulness before You, perhaps

הֲתִשְׁכַּח אִשָּׁה עוּלָהּ, מֵרַחֵם בֶּן בִּטְנָהּ?

hands; your walls [of Jerusalem] are always before Me.

Lift up your eyes, [look] around you and see: All of them gather themselves together and come to you. Your lost children shall yet say to you: "The land is too small to hold us; give us a little place so that I may live there." Then shall you say to yourself: "Who has begotten all these for me? I was bereaved and alone, exiled and wandering. Who has reared these [my children]? I was left alone. Where did they come from?" So said the Lord: "I will lift up My hand to the nations and I will give them a signal; and they shall bring your sons in their bosom and they shall carry your daughters on their shoulders."

CYRUS, THE ANOINTED OF THE LORD

THUS SAYS THE LORD to his anointed, Cyrus, whose right hand I grasp, subduing nations before him, and making kings run in his service, opening doors before him and leaving the gates unbarred: I will give you treasures out of the darkness, and riches that have been hidden away, that you may know that I am the Lord, the God of Israel who calls you by name. For the sake of Jacob My servant, of Israel My chosen one, I say of Cyrus: My shepherd who fulfills My every wish, he shall say of Jerusalem, "Let her be rebuilt," and of the Temple, "Let its foundations be laid."

THE IN-GATHERING OF EXILES

WHO ARE THOSE that fly like clouds and like doves to their cotes? Surely the people of the Islands are waiting with their ships of Tarshish to bring your sons from afar, their silver and gold with them, in honor of your God, because He has glorified you. Aliens shall build your wall and their kings shall minister to you. In My wrath I punished you; but in My mercy I had compassion on you.

Sing, O you heavens, for what the Lord has done! Shout, O depths of the earth! Break into song, you mountains,

---

You will forget our conduct at Sinai when You revealed Yourself and declared: 'I am the Lord your God.'"

"That," the Lord declared, "will not be forgotten."

To forget is to lose the recollection of something or to put it out of one's memory. To forsake is to renounce something dear to one. How does the Lord promise to forget but not to forsake?

עוֹד יֹאמְרוּ בְאָזְנָיִךְ בְּנֵי שִׁכֻּלָיִךְ: צַר לִי הַמָּקוֹם, גְּשָׁה לִּי וְאֵשֵׁבָה.

you forest and every tree in it; for the Lord has redeemed Jacob and glorifies Himself in Israel.

Arise, shine for your light has come. The glory of the Lord has risen and shone upon you. Darkness still covers the earth and gross darkness envelops the people; but upon you the Lord will shine forth and His glory shall be seen upon you. Nations shall walk by your light and kings by the brightness of your glow.

Who hath wrought and done it? He that called the generations from the beginning. I, the Lord, who am the first, and with the last am the same. The isles saw and feared; the ends of the earth trembled; they drew near and came.

Go forth from Babylon. Flee from the Chaldeans. With a voice of singing, declare, tell, speak this even to the end of the earth. Say: "The Lord has redeemed His servant Jacob."

THE IMAGE WORSHIPERS

TO WHOM WILL YOU COMPARE GOD? [4] To what image will you liken Him? To the image which a craftsman has cast and a goldsmith covered over with gold and a silversmith adorned with silver chains? To whom then will you liken Me that I should be equal? says the Holy One.

One artisan helps the other. Every one says to the other: Be diligent. The crafts-

---

[4] TO WHOM WILL YOU COMPARE GOD: The Torah and prophets explicitly state that the Lord is not corporeal. Maimonides states that it is written: "God is in heaven above and upon earth below" (Deuteronomy 4:39). A corporeal being cannot be in two places at the same time. It is also written: "For you saw no image, no form of any figure" (Deuteronomy 4:15).

If the Lord had a body it would be possible to compare Him to other bodies. If this is so, why does the Torah, in speaking of the vision of God granted to the Elders of Israel, state: "Under His feet was a floor of sapphire and like the heavens themselves for brightness" (Exodus 24:10)? And why are there similar references to God's hands, ears, and so on? Maimonides explains that all such passages are designed for those people who can only grasp what is concrete so that Scripture speaks as human beings can understand.

קוּמִי אוֹרִי כִּי בָא אוֹרֵךְ וּכְבוֹד יְיָ עָלַיִךְ זָרָח.

man encourages the goldsmith; he that smooths with a hammer encourages him who strikes the anvil and says to the solderer: "It is good." And fastens it with nails so that it should stand firm. He chooses an oak [5] tree which does not rot. Then he seeks a skillful craftsman to set up an image that shall not reel.

The smith makes an ax, he works it over the coals, fashions it with hammers. He works with his strong arm, [he does not eat] even when he grows hungry and loses strength. He does not drink any water and he grows faint. The wood worker draws a measuring line. He marks it out with a pencil, works on it with planes and shapes it into the likeness of a man, like a man beautifully adorned, to sit in the god's house.

Or a man goes and cuts himself a cedar. He plants himself a tree and the rain makes it grow. The man uses part of it for fuel. He kindles a fire, warms himself, bakes bread [on its coals]. From what is left he then makes a god and prostrates himself before it. Half of it he burned in the fire and in its embers he roasted meat. He ate the roast, was satisfied and also warmed himself, exclaiming: "Aha, I am warm, I feel the fire." Before the rest, of which he made the idol, he prostrates himself, worships it, prays to it, saying: "Save me, for you are god." They know not, neither do they understand, for their eyes are bleared [6] and they cannot see, and their hearts cannot understand to say: "Half of it I used as fuel and on its embers I have baked bread, roasted meat and eaten it. How can I make the rest of it an abomination and prostrate myself before a block of wood?"

ᴥᴣ [5] HE CHOOSES AN OAK: *Idolatry is the worship of the work of man's hands, however skillful.*

ᴥᴣ [6] THEIR EYES ARE BLEARED: Reb Yehudah has written that generations of mankind who do not as a rule learn from the experience of previous generations have their eyes bleared. The generation of the Deluge did not learn from the generation of Enoch, when the Lord had flooded a third of the world as a warning to the people for their transgressions.

יִסְגָּד־לוֹ וְיִשְׁתַּחוּ וְיִתְפַּלֵּל אֵלָיו וְיֹאמַר: הַצִּילֵנִי כִּי אֵלִי אָתָּה.

THE LORD'S PEOPLE AND HOUSE OPEN TO ALL

LET NOT THE ALIEN SAY, when he would join himself to the Lord: "The Lord will surely exclude me from His people." For the foreigners who join themselves to the Lord, ministering to Him, loving the name of the Lord, and becoming His servants, all who keep the Sabbath free from profanation and hold to My covenant, I will bring them to My holy mountain and make them joyful in My house of prayer. Their burnt-offerings and sacrifices will be acceptable on My altar, for My house shall be called a house of prayer for all people. Thus says the Lord God, who gathers the dispersed of Israel: others will I gather to him besides those already gathered.

THE VANITY OF GRAVEN IMAGES

LET THEM BRING THEM FORTH and declare to us the things that shall happen; the former things, what are they? Declare you that we may consider and know the end of them; or announce to us things to come. Declare the things that are to come hereafter that we may know you are gods. Yes, do good or do evil that we may be dismayed and behold it together. Behold, you are nothing and your work a thing of nought. An abomination is he that chooses you. Their works are vanity and nought; their molten images are wind and confusion.

Thus says the Lord, the King of Israel, and his Redeemer the Lord of hosts: I am the first, and I am the last, and beside Me there is no God.

The people of Sodom and Gomorrah did not learn anything from the generation which built the Tower of Babel, and that was a great surprise because then all mankind spoke a single language and could easily communicate one with the other. Yet that generation too made the same mistakes as their predecessors.

Blindness of self-love and self-involvement are themselves idol worship; they worship the present and the self, and therefore cannot learn from others or from the past, and so cannot change the future or themselves.

אֲנִי רִאשׁוֹן וַאֲנִי אַחֲרוֹן, וּמִבַּלְעָדַי אֵין אֱלֹהִים.

CREATOR OF THE ENDS OF THE EARTH

KNOW YOU NOT? Hear you not? Has it not been told you from the beginning? Have you not understood from the foundations of the earth? It is He that sits above the circle of the earth, and the inhabitants thereof are as grasshoppers; He that brings princes to nothing. He makes the judges of the earth as a thing of nought. Scarcely are they planted, scarcely are they sown, scarcely has their stock taken root in the earth; when He blows upon them and they wither, and the whirlwind takes them away as stubble. To whom then will you liken Me, that I should be equal? says the Holy One.

Why do you say, O Jacob, and speak, O Israel: "My way is hid fron the Lord, and my right is passed over from my God?" Have you not known that the Lord, the Creator of the ends of the earth does not faint nor is weary? His discernment is past searching out. He gives power to the faint; and to him that has no might he increases strength. Even the youths shall faint and be weary and the young men shall utterly fall; but they that wait for the Lord shall renew their strength. They shall mount up with wings as eagles. They shall walk and not faint.

MAN IS GRASS

WOE TO HIM that strives with his Maker, as a potsherd among the potsherds of the earth! Shall the clay say to him that fashions it: "What are you making?" Or: "Your work, it has no hands?" Woe to him that says to his father: "Why do you beget?" Or to a woman: "Why do you labor so?"

Hark! one says: "Proclaim!" And I said: "What shall I proclaim? All flesh is grass, and all the goodliness therof is as the flower of the field. The grass withers, the flower fades; because the breath of the Lord blows upon it. Surely the people is grass. The grass withers, the flower fades; but the word of our God shall stand forever."

Thus says the Lord: I, even I, have made the earth, and created man upon it, even My hands have stretched out the heavens, and all their host have I commanded. I have roused him up in victory, and I make level all his ways. He shall build My city, and he shall let My exiles go free, nor for any price or reward. O, Israel, that are saved by the Lord with an everlasting salvation: You shall not be ashamed nor confounded world without end.

יָבֵשׁ חָצִיר, נָבֵל צִיץ, וּדְבַר אֱלֹהֵינוּ יָקוּם לְעוֹלָם.

THE HIDDEN GOD

I AM THE LORD and there is none else. Beside Me there is no god. I have strengthened you though you are not aware of Me, so that they may know from the rising sun and from the west that there is none beside Me. I am the Lord and there is none else. I form the light and create darkness. [7] I make peace and create evil, I am the Lord that does all those things.

My thoughts are not your thoughts, nor My ways your ways, says the Lord. As the heavens are higher than the earth, so are My ways higher than your ways, and My thoughts than your thoughts.

Truly, You are a hidden God, [8] but You are also the God of Israel, the Savior.

Seek the Lord while He may be found. Call upon Him while He is near. Let the wicked forsake his way and the unrighteous man his thoughts. Let them return to the Lord and He will have compassion upon them. Return to our God because He pardons abundantly.

Thus said the High and Lofty One who inhabits eternity, whose name is holy: I dwell in the high and holy place but I am with him that is conscience

---

&⸗ [7] I FORM THE LIGHT AND CREATE DARKNESS: Rabbi Hezekiah says that the command for peace is greater than any other *mitzvah* in the Torah. Darkness and light are the basis of creation, and peace is as important as both of them. Peace is so great it balances all creation. Of all other commands it is written, "If you chance," or "If you see," so that "If you chance upon your enemy's ox or donkey going astray, you must be sure to lead it home" (Exodus 23:4). In short, if you see it, you must obey the command; but if you don't, you need not seek out the opportunity. But about peace it is written: "Seek peace and pursue it in any other place, everywhere."

&⸗ [8] YOU ARE A HIDDEN GOD: *Man can never know God, although he must forever strive to do so. In remaining a hidden God, the Lord keeps men from making an idol of Him.*

אָכֵן אַתָּה אֵל מִסְתַּתֵּר, אֱלֹהֵי יִשְׂרָאֵל מוֹשִׁיעַ.

stricken and humble in spirit, [9] to re-
vive the spirit of the humble and to re-
vive the heart of the penitent.

THE LORD'S SALVATION

THUS SAYS THE LORD: In an acceptable
time I have answered you, and in a day
of salvation I have helped you. I will
preserve you and give you for a covenant of the people, to raise up the land,
to cause to inherit the desolate heritages;
saying to the prisoners: "Go forth." To
them that are in darkness: "Show yourselves." They shall feed in the ways and
in all high hills [10] shall be their pasture.

They shall not hunger or thirst, neither
shall the heat nor the sun smite them; for
He that has compassion on them will
lead them, even by the springs of water
will He guide them. I will make all My
mountains a way, and My highways
shall be raised on high. Behold, these
shall come from far.

Behold, I make you a new threshing-
sledge with sharp teeth. You shall thresh
the mountains and beat them small and
shall make the hills as chaff. You shall
fan them and the wind shall carry them
away, and the whirlwind shall scatter
them. And you shall rejoice in the Lord,
you shall glory in the Holy One of
Israel.

ഏ [9] HUMBLE IN SPIRIT: Raþbi Huna and Rabbi Hisda disputed the meaning of the verse. One said that the Lord raises the humble man to His
level before the Lord is with him. The other maintained that God descends to the level of the most humble.

Not only does the Lord not reject the poor, the despairing, the broken in spirit, but He declares that He is always near them. As the Psalms
(34:18) say: "The Lord is near the broken-hearted and He helps the
crushed in spirit." Rabbi Alexander said that the ordinary man throws
out chipped or broken utensils, but the Lord cherishes those of his vessels who are hurt or damaged.

ഏ [10] IN ALL HIGH HILLS: Out of Zion the beauty of the world has been
and shall yet be made perfect.

כֹּה אָמַר יְיָ: בְּעֵת רָצוֹן עֲנִיתִיךָ וּבְיוֹם יְשׁוּעָה עֲזַרְתִּיךָ.

5. ISAIAH [42–66]

JACOB THE SUFFERING SERVANT

BEHOLD, [Jacob is] My servant [1] whom I uphold, My chosen one, in whom I delight. I have put My spirit upon him, he shall make justice go forth to the nations. He shall not shout nor raise his voice. He shall not make his voice heard in the streets. A bruised reed he shall not break and a dimly flickering wick he shall not quench. He will establish justice according to the truth. He shall not be quenched nor crushed until he shall establish justice on earth; and the faraway islands will wait longingly for his teaching.

Listen to me, O islands, hearken people from afar: the Lord called me from my birth, before I was born He appointed my destiny. He made my mouth like a sharp sword, the shadow of His hand

---

[1] JACOB IS MY SERVANT: *Jacob may be understood variously to mean the prophet, the faithful remnant of Israel, and an idealized people of Israel.*

לֹא יִצְעַק וְלֹא יִשָּׂא וְלֹא יַשְׁמִיעַ בַּחוּץ קוֹלוֹ.

protected me. He has made me a polished arrow in His quiver. He has concealed me. He said to me: "You are My servant, Israel, through whom I will be glorified." [2] And I thought: "In vain I have labored, I have spent my strength for nothing and uselessly. But in truth my reward is with the Lord and my recompense with my God. Now the Lord that made me His servant even before I was born, to bring Jacob back to Him, and that Israel shall be gathered to Him, for I am honored in the eyes of the Lord and my God has become My strength. Then He said: "It is too slight a thing for you that you should be My servant and merely raise the tribes of Israel and restore the survivors of Israel. I will also make you a light to the nations [3] that My salvation may reach the end of the earth." Thus said the Lord, the Redeemer of Israel, his Holy One, to him who is despised by men, [4] abhorred by nations, the slave of rulers. Kings shall rise

---

⋲§ [2] I WILL BE GLORIFIED: *The prophet as servant of God and personification of Israel was predestined to carry out the Lord's mission, was given sharp words by the Lord to do so, and was protected by Him.*

⋲§ [3] A LIGHT TO THE NATIONS: *The suffering servant (and Israel) will be an example and a symbol to all the nations.*

⋲§ [4] WHO IS DESPISED BY MEN: Akilos, the son of the Roman Emperor Hadrian's sister, wished to become a Jew. So he went to his uncle and told him that he wanted to go into business. Hadrian said: "I like your ambition. If you need money, my treasury is open to you." Akilos replied: "I need no money, but I need advice. What kind of merchandise shall I buy to make a profit?" The Emperor answered: "Merchandise which has fallen so low in price it seems to be buried. Don't hesitate; buy it. Eventually it will rise beyond the original price."

Akilos went to the land of Israel and was there converted to Judaism. He studied Torah diligently and became a great scholar. When he

וַיֹּאמֶר לִי: עַבְדִּי אַתָּה, יִשְׂרָאֵל אֲשֶׁר בְּךָ אֶתְפָּאָר.

when they see you, princes shall pros-
trate themselves before you, because the
Lord who is faithful, the Holy One of
Israel, has chosen you.

HOPES AND TRIUMPHS

THE LORD endowed me with fluent speech
that I should know how to comfort

---

returned to Rome his uncle asked, "Why is your face so changed? Have
you lost your money or has someone insulted you? If you have lost
your money, do not be concerned; I shall give you more, as much as
you need. And if anyone has affronted you, tell me and I shall punish
him."

"I have neither been insulted nor have I lost money," Akilos said.

"Then why has your appearance changed so much?" the Emperor
inquired.

"Because I studied Torah diligently and was circumcised."

"Who gave you permission to do that?" the Emperor Hadrian asked.

"I took your advice, Uncle. You told me to buy merchandise which
had declined so far in price it seemed to be buried. No nation is more
despised than the Jews, but their greatness will not only be restored, but
will rise far higher than it was before."

"Truly, is that why you did it?"

"I wanted to study Torah," Akilos confessed.

"But why did you have to circumcise yourself and become a Jew to
do that?"

"Because," Akilos replied, "only in that way can you understand
the Torah."

*Akilos understood that only by putting himself genuinely and irreversibly
into the postion of Jews, i.e., by being circumcised, could he truly know what
it was to be a Jew and walk in the way of the covenant.*

לְמַעַן יְיָ אֲשֶׁר נֶאֱמָן, קְדוֹשׁ יִשְׂרָאֵל וַיִּבְחָרֶךָ.

with words those who are weary. The
Lord God opened my ear [to hear His
message]. I did not rebel, nor turn away
[from the heavy burden]. I gave my
back to the lasher [5] and my cheek to
those who plucked off the hair. I did not
hide my face from those who shamed me
or spat on me. I have not been confounded, [6] for the Lord will help me.
Therefore I have set my face like a flint
and I know that I shall not be ashamed.
My vindicator is near. Who will contend with me? Who is my adversary?
Let him come near me. Behold, the Lord

ᴇᴅ [5] MY BACK TO THE LASHER: Our Rabbis declare that this phrase does
not mean that man has license to do what he wishes with his own body
or property if he wishes to abuse himself or destroy his property wantonly. The verse means that the prophet knew that when he went to
reprove the people he would be scorned and abused, but he was prepared for it. A man who stands up for justice and righteousness must
be ready to suffer contumely and danger. But anyone who abuses his
body or wantonly destroys his property is brought to account. As it is
written (Genesis 9:5): "For your own life's blood, I shall require an
account," and (Deuteronomy 4:5): "Guard yourself well."

*The prophet (and Israel) as suffering servant of the Lord willingly endures
the pain and humiliation imposed by the Lord's mission.*

ᴇᴅ [6] I HAVE NOT BEEN CONFOUNDED: Rabbi Bahay said: "Whoever trusts
and relies on God is not confounded. He sets his face like flint and is not
afraid of those who oppose him." The man who trusts in God is peaceful and tranquil, self-assured and self-reliant. He knows on whom he
can rely.

If a man does not trust in the Lord he usually relies on idols made by
the hands of men, or makes of man himself an idol. "Cursed is the man
whose heart is departed from the Lord and puts his trust in man and
makes flesh his strength."

עַל־כֵּן שַׂמְתִּי פָנַי כַּחַלָּמִישׁ וָאֵדַע כִּי לֹא אֵבוֹשׁ.

God helps me. [7] Who shall prove me wrong? They are all like worn-out garments which fall apart because moths have eaten them up.

Behold, My servant shall prosper; he shall be exalted and lifted up and shall be very high. As many were appalled at you because his face was so marred that it was unlike that of a man, [8] his form unlike that of the sons of Adam, so shall he startle many nations, their kings shall shut their mouths because of him. They shall see more than what was told to them and discern more than has been heard.

Who could have believed what we heard? [We saw that] he grew like a sapling before us and as a root out of dry ground. He had no form nor comeliness that we should notice him. He had no beauty that we should admire him. He was despised and rejected of men, a man of pains and intimate with disease, as one from whom men hide their faces. He was despised and we took no heed of him.

THE SMITTEN OF GOD

YET OUR SICKNESS did he bear, our pains

&§ [7] THE LORD GOD HELPS ME: Our Sages tell us that communal worship and group study strengthen and exalt a man much more than if he prayed or studied alone. To what can we compare communal prayer and group study? To ten people who make a party. Each brings a different delicacy for the celebration: one brings fish, another meat, a third vegetables, a fourth fruit and desserts. When the ten dined together, each ate not only the delicacy he had himself brought but the delicacies of all the other nine. The same results from communal prayer and group study; each individual returns home with ten different thoughts and feelings about what has been studied or prayed.

&§ [8] UNLIKE THAT OF A MAN: *The suffering servant's (and Israel's) mission shall be a martyrdom whose agonies will scar him for life, making him different from all men. Yet, at the last, he shall overcome his pains and be exalted.*

הִנֵּה יַשְׂכִּיל עַבְדִּי, יָרוּם וְנִשָּׂא וְגָבַהּ מְאֹד.

he carried. [9] We thought him smitten of God [10] but he was pierced and mortally wounded because we had sinned. Our iniquities crushed him. He was chastised for our transgressions and by his bruises were we healed. Like sheep we have all gone astray, every one turned his own way, and on him the Lord laid the guilt of all of us.

When he was oppressed, he was submissive and opened not his mouth. Like a lamb is led to the slaughter and like a sheep that is dumb before her shearers, he did not open his mouth. [11] For lack of justice he was oppressed. He was cut off from the living because of the punishment due to My people for their transgressions. They dug his grave with the wicked, his tomb with the evildoers. Although he had done no violence, neither was deceit in his mouth, their iniquities he did bear.

Therefore will I give him a portion among the great and with the mighty shall he share the honor, for he bared his soul to death and was numbered with the transgressors. Yet he bore the sin of many and interceded for transgressors.

❧ [9] OUR PAINS HE CARRIED : *The suffering servant (and Israel) is punished for sins which he did not commit; the victim suffers for those who victimized, the innocent suffers for those who transgressed.*

❧ [10] SMITTEN OF GOD : Why should one man bear the sin and sickness of his generation? Is not every individual responsible for himself? Is it not written (Jeremiah 31:30): "Every one shall die for his own iniquity"?

These verses refer to the people of Israel in the Diaspora over many centuries. Nations thought that Jews suffered because they were rejected by God and therefore they were "despised by men, abhorred by nations and the slaves of rulers." In truth, they suffered because none cared, because "everyone turned his own way." The Jew did not conform. He cared about the guilt of his generation, suffered and was humiliated because of it. For lack of justice, "our iniquities crushed him."

❧ [11] HE DID NOT OPEN HIS MOUTH : *In the face of persecution and slaughter, the suffering servant (Israel) is gentle, meek and unprotesting.*

כַּשֶּׂה לַטֶּבַח יוּבָל וּכְרָחֵל לִפְנֵי גוֹזְזֶיהָ נֶאֱלָמָה, וְלֹא יִפְתַּח פִּיו.

BABYLON AND CHALDEA

COME DOWN and sit in the dust, O virgin daughter of Babylon, sit on the ground without a throne, O daughter of the Chaldeans; for you shall no longer be called delicate and tender. Take the millstones and grind meal; remove your veil, strip off the train, uncover the leg, pass through the rivers. Your nakedness shall be uncovered, [12] yes, your shame shall be seen. I will take vengeance and will let no man intercede. Our Redeemer, the Lord of hosts is His name, the Holy One of Israel.

Sit silent and get into darkness, O daughter of the Chaldeans; for you shall no longer be called the mistress of kingdoms. I was angry with My people, I profaned My inheritance, and gave them into your hand; you showed them no mercy. Upon the aged you have laid your heavy yoke.

And you have been secure in your wickedness. You have said: "No one sees me." [13] Your wisdom and your knowledge have perverted you. And you have said in your heart: "I am and there is none else beside me." Yet shall evil come upon you. You shall not know how to charm it away. And calamity shall fall upon you. You shall not be able to fend it off. And ruin shall come upon you suddenly before you know.

I have long time held My peace, I have been still and refrained Myself. Now will I cry like a woman in labor, gasping and panting at once. I will make waste mountains and hills, and dry up all their herbs. I will make the rivers islands and will dry up the pools. I will bring the blind by a way that they knew not, in paths that they knew not will I lead them. I will make darkness light before them and rugged places plain. These things will I do and I will not leave them

---

[12] YOUR NAKEDNESS SHALL BE UNCOVERED: *Babylonia, Chaldea, and all tyrannies shall finally be stripped of grandeur and pretense, their sins exposed and punished.*

[13] NO ONE SEES ME: *One of the most common human delusions: If no one sees me sin, then no one knows, and nothing has happened. No sin has been committed and no wickedness need be repented.*

גֹּאֲלֵנוּ יְיָ צְבָאוֹת שְׁמוֹ, קְדוֹשׁ יִשְׂרָאֵל.

undone. They shall be turned back, greatly ashamed, that trust in graven images, that say unto molten images, "You are our gods."

THE FAST AND THE FUTURE

THE PEOPLE ASK: "Why have we fasted [14] and You took no heed of it? Why have we afflicted our souls and You took no knowledge of it?" It is because in the day of your fast you pursue your desire and oppress all who labor for you. You fast for the sake of strife and contention, and you strike with the fist of wickedness. Is such the fast I have chosen? The day of a man to afflict his soul? Is it to bow down his head as a bulrush and spread sackcloth and ashes under him? Will you call this a fast [15] and an acceptable day for the Lord? This is the fast I have chosen: To loosen the fetters of wickedness, to undo the bands of the yoke, and to let the oppressed go free. You shall break every yoke, share your bread with the hungry and bring into your house the homeless. [16] When you see a naked man, you shall cover him and not hide yourself from your own flesh. [17] Then you shall call and the Lord will answer you. Then you shall cry and he will say: "Here I am."

⤐ [14] WHY HAVE WE FASTED: All the virtue of fasting lies in the giving of charity which accompanies it.

⤐ [15] WILL YOU CALL THIS A FAST: *Formal fasting is unacceptable to the Lord: It is not ceremonials the Lord desires but the substance of virtue, good deeds.*

⤐ [16] HOUSE THE HOMELESS: *True fasting is to perform the mitzvot of feeding the hungry, clothing the naked, abolishing slavery and oppression.*

⤐ [17] NOT HIDE YOURSELF FROM YOUR OWN FLESH: Rabbi Jose the Galilean was married to a shrew. Students, colleagues and friends advised him to

הֲלוֹא פָרֹס לָרָעֵב לַחְמֶךָ וַעֲנִיִּים מְרוּדִים תָּבִיא בָיִת, כִּי תִרְאֶה עָרֹם וְכִסִּיתוֹ וּמִבְּשָׂרְךָ לֹא תִתְעַלָּם.

Thus said the Lord: "The heaven is My throne and the earth My footstool. What is the house that you may build for Me? And what manner of place as My residence? My hand made all these things and so all these things came to be.

---

divorce her, but he could not, because her dowry was too great for him to repay. His friends pitied him so much that they raised the money for the dowry and so enabled Rabbi Jose to divorce her.

In time, the wife married a city watchman who abused her, beat her and took all her money. The wife might have brought the watchman to court, but since her former husband was one of the judges, she was ashamed to display her distress before him.

The watchman became blind and could not work, and his wife was obliged to go from house to house begging with him. In doing so she avoided the street on which her former husband lived. The watchman, though blind, knew the city by heart and asked her why she always avoided that particular street. She always made excuses until finally the blind man realized that she was avoiding Rabbi Jose's street.

The next day, when they went begging, he began to beat her with his cane and insist that she take him to that street. She did so, and while they went from house to house, he abused her and struck her with his cane. Rabbi Jose, hearing the tumult, looked out of the window and saw her distress. Immediately he called the court into session and set a monthly pension for her so that she would not have to beg any longer. When his friends asked him why he was so compassionate to someone who had tormented him for so many years, Rabbi Jose replied: "It is written: 'You shall not hide yourself from your own flesh.' And it is also written (Genesis 2:24) that when a man marries, he leaves his father and mother and clings to his wife and they become as one flesh."

הַשָּׁמַיִם כִּסְאִי וְהָאָרֶץ הֲדֹם רַגְלָי – אֵי־זֶה בַיִת אֲשֶׁר תִּבְנוּ לִי וְאֵי־זֶה מָקוֹם מְנוּחָתִי?

Yet on this man will I look, on the humble and the contrite spirit, [18] and on him who stands in awe at My word."

Drop down, you heavens, from above, and let the skies pour down righteousness; let the earth open that they may bring forth salvation, and let her cause righteousness to spring up together; I the Lord have created it.

And they that shall be of you shall build the old waste places. You shall raise up the foundations of many generations and you shall be called the repairer of the breach, the restorer of paths to dwell in.

Then you shall delight yourself in the Lord, and I will make you to ride upon the high places of the earth and I will feed you with the heritage of Jacob your father. For the mouth of the Lord has spoken it.

THE NEW JERUSALEM

REJOICE AND EXULT FOREVER in what I create; for, behold, I shall create a Jerusalem which will have in her only exultation and people of joy. I will rejoice with Jerusalem and joy in My people. The voice of weeping shall no more be heard in her, nor the voice of crying. There shall not be an infant nor an old man who has not lived out his years of life. The youngest shall die a hundred years

---

[18] THE HUMBLE AND CONTRITE SPIRIT: Rabbi Okybia was sick and near to death. His son said to him: "Father, command your friends to befriend me. Tell them how good and able I am." His father refused, replying, "I shall not say a word to them." "Why, Father," his son asked, "have I done something wrong?" Then Rabbi Okybia replied: "No, my son, but your deeds will bind them to you or estrange them from you."

No one is given the delights of the world-to-come because of his father's virtues.

Our Sages remind us that he who loves his neighbors, gives charity in the hour of their need, studies Torah and performs good deeds humbly, to him the Lord promised: "He shall call and I will answer." Of that man too the Lord said: "I am with the contrite and humble spirit."

וְגַלְתִּי בִירוּשָׁלִַם וְשַׂשְׂתִּי בְעַמִּי, וְלֹא יִשָּׁמַע בָּהּ עוֹד קוֹל בְּכִי וְקוֹל זְעָקָה.

old. He who will die short of a hundred years shall be deemed accursed. They shall build houses and inhabit them. They shall plant vineyards and eat the fruit of them. They shall not build and another inhabit, nor shall they plant and another eat. For as the days of a tree so shall be the days of My people, and My chosen ones shall enjoy the work of their hands.

The wolf and the lamb shall feed together, and the lion shall eat straw like an ox. They shall not hurt nor destroy on My holy mountain, says the Lord.

For brass I will bring gold and for iron I will bring silver, and for wood brass and for stones iron. I will also make your officers peace, and righteousness your magistrates. Violence shall no more be heard in thy land, desolation nor destruction within your borders. But you shall call your walls Salvation and your gates Praise.

The sun shall no more go down, [19] neither shall your moon withdraw itself. For the Lord shall be your everlasting light and the days of your mourning shall be ended.

❧ [19] THE SUN SHALL NO MORE GO DOWN: Rabbi Simeon ben Lakish said: "In the time to come there will be no Gehenna. God will take the sun out of its orbit and its heat will heal the righteous and consume the wicked."

לֹא יָבוֹא עוֹד שִׁמְשֵׁךְ וִירֵחֵךְ לֹא יֵאָסֵף, כִּי יְיָ יִהְיֶה לָּךְ לְאוֹר עוֹלָם וְשָׁלְמוּ יְמֵי אֶבְלֵךְ.

6. JEREMIAH [1–16] II KINGS [22, 23]

THE PROPHET'S MISSION

THE WORDS OF JEREMIAH, [1] the son of Helkiah, of the priests that were in Anathoth in the land of Benjamin. The word of the Lord came to him in the days of Josiah, king of Judah, in the thirteenth year of his reign. It also came in the days of Jehoiakim, the son of Josiah, the king of Judah. It continued to come to him until the end of the eleventh year of Zedekiah, the son of Josiah, king of Judah, when Jerusalem was carried into exile in the fifth month.

The word of the Lord came to me, saying: "Before you were born I sanctified you and appointed you a prophet to

[1] JEREMIAH: The name means "The Lord hurls," or "The Lord founds," or "the appointed of the Lord."

[handwritten notes:] didn't want to be prophet – no did – chosen before birth, thought wasnt good enough, tell – true prophet from false, people wont like you

Jer went to Egypt, tells people that God really likes them.

Babolonia conquer them (from north), some people moved south (Yemen)

וּבְטֶרֶם תֵּצֵא מֵרֶחֶם הִקְדַּשְׁתִּיךָ, נָבִיא לַגּוֹיִם נְתַתִּיךָ.

the nations." [2] Then I said: "Woe, Lord God, I cannot speak for I am so young." The Lord said to me: "Do not say 'I am so young' [3] for I am sending you. Therefore, to whomsoever I shall send you, you shall go, and whatsoever I shall command you, you shall speak. Be not afraid of them for I am with you to deliver you." Then the Lord stretched out His hand and touched my mouth [4] and said to me: "Behold, I have put My word in your mouth. See, this day I have set you over the nations and the kingdoms to uproot and pull down, to destroy and overthrow, to build and to plant."

The word of the Lord came also to me, saying: "You shall not take yourself

---

⋐§ [2] TO THE NATIONS: *Jeremiah is appointed a prophet not only to the people of Israel but to all the peoples of the world.*

⋐§ [3] I AM SO YOUNG: Our Sages say that Jeremiah complained: "O Lord, was there any prophet who came to Your people who was not jeered by them? They even wanted to kill the prophet of prophets, Moses. As it is written: 'But all the congregation bade stone them with stones' (Numbers 14:10). When Elijah came to them, they mocked him by calling him 'the hairy one' (II Kings 1:8). Elisha they nicknamed 'baldhead' (II Kings 2:23). The prophet Amos, who hesitated in his speech, they derided as 'the stammerer.' And I am so young, O Lord, without experience, and not wise in the ways of the world. Lay not so heavy a burden upon me."

Then the Lord replied: "Because you are young have I chosen you. In your youthful innocence and naiveté you will dare and be bold in action. I love youth. As it is written: 'When Israel was young, then I loved him' (Hosea 11:1). Because you are young I have chosen you for this difficult task."

⋐§ [4] TOUCHED MY MOUTH: *Henceforth Jeremiah will speak with a tongue imbued with the poetry of God's words and intentions.*

רְאֵה, הִפְקַדְתִּיךָ הַיּוֹם הַזֶּה עַל הַגּוֹיִם וְעַל הַמַּמְלָכוֹת לִנְתוֹשׁ וְלִנְתוֹץ וּלְהַאֲבִיד וְלַהֲרוֹס, לִבְנוֹת וְלִנְטוֹעַ.

a wife, [5] neither shall you have sons or daughters in this place." For thus says the Lord concerning the sons and daughters born in this place, and concerning their mothers that bore them, and concerning their fathers that begot them in this land: They shall die grievous deaths; they shall not be lamented, neither shall they be buried; they shall be as dung upon the face of the ground; and they shall be consumed by the sword, and by famine; and their carcasses shall be meat for the fowls of heaven, and for the beasts of the earth.

Enter not into the house of mourning, neither go to lament, neither bemoan them; for I have taken away My peace from this people, says the Lord, even mercy and compassion. Both the great and the small shall die in this land; they shall not be buried; neither shall men lament for them; neither shall men break bread for them in mourning, to comfort them for the dead; neither shall men give them the cup of consolation to drink for their father or for their mother. And you shall not go into the house of feasting to sit with them, to eat and to drink.

THE ALMOND TWIG

THEN THE WORD OF THE LORD came to me, saying: "What do you see, Jeremiah?" And I said: "I see the twig of an almond tree." And the Lord said to me: "You have seen well, for I am wakeful [6] upon My word and hasten to perform it."

And the word of the Lord came to me again: "What do you see?" I said: "I see a seething cauldron and the seething began

---

⋙ [5] YOU SHALL NOT TAKE YOURSELF A WIFE: *For those who wish to change society, for those who wish to be moral exemplars, saints and prophets, having a wife and family, friends and acquaintances, can be a great burden and make more difficult the sacrifices a prophet must make.*

⋙ [6] I AM WAKEFUL: *The Hebrew here is a pun.* Shoked *means alert, watchful, quick, or hasten; while* shaked *means almond tree. The almond tree in Israel is the first to blossom after winter is past. It awakens from the winter earlier than any other tree. So too will the Lord be quick to perform, hasten to carry out his word. The Lord promises that when there is the first blossom of moral*

הֵיטַבְתָּ לִרְאוֹת, כִּי שֹׁקֵד אֲנִי עַל דְּבָרִי לַעֲשֹׂתוֹ.

from the north." The Lord said: "Out of the north calamity shall break forth upon all the inhabitants of the land. I will call all the families of all the kingdoms of the north and they shall come and each shall set his throne at the entrance of the gates of Jerusalem and against the walls all around and against all the cities of Judah. I will pronounce My judgment against them for all their wickedness; because they have forsaken Me and have offered sacrifices to other gods and worshiped the works of their hands. Therefore, gird up your loins and arise, and speak to them all that I command you. Do not be dismayed before them, for I made you a fortified city, an iron pillar, a brazen wall against the whole land, against the kings of Judah, against the princes, against the priests and against the people of the land. They shall fight against you, but they shall not overcome you, for I am with you to deliver you."

ISRAEL ASSAYED

THE WORD OF THE LORD came to me, saying: "Go and cry in the ears of Jerusalem, [7] saying: 'Thus said the Lord: I remember the affections of your youth, the love of your bridal days, how you followed me in the wilderness in a land

---

and spiritual rebirth, He will recognize it and hasten to fulfill His promises to the people of Israel.

[7] IN THE EARS OF JERUSALEM: Why do the prophets so often appeal to men's ears? "Go cry in the ears of Jerusalem." "Hear you the word of the Lord." Isaiah says: "Incline your ears and come to me. Hear and your soul shall live" (Isaiah 55:3). How can man, by hearing, make his soul live?

Our Rabbis explain that when the human being is soiled by sin, the ear hears the castigation, the man becomes aware of his sin and repents, and then the whole body acquires a new life. The best way to communicate is by speech; if the ear will hear, the whole body will live.

It is through speech that men communicate the sense of sin and virtue, acceptance and repentance. It is speech, the voice and the ear, that differentiates men from other animals.

זָכַרְתִּי לָךְ חֶסֶד נְעוּרַיִךְ, אַהֲבַת כְּלוּלֹתָיִךְ, לֶכְתֵּךְ אַחֲרַי בַּמִּדְבָּר, בְּאֶרֶץ לֹא זְרוּעָה.

[handwritten margin notes:]
Israel special to God.
Israel was Gods first child
1st fruit - wait 3yrs.
Maaser - 10th of the
sacrifices - no more
no more Temple
let food full not aloud to eat
it belongs to God
love you more if you were good

unsown. Israel was the Lord's sacred portion, [8] the first-fruits of the harvest. Whoever devours him is guilty, and evil shall come upon him.'"

Now, thus said the Lord: "What did your fathers find wrong with Me that they have removed themselves so far from Me? They have followed nought and become nought. They asked not: 'Where is the Lord that brought us up from the land of Egypt, who led us through the wilderness, through a land of deserts and pits, through a land of drought and of the shadow of death, through a land that no man passed through and where no man dwelt.'

"I brought you to a land of fertile fields, to eat its fruits and good things. But you came and defiled My land and made My heritage an abomination. Therefore will I contend against you, against your children's children will I contend. My people have committed two evils: They have forsaken Me, the fountain of living waters, to hew for themselves broken cisterns that cannot hold water. Your own wickedness [9] will punish you and your own unruliness

---

᠁ [8] THE LORD'S SACRED PORTION: Why, on one hand, does Jeremiah castigate Judah, prophesying calamity, and on the other declare that "Israel is the Lord's sacred portion... Whoever devours him is guilty and evil shall come upon him"? The Rabbis explain with a parable: A king once married a woman whom he continually praised. When friends visited her, they saw her unkempt and her living quarters in disorder, so they said: "Even now when you are so slovenly, in such disarray, even sordid, your husband still adores and praises you before everyone. Think how much more he would love and admire and praise you if you were neat and clean and orderly."

So it was with Jeremiah's generation. The prophet told the people that the Lord still remembered the affection of their youth, of their bridal days, saying: "If you heard and obeyed me, then the Lord's bounty to you would be limitless because of His great love for you."

᠁ [9] YOUR OWN WICKEDNESS: Rabbi Eliezer said: "The righteous are judged by their good inclination (*yetzer tov*), the wicked by their evil

קֹדֶשׁ יִשְׂרָאֵל לַיְיָ, רֵאשִׁית תְּבוּאָתֹה, כָּל אֹכְלָיו יֶאְשָׁמוּ.

reprove you. You will know and see
how evil and bitter a thing it is that you
have forsaken the Lord, [10] your God.
Upon the hem of your garments is the
blood of the souls of the innocent. Yet
you say I am innocent, His anger has
turned away from me. I will judge you
for saying: 'I have not sinned.' [11]

---

inclination *(yetzer hara).*" In man the evil impulse will judge the man
itself. Rabbenu Bachya explains that when a man seeks only pleasure
he cannot really enjoy it, because pleasure becomes its own law which
he is forced to obey and so pleasure itself becomes a burden to him. In
that way his own sins come, in time, to punish him. The Gaon of Vilna
comments further: "The man who devotes himself to worldly pleasure
alone is like one who drinks salt water to quench his thirst; the more
he drinks, the thirstier he becomes."

[10] FORSAKEN THE LORD: A prince always accompanied his father the
king everywhere, and was respected and honored by the people. One
day the prince abandoned his father and went out into the world.
There he was insulted and abused by the people who did not know he
was a prince. When he returned to the palace, he complained to his
father that the people had shown him neither respect nor honor. The
king then told him: "By abandoning me, you were no longer known
as a prince. You behaved like a common man and therefore you were
treated no better."

So it is with Israel. When Israel walks in the way of the Lord, the
nations of the world consider it chosen and are in awe of it. When
Israel transgresses and abandons its King, then nations lose their respect
and their awe of Israel.

[11] I HAVE NOT SINNED: Rabbi Shmuel, son of Rav, said: "The Lord
punishes man for sin only when man insists that he committed no sin."
But Rabbi Chanina objected: "Whoever says the Lord is indulgent
and does not punish sinners is a fool. The Lord is gracious and long-

הִנְנִי נִשְׁפָּט אוֹתָךְ עַל אָמְרֵךְ לֹא חָטָאתִי.

"I made you an assayer among My people. You shall assay and you shall find out their ways. All of them are hardened rebels, going about with slanders. They are brass and iron. All of them are corrupted. The bellows blows fiercely, the lead is consumed by the fire. But in vain does the founder refine, for the dross is not separated." Rejected silver they call them, because the Lord has rejected them.

EVIL FROM THE NORTH

"TELL IT IN JUDAH and let it be known in Jerusalem, and say: Blow the *shofar* through the land, cry aloud and say: Gather and let us go into the fortified cities. Raise up a standard toward Zion; assemble in a safe place; do not tarry; for I will bring evil from the north, a great destruction. A lion has come up from his thicket and a destroyer of nations has set out, gone forth from his place to make your land a desolation, so that your cities be laid waste, left without inhabitants. For this, gird on a sackcloth, lament and wail, for the fierce

anger of the Lord has not turned away from us.

"See, he comes up like a cloud and his chariots are as the whirlwind; his horses are swifter than eagles. Woe to us for we are devastated. O Jerusalem, wash wickedness from your heart that you may be saved. How long shall your evil thoughts lodge within you? For hear, a voice calls out from Dan and a calamity is proclaimed from the hills of Ephraim. Make it known to the nations, announce it to Jerusalem: Besiegers are coming from a distant land and their voices are raised against the cities of Judah. Like keepers of a field they ring her about. Your way, and your doings brought these things upon you. This is the fruit of your wickedness. It is bitter and it pierces your heart."

Thus said the Lord: "Behold, a people comes from the north, a mighty nation shall be stirred up from the uttermost parts of the earth. They are armed with bow and spear. They are cruel and have no compassion. Their voice is the roaring of the sea. They ride upon horses arrayed as men for war against you, O daughter

---

suffering, he waits patiently for sinners to repent, but eventually he punishes those who do not."

בָּחוֹן נְתַתִּיךָ בְעַמִּי, מִבְצָר. וְתֵדַע וּבָחַנְתָּ אֶת דַּרְכָּם.

of Zion." When we only heard of them, our hands waxed feeble; anguish took hold of us and pain as a woman in travail. "Go not in the field nor walk in the road, for there is the sword of the enemy and terror on every side. O daughter of My people, gird on sackcloth, wallow in ashes, and mourn as for an only son, most bitter lamentation, for the spoiler shall come suddenly upon us."

THE ANGUISHED OUTCRY

MY INNARDS! My innards! O the walls of my heart! My heart moans within me. I cannot keep silent because I heard the sound of the *shofar*, the alarm of war. Calamity follows calamity, the whole country is despoiled. Suddenly my tents are utterly destroyed. [12] In an instant the curtains of my tent are ruined. How long shall I see my standard, shall I hear the sound of the *shofar*? It is because My people are foolish; they know Me not. They are stupid children and have no understanding. They are wise to do evil, but ignorant to do good.

I looked at the earth and it was waste and void; and the heavens had no light. I looked at the mountains, and they trembled and all the hills swayed. I looked and there was no man and all the birds of heaven had fled. I looked and the fruitful field was a wilderness and all the cities were rubble because of His fierce anger. But, thus said the Lord: "The whole land shall be desolated, yet will I not make a full end."

I try to overcome my sorrow, but my heart aches within me. Behold the cry of the daughter of my people from a far off land: "Is not the Lord in Zion? Is not her King in her?"—"Why have they angered Me with their graven images and with foreign vanities?"—"The harvest is past, the summer is ended, and we are not saved."

⋖§ [12] MY TENTS ARE UTTERLY DESTROYED: Rabbi Elijah remarks that as tents collapse when the pegs are removed, so by having its scholars murdered the tent of Israel was destroyed. None remained to teach the people the Law what was permitted and forbidden, so Israel ceased to be a holy community.

The cornerstone of a society is its laws and ethical precepts; without them the entire edifice of the society collapses.

מֵעַי מֵעַי אוֹחִילָה, קִירוֹת לִבִּי הוֹמֶה לִי לִבִּי, לֹא אַחֲרִישׁ.

[handwritten annotation: punish people who dont know you]

[handwritten annotation: punish babylonians]

NO BALM IN GILEAD

The calamity which overtook my
people broke my heart;
Gloom and desolation have envel-
oped me.
Is there no balm in Gilead?
Is there no physician there?
Why is there no recovery for
  my people?
I would that my head turned into
  water,
And my eyes into a fountain of tears
That I might weep day and night
  for the slain of my people.
Woe is me for my hurt!
How grievous is my wound!
I thought this but a sickness
Which I could bear,
But my tent is cut down
And all its cords are broken;
My children are gone from me,
And they are no more;
There is none to pitch my tent
  again,
And to spread my tent flaps,
For the shepherds are become brut-
ish,
And have not inquired of the Lord.
O Lord, I know that a man's way is
  not his own;
It is not [always] in man's power to

direct his steps as he walks.
O Lord, punish me, but in judgment,
Not in anger, lest Thou bring me to
  nothing.
Pour out Thy wrath upon the na-
  tions that know Thee not, *[handwritten: Passover seder]*
And upon the families that invoke
  not Thy name;
For they have devoured Jacob,
They have consumed him,
And have made his habitation des-
  olate.

JOSIAH AND THE SCROLL

[handwritten annotation: honest King who was he?]

JOSIAH WAS eight years old when he began to reign, and he reigned thirty-one
years in Jerusalem. He did right in the
eyes of the Lord, and walked in the way
of David.

In the eighteenth year of King Josiah,
the king sent Shaphan, the scribe, to the
House of the Lord saying: "Go to Hilkiah, the High Priest, and see that he
shall take money which the keepers of
the doors have gathered from the people
and deliver it into the hands of the work-
ers who have supervision of the House
of the Lord, that they may hire the car-
penters, the builders, and the masons, to
make repairs on the House."

Now when they brought out the money that had been taken to the House of

הַצֳרִי אֵין בְּגִלְעָד אִם רוֹפֵא אֵין שָׁם, כִּי מַדּוּעַ לֹא עָלְתָה אֲרוּכַת בַּת עַמִּי?

the Lord, Hilkiah, the priest, found a scroll of the Torah of the Lord given to Moses.

Then Hilkiah said to Shaphan, the scribe: "I have found the scroll of the Torah in the House of the Lord." Then Shaphan carried the scroll to the king, and said: "Hilkiah, the priest, has given me a scroll." Then Shaphan read it before the king.

And the king commanded Hilkiah, the priest, and Shaphan, the scribe: "Go inquire of the Lord for me and for all Judah concerning the words of this book that is found; for great is the anger of the Lord against us, because our fathers have not hearkened to the words of this scroll, to do all in it that is written concerning us."

So Hilkiah and Shaphan went to Huldah, the prophetess, the wife of Shallum, the son of Tikvah. And she said to them: "Thus says the Lord: Tell the man that sent you to me: Behold, I will bring evil upon this place because they have forsaken Me, and have sacrificed to other gods. My wrath shall be kindled against this place, and it shall not be quenched. But to the king of Judah who sent you to inquire of the Lord, say to him: The Lord, God of Israel, says: Because your heart was tender and you did humble

yourself before the Lord when you heard what I spoke against this place and its people, that they should become an astonishment and a curse, and have rent your clothes and wept before Me, I have also heard you. Therefore, I will gather you to your fathers in peace, neither shall your eyes see all the evil which I will bring upon this place." And they brought back word to the king.

A COVENANT BEFORE THE LORD

THEN THE KING gathered all the elders of Judah and Jerusalem. The king went up to the House of the Lord, together with all the men of Judah, and all the priests and prophets, and all the people small and great, and he read in their hearing all the words of the scroll of the covenant which was found in the House of the Lord.

Then the king stood on a platform, and made a covenant before the Lord, to follow the Lord and keep His commands, His decrees and His statutes, with all his heart, and with all his soul, and to confirm the words of the covenant that were written in this scroll. And all the people accepted the covenant, and did according to the covenant of the God of their fathers.

לְכוּ דִרְשׁוּ אֶת יְיָ בַּעֲדִי וּבְעַד הָעָם וּבְעַד כָּל יְהוּדָה עַל דִּבְרֵי הַסֵּפֶר הַנִּמְצָא הַזֶּה.

JOSIAH'S REFORMS

THEN THE KING commanded the priests
to bring out of the Temple of the Lord
all the vessels which were made for the
Baal and the Asherah, and he burned
them outside Jerusalem, in the limekilns
at Kidron. He also did away with those
idolatrous priests whom the kings of
Judah had ordained to offer sacrifices to
the Baal, to the sun, to the moon, and
to all the host of heaven. He destroyed
the Topheth which was in the valley of
Ben-Hinnom, so that no man might
make his son or daughter pass through
the fire of Molech.

scroll in book of Deuteronomy

gentiles through children in fires

וְטִמֵּא אֶת הַתֹּפֶת אֲשֶׁר בְּגֵי בֶן־הִנֹּם, לְבִלְתִּי לְהַעֲבִיר אִישׁ אֶת בְּנוֹ וְאֶת בִּתּוֹ
בָּאֵשׁ לַמֹּלֶךְ.

7. JEREMIAH   [5–26] II CHRONICLES [35, 36] LAMENTATIONS [4]

JEREMIAH AND THE COVENANT

ALL JUDAH and Jerusalem mourned for Josiah. And Jeremiah lamented after him: "The breath of our nostrils, the anointed of the Lord, of whom we said, 'Under His shadow shall we live among the nations,' was trapped in their pit. But weep not for him that is dead, neither bemoan him."

Then the people took Jehoahaz, the son of Josiah, and made him king in his father's place. Jehoahaz was twenty-three years old when he began to rule; and he reigned three months in Jerusalem. Then [Necoh] the king of Egypt deposed him and fined the land a hundred talents of silver and a talent of gold. The king of Egypt made his brother Eliakim king over Judah and Jerusalem and changed his name to Jehoiakim. And Necoh took Jehoahaz, his brother, and carried him away to Egypt.

[And Jeremiah said:] "But weep bitterly for him that goes away, for he shall return no more. For thus said the Lord concerning Jehoahaz who went forth into exile: 'He shall not return here any more, but he shall die in the place to

רוּחַ אַפֵּינוּ, מְשִׁיחַ יְיָ, נִלְכַּד בִּשְׁחִיתוֹתָם, אֲשֶׁר אָמַרְנוּ בְּצִלּוֹ נִחְיֶה בַגּוֹיִם.

which they have taken him captive, and he shall see this land no more.'"

Jehoiakim was twenty-five years old when he began to reign. He reigned eleven years in Jerusalem and he did evil in the sight of the Lord.

The Lord said to me: "Proclaim all these words in the cities of Judah and in the streets of Jerusalem, saying: 'Hear the words of the covenant and do them.'" But they did not observe them.

The Lord said to me: "Treason is found among the men of Judah and among the inhabitants of Jerusalem. They have turned back [1] to the sins of their forefathers, who refused to hear My words; they have run after other gods to serve them. They have broken My covenant which I made with their fathers. Therefore will I bring disaster upon them which they shall not be able to escape. Though they shall cry to Me, I shall not listen to them.

And you! Do not pray for this people, [2] neither lift up a cry [3] on their behalf, because I will not listen to them when they cry to Me in time of their distress.

JERUSALEM CORRUPTED

SEE YOU NOT what they do in the cities of Judah and in the streets of Jerusalem? The children gather wood [4] and the fathers make the fire, and the women

---

◦§ [1] THEY HAVE TURNED BACK: The greatest sinner is he who regrets his former goodness.

◦§ [2] DO NOT PRAY FOR THIS PEOPLE: He who is compassionate when he should be severe ends by being severe when he should be compassionate.

◦§ [3] NEITHER LIFT UP A CRY: Have you done good to the evil? Then you have done evil.

◦§ [4] THE CHILDREN GATHER WOOD: *Everyone, men, women and children, take part in the rites of idolatry.*

וְאַתָּה אַל תִּתְפַּלֵּל בְּעַד הָעָם הַזֶּה, וְאַל תִּשָּׂא בַעֲדָם רִנָּה וּתְפִלָּה.

knead the dough, to make cakes to the queen of heaven, [5] and to pour out drink offerings to other gods, that they may provoke Me to anger. Do they provoke Me? said the Lord. Do they not provoke themselves to the confusion of their own faces? My anger and My fury [6] shall be poured out upon this place: upon man, upon beasts, upon the trees in the field and upon the fruit of the land; and it shall burn without being quenched.

Wander through the streets of Jerusalem, look and see, search her squares; if you can find a man, [7] if there is one who does justice and seeks truth, then I will forgive her. Even when they swear, "As the Lord lives," they swear falsely. O Lord, are not Your eyes looking for truth? You have stricken them, [8] but

---

⋗ [5] QUEEN OF HEAVEN: *Probably Ishtar, the goddess of Babylon, and also a reference to Babylonian astrology.*

⋗ [6] MY ANGER AND MY FURY: *God's moral indignation at Israel's sinfulness is so great that He will punish men, animals and land.*

⋗ [7] IF YOU CAN FIND A MAN: When the Lord saw that the sins of Sodom and Gomorrah had grown so heinous that the cities would have to be destroyed, lest they corrupt the rest of the world, He told Abraham of His intention so that the Patriarch might plead for them. When the Lord saw the great iniquity of Jerusalem which He had to punish, He told Jeremiah to search out even a single just man, because He wanted Jeremiah to be able to plead the cause of Jerusalem.

⋗ [8] YOU HAVE STRICKEN THEM: Maimonides points out that the man who remains unaware of wrongdoing, and does not consider repentance, cannot see or understand the great order of law in nature and society. People's belief that their troubles are mere accidents impels them to continue in their evil ideas and wicked behavior.

שׁוֹטְטוּ בְּחוּצוֹת יְרוּשָׁלַיִם וּרְאוּ־נָא וּדְעוּ, וּבַקְּשׁוּ בִרְחוֹבוֹתֶיהָ אִם תִּמְצְאוּ אִישׁ.

they were not affected. You almost destroyed them, but they did not heed the warning. They made their faces harder than rock, and have refused to repent.

I said: "They are poor people, [9] they are foolish, and they know not the ways of the Lord, nor the ordinances of their God. I will go to the great ones [10] and speak to them, for they know the ways of the Lord, and the ordinances of their God." But they too have broken the yoke and burst the bonds. [11] They pry, as fowlers lie in wait; they set a trap, they catch men. As a cage is full of birds, so are their houses full of deceit, therefore they became great and rich. They grew fat and sleek, they overstepped all bounds of wickedness. [12] They did not plead the cause of the fatherless and did not defend the rights of the needy. Shall I not punish them for these things, said the Lord; shall not My soul be avenged on such a nation as this?

◦§ [9] THEY ARE POOR PEOPLE: *Jeremiah pleads that poverty and ignorance have made the people sin.*

◦§ [10] TO THE GREAT ONES: Rabbi Johanan ben Zakkai said: "Happy is that generation whose leaders bring atonement for its unintended sins. If the leader does so, the common man will surely do likewise. And if they atone for their unintended sins, how much more readily will they repent for their deliberate transgressions."

◦§ [11] BURST THE BONDS: *The people have thrown off the restraints of religion and morality; the yoke of Torah is broken and the bonds of God's commandments.*

◦§ [12] BOUNDS OF WICKEDNESS: Rabbi Johanan ben Nuri said: "The art of the evil inclination *(yetzer hara)* is that today it says to man: Do this! and the next day, Do that! until at last it commands: Worship other gods! And then man obeys and does that."

כִּכְלוּב מָלֵא עוֹף כֵּן בָּתֵּיהֶם מְלֵאִים מִרְמָה.

THE FIERCE ENEMY

THE HOUSE OF ISRAEL and the house of Judah committed treason against Me, says the Lord. They have denied the Lord and said: "It is not from Him that comes evil [or good], neither shall we see sword or famine. And the prophets are mere wind, no true word is in them. As they have spoken to us, so let it be done to them." Therefore, says the Lord, God of the host, because they have spoken this word, I will make My word in your mouth fire and this people wood, and it shall devour them.

O house of Israel, said the Lord, I shall bring upon you a nation from afar, a mighty nation, an ancient nation, a nation whose language you do not know, so you will not understand what they say. Their quiver is an open grave, they are all mighty warriors. They shall eat up your harvest and your bread; they shall eat up your sons [13] and daughters; they shall eat up your flocks and your herds; they shall eat up your vines and your fig-trees. They shall batter down your fortified cities in which you trust. But even in those days I shall not destroy you completely.

When men shall ask you, "Why is it that the Lord, our God, does all these things to us?" you shall say to them: "Thus said the Lord: As you have forsaken Me and served strange gods in your land, so shall you serve strangers in a land that is not yours."

THE TEMPLE SHALL BE DESTROYED

THE WORD that came to Jeremiah from the Lord, saying: "Stand in the gate of the Lord's house and proclaim there this word: Hear the word of the Lord, all you men of Judah, who enter this gate

---

⤙ [13] THEY SHALL EAT UP YOUR SONS: Our Sages ask what the relationship is between eating up the harvest and bread, and eating up sons and daughters. Rabbi Jonathan explains: "If a man deprives another man of his property, he is in a sense depriving him of his life."

In taking another man's food, clothing, shelter and means of livelihood away, one may not only kill him, but kill his children as well.

הִנְנִי נֹתֵן דְּבָרַי בְּפִיךָ לְאֵשׁ וְהָעָם הַזֶּה עֵצִים וַאֲכָלָתַם.

to worship the Lord. Thus said the Lord of the host, the God of Israel:

Amend your ways and your doings and I will let you dwell in this land. Trust not in such lying words as: "The temple of the Lord, the temple of the Lord, the temple of the Lord." [14] These are deceptive words. If you will thoroughly amend your ways and your doings, if you see justice done between a man and his neighbor, if you oppress not the stranger, the fatherless and the widow, and shed no innocent blood in this land, and do not follow other gods to your own injury, [15] then will I let you dwell in this place, in the land I gave to your fathers, forever and ever. But you trust in lying words which are of no value.

Will you steal, murder, commit all kinds of sin, swear falsely, and sacrifice to Baal, and follow after gods whom you know not? Then you come and stand before Me in this house which bears My name and say: "We are safe, safe to do all these abominations." Is this house which bears My name become a den of thieves in your eyes? Go now to My place which was in Shiloh, [16] where first I caused My name to dwell and see what I did to it, because of the wickedness of My people Israel. Now, because you did the same deeds, I spoke to you again, and you did not listen. I called, but you did not answer. Therefore, will I do to this house which bears My name, in which you trust, and to the land which

---

  [14] THE TEMPLE OF THE LORD: *Unless the people mend their ways, cease to sin and begin to do justice, the presence of the Temple among them will not save them from destruction and disaster. They will be punished and driven from the land.*

  [15] TO YOUR OWN INJURY: *To follow false gods is to follow false values; to live by those false values is to do yourself irreparable injury.*

  [16] SHILOH: *Once before, when Israel transgressed, the Lord had destroyed His sanctuary at Shiloh. If Israel continues to make the Lord's house a den of thieves, He will not hesitate to destroy the Temple.*

הֵיטִיבוּ דַרְכֵיכֶם וּמַעַלְלֵיכֶם וַאֲשַׁכְּנָה אֶתְכֶם בַּמָּקוֹם הַזֶּה.

I gave to you and to your fathers, as I have done to Shiloh. [17] I will cast you out of My sight as I have cast out your brethren, the children of Ephraim.

FALSE PROPHETS

BOTH PROPHET AND PRIEST [18] are ungodly. Yes, in My house, have I found their wickedness, says the Lord. And I have seen unseemliness in the prophets of Samaria: They prophesied by Baal and caused My people Israel to err. But in the prophets of Jerusalem I have seen a horrible thing: They commit adultery and walk in lies and they strengthen the hands of evil-doers, so that none returns from his wickedness. From the prophets of Jerusalem ungodliness is gone forth into all the land.

I have not sent these prophets, yet they ran; I have not spoken to them, yet they prophesied. But if they have stood in My council, then let them cause My people to hear My words, and turn them from their evil ways and from the evil of their doings.

GOOD DEEDS NOT SACRIFICES

HEAR, O EARTH, I will bring a calamity upon this people, the fruit of their own scheming, [19] because they have not given heed to My words and have rejected My teaching. Of what value to Me is the frankincense that comes from Sheba, and the sweet cane from a far country? I do not desire your burnt-offerings, [20] and your sacrifices are not pleasing to Me.

✑ [17] AS I HAVE DONE TO SHILOH: From the day the Temple was destroyed, God knows no laughter.

✑ [18] BOTH PROPHET AND PRIEST: *False prophets and corrupt priests have led the people astray and have themselves set evil examples.*

✑ [19] THE FRUIT OF THEIR OWN SCHEMING: *Calamity will come to Israel as the result of its own sins, its failure to walk in the ways of the Lord amd His Torah.*

✑ [20] YOUR BURNT-OFFERINGS: He who practices charity is more virtuous than all the sacrifices.

לֹא שָׁלַחְתִּי אֶת הַנְּבִיאִים וְהֵם רָצוּ, לֹא דִבַּרְתִּי אֲלֵיהֶם וְהֵם נִבָּאוּ.

For on the day I brought your fathers out of the land of Egypt, I did not speak to them, nor commanded them, about burnt-offerings or sacrifices. But this I commanded them, saying: "Listen to My voice and I will be Your God and you shall be My people. You walk in all the ways I command you that it may be well with you."

For the children of Judah have done that which is evil in My sight, said the Lord; they have set their detestable things in the house whereon My name is called, to defile it. And they have built the high places of Topheth, which is in the valley of the son of Hinnom, to burn their sons [21] and their daughters in the fire; which I commanded not, neither came it into My mind. Therefore, behold, the days come when it shall be no longer called Topheth, but the valley of slaughter; for they shall bury in Topheth for lack of room. And the carcasses of this people shall be food for the fowls of the heaven, and for the beasts of the earth; and none shall frighten them away. Then will I cause to cease from the cities of Judah and from the streets of Jerusalem the voice of mirth and the voice of gladness, the voice of the bridegroom and the voice of the bride; and and the land shall be desolate.

❧ [21] TO BURN THEIR SONS: The citizens of Jerusalem taunted Jeremiah by saying: "Did not the Lord command the Patriarch Abraham to sacrifice his beloved son Isaac as a burnt-offering? (Genesis 22:2) Did not Jephthah vow to give as a burnt-offering the first thing that came out of his house to greet him, and then sacrifice his only daughter to the Lord? (Judges 11:31, 39) Did not Mesha, king of Moab, sacrifice his eldest son for a burnt-offering on the walls of his city?" (II Kings 3:27).

To which the prophet replied: "The Lord never commanded Jephthah to sacrifice his daughter. He never spoke to the pagan king of Moab. Nor did it come to His mind that Abraham should sacrifice Isaac. The Lord wished only to test Abraham."

The Lord tested Abraham and Isaac in the akedah *specifically to warn Israel against child sacrifice and to prohibit it. Child sacrifice was one of the "ways of the nations" against which the prophets warned most vehemently.*

שִׁמְעוּ בְקוֹלִי וְהָיִיתִי לָכֶם לֵאלֹהִים וְאַתֶּם תִּהְיוּ לִי לְעָם.

THE EARTHEN FLASK

THUS SAID THE LORD to Jeremiah: "Go and buy a potter's earthen flask and take with you the elders of the people and the elders of the priests. Then go out to the valley of Ben-Hinnom and you shall say: Hear the words of the Lord, [22] O king of Judah, and inhabitants of Jerusalem. I will bring disaster on this place that whoever hears it, his ears shall ring, because you have forsaken Me and have desecrated this place and offered sacrifices to other gods and filled this place with the blood of the innocent.

"Then you [Jeremiah] shall break the flask in the sight of the men that went with you, and you shall say to them: 'Thus said the Lord of the host: As one breaks an earthen vessel that cannot be made whole again, so will I break this people and this city.'"

When Jeremiah came from Topheth where the Lord had sent him, he stood in the court of the Lord's house and said to all the people: "Thus said the Lord, the God of Israel: I will bring upon this city and all the towns [around it] the great calamity that I have pronounced against them because the people have made their necks stiff that they might not listen to My words."

Now when Pashhur the priest, the son of Immer, who was the chief officer in the house of the Lord, heard Jeremiah prophesying these things, Pashhur struck Jeremiah the prophet and put him into the stocks. Then Jeremiah said: "Thus said the Lord: I will make you a terror to yourself and to all your friends. They shall fall by the sword of their enemies, and you shall see them fall. I will also give all Judah into the hand of the king of Babylon, and he shall carry them captive to Babylon or shall slay them. And you, Pashhur, and all your household, shall go into exile. You shall be brought to Babylon and there you shall die and there you shall be buried, you and all your friends to whom you have prophesied falsely."

THE TRIAL

IN THE BEGINNING of the reign of Jehoiakim, the son of Josiah, king of Judah came the word of the Lord [to Jere-

---

⋘ [22] HEAR THE WORDS OF THE LORD: God does not punish unless He first gives warning.

כָּכָה אֶשְׁבֹּר אֶת הָעָם הַזֶּה וְאֶת הָעִיר הַזֹּאת, כַּאֲשֶׁר יִשְׁבֹּר אֶת כְּלִי הַיּוֹצֵר אֲשֶׁר לֹא יוּכַל לְהֵרָפֵה עוֹד.

miah], saying: "[Now] stand in the court of the Lord's house and speak to all the people of Judah who come to worship in the house of the Lord, all that I commanded you to speak to them, do not keep back a single word."

When Jeremiah had finished speaking all the Lord had commanded him to speak, the priests and the [false] prophets laid hold of him and said: "You shall surely die. How dare you prophesy in the name of the Lord that his house shall become like Shiloh and this city desolate, without an inhabitant?"

When the princes of Judah heard this, they came up from the king's house to the house of the Lord and sat in the entrance of the new gate of the Lord's house. Then the priests and the [false] prophets spoke to the princes and to all the people, saying: "This man deserves death, for he has prophesied against this city, as the people have heard with their own ears."

Then Jeremiah said to all the princes and to all the people: "The Lord sent me to prophesy against this house and against this city, all the words that you have heard. Therefore, now, amend your ways and your doings, and heed the voice of the Lord, your God; then the Lord will repent [23] of the evil which He has pronounced against you. As for me, I am in your hands; do with me whatever you think is right and proper. Only you should know that, if you put me to death, you will bring innocent blood upon yourself and upon the city, for in truth the Lord has sent me to speak all the words in your ears."

DEFENSE AND PROSECUTION

THEN SOME OF THE ELDERS of the land rose up and spoke to all the assembly, saying: "Micah, the Morashtite, prophesied in the days of Hezekiah, king of Judah, and he [also] said: 'Zion shall be plowed like a field and Jerusalem shall become a heap of ruins, and the mountains of the house of the Lord a high place in the forest.' Did Hezekiah, king of Judah, put him to death? He feared the Lord and entreated Him, and the Lord repented of the evil which He pronounced against them. This man does not deserve death because he has spoken to us in the name of the Lord our God."

⋙ [23] THE LORD WILL REPENT: Even in His anger the Lord remembers to send a share of His mercies.

אֵין לָאִישׁ הַזֶּה מִשְׁפַּט מָוֶת כִּי בְּשֵׁם יְיָ אֱלֹהֵינוּ דִּבֶּר אֵלֵינוּ.

[But the other elders said:] "There was another man who prophesied in the name of the Lord. Uriah, the son of Shemaiah, also prophesied against this city and against this land, just as Jeremiah has prophesied. Then Jehoiakim, the king, and all his valiant men, and all the princes heard it, and the king sought to put him to death. Uriah heard of it and fled to Egypt. But Jehoiakim, the king, sent men to Egypt and they fetched Uriah from Egypt and brought him before King Jehoiakim who had him slain with the sword and cast his dead body in a grave in the public burying ground."

But Ahikam, [24] the son of Shaphan, protected Jeremiah and saved him from those who wanted to put him to death.

---

[24] AHIKAM: *Ahikam was one of the men Josiah sent with the scroll to consult the prophetess Huldah when it was discovered in the wall of the Temple. Ahikam protected Jeremiah, as did his son Gedaliah, later governor of Judah under Babylon.*

אַךְ יַד אֲחִיקָם בֶּן שָׁפָן הָיְתָה אֶת יִרְמְיָהוּ לְבִלְתִּי תֵּת אוֹתוֹ בְיַד הָעָם לַהֲמִיתוֹ.

8. JEREMIAH [11-36]

A KING MUST BE RIGHTEOUS

THUS SAID THE LORD: "Go down to the house of the king of Judah and speak there these words, saying: 'Hear the word of the Lord, O King of Judah, who sits on the throne of David. You and your servants and the people who enter this gate. Thus said the Lord: Do justice [1] and righteousness, deliver the oppressed from the hand of the oppressor. Do no wrong, do no violence to the stranger, [2] the fatherless nor to the widow; neither shed innocent blood in this place. If you do these things, then

---

[1] DO JUSTICE: When mercy is not a part of justice, the world is overcome by hunger.

[2] TO THE STRANGER: *In ancient times strangers were the subject of hostility and suspicion, and this still remains true in many parts of the world. The Bible was especially concerned to protect the rights and privileges of strangers.*

עֲשׂוּ מִשְׁפָּט וּצְדָקָה וְהַצִּילוּ גָזוּל מִיַּד עָשׁוֹק.

shall there enter by the gate of this house kings sitting upon the throne of David, riding in chariots and on horses, he and his servants and his people. But if you do not heed these words, I swear by Myself, [3] says the Lord, that this house shall become desolation.'

"Woe to him [4] who builds his house by unrighteousness and his chamber by injustice, that makes his neighbor work without wages [5] and give him not his hire, that says, 'I shall build me a spacious house with roomy chambers, wide windows, paneled with cedar and painted with vermilion.' Would you play the king by vying with other kings in cedar? Your father ate and drank [6] and also did justice and righteousness. Then was it all well with him. He defended the poor and needy; it was well with him. Is this not to know me? [7] says the Lord. But your eyes and your heart are set on nothing but your covetousness, on shedding innocent blood, on oppression and on violence. Therefore said the Lord concerning Jehoiakim, the son of Josiah, king of Judah: They shall not lament for him. He shall be buried with the burial of a donkey, dragged and cast out beyond the gates of Jerusalem."

---

[3] SWEAR BY MYSELF: *This is the most awesome vow that may be sworn in Scripture. It is, in fact, a metaphor for God declaring His ethical nature and purpose.*

[4] WOE TO HIM: *Censure of King Jehoiakim.*

[5] WORK WITHOUT WAGES: *The prophets all condemned forced labor. Even the king was prohibited from requiring work without wages, though many of the kings violated the prohibition.*

[6] ATE AND DRANK: *Josiah concentrated on the ethical duties of a king, not on the material comforts and luxuries of monarchy.*

[7] IS THIS NOT TO KNOW ME: *The moral nucleus of Judaism: To do justice, to behave righteously, to protect the poor, is to know God.*

דָּן דִּין עָנִי וְאֶבְיוֹן, אָז טוֹב. הֲלֹא הִיא הַדַּעַת אוֹתִי, נְאֻם יְיָ.

THE BURNED SCROLL

IN THE FOURTH YEAR of Jehoiakim, the son of Josiah, king of Judah, this word came to Jeremiah from the Lord: "Take a scroll and write on it all the prophecies I have spoken to you against Israel, against Judah and against all the nations, from the first I spoke to you in the days of Josiah to this day. Perhaps when Judah will hear all the calamities which I propose to bring upon them, they may return from their evil ways [8] and I will forgive them their iniquity and their sins."

So Jeremiah called Baruch, the son of Neriah, and Baruch wrote upon a scroll from the mouth of Jeremiah all the prophecies which the Lord had spoken to him. Then Jeremiah said to Baruch: "I am forbidden from going into the house of the Lord. Therefore you go and read from the scroll the prophecies of the Lord to the people in the Lord's house who gather there upon a fast-day." Baruch did according to all that Jeremiah the prophet commanded him.

When Micaiah had heard all the words that Baruch read, he told it all to the princes who were in the scribe's chamber. Then they sent Jehudi, the son of Nethaniah, to Baruch, saying: "Take the scroll from which you read to the people and come to us." So Baruch took the scroll in his hand and came to them, and read it to them.

When they had heard it, they turned in fear to one another, and they asked: "Tell us, how did you write all this? [9] Baruch answered them: "He pronounced all these prophecies to me with his mouth and I wrote them with ink on the scroll." The princes said to Baruch: "Go and hide yourself, you and Jeremiah, and let no man know where you are. And we will tell the king these prophecies."

---

   [8] FROM THEIR EVIL WAYS: He who justifies himself below is justified above.

      Those who live righteously and perform deeds of lovingkindness in this world will need no other justification in the world to come.

   [9] HOW DID YOU WRITE ALL THIS: To discover if the scroll contained the words of God, the princes asked Baruch if he had transcribed Jeremiah's words exactly. Baruch told them that he had.

מִפִּיו יִקְרָא אֵלַי אֵת כָּל הַדְּבָרִים הָאֵלֶּה, וַאֲנִי כּוֹתֵב עַל הַסֵּפֶר בַּדְּיוֹ.

They deposited the scroll in the chamber of Elishama the scribe and they came to the king in the court and told him the whole matter. Then the king sent Jehudi to bring the scroll. Jehudi went and brought the scroll and read it before the king and all the princes.

Now the king was sitting in the winter-house because it was the ninth month of the year. [10] The fire of the brazier was burning before him. And when Jehudi had read three or four columns, the king would cut it off with a penknife and cast it into the fire [11] that was in the brazier until the whole scroll was consumed in the fire. Elnathan and De-laiah and Gemariah entreated the king not to burn the scroll, but he would not listen to them. And the king commanded that Baruch the scribe and Jeremiah the prophet be taken, but the Lord hid them.

THE PLOT AGAINST JEREMIAH

I WAS LIKE A DOCILE LAMB that is led to the slaughter. I knew not [12] that they plotted against me: "Let us put poison that kills into his food and let us cut him off from the land of the living that his name may be no more remembered." The men of Anathoth [13] that sought my

---

◄§ [10] THE NINTH MONTH: *About the same time as our month of December. This month was subsequently called Kislev in the Jewish calendar.*

◄§ [11] CAST IT INTO THE FIRE: When a great man says something which appears illogical, do not laugh at it. Instead, try to understand it.

◄§ [12] I KNEW NOT: A man who intends to do evil to others does not generally reveal his intention, but God discloses it.

◄§ [13] THE MEN OF ANATHOTH: Anathoth was a village of priests descended from Abiathar who had been expelled from the Temple by King Solomon. People considered the priests of Anathoth rejected, and only the poorest folk brought them their sacrifices. As a result they were so poor they often had to beg to live.

וְלֹא יָדַעְתִּי כִּי עָלַי חָשְׁבוּ מַחֲשָׁבוֹת: נַשְׁחִיתָה עֵץ בְּלַחְמוֹ וְנִכְרְתֶנּוּ מֵאֶרֶץ חַיִּים.

life said: "You shall not prophesy [14] in the name of the Lord lest you die by our hands." But, Lord of hosts who judges righteously, who tests the heart and the innermost thoughts and feelings: Let me see Your vengeance on them, for to You I have revealed my cause.

Then they said: "Come let us hatch a plot against Jeremiah; for instruction shall not perish [15] from the priest nor counsel from the wise nor prophecy from the prophet. Come, let us malign him [16] and let us pay no heed to his prophecies."

Give heed to me, O Lord, and listen to the voice of those that contend with me. Shall evil be repaid for good? They have dug a pit for my life. Remember how I stood before You to speak good for them, [17] to turn away Your wrath

---

When Josiah destroyed all the high places in Judah, the one at Anathoth was among them. Jeremiah's support of Josiah's reform earned him the enmity of his neighbors, not only because their shrine was desecrated but because they were thereby deprived of their meager livelihood.

ı§ [14] YOU SHALL NOT PROPHESY: *Tyrannies always try to suppress free speech, by threat of death, by slander, by entrapment, by any devious or dubious means at hand which seems to them effective.*

ı§ [15] FOR INSTRUCTION SHALL NOT PERISH: *The people thought they had no need of Jeremiah's prophecy, instruction or counsel; they considered themselves and their wise men sufficiently instructed and enlightened.*

ı§ [16] LET US MALIGN HIM: *God accepts repentance for all sins, except that of abusing another with a bad name.*

[17] SPEAK GOOD FOR THEM: *The ideal man has the strength of a male and the compassion of a female.*

Jeremiah had often, out of compassion, interceded for them with God.

לְכוּ וְנַחְשְׁבָה עַל יִרְמְיָהוּ מַחֲשָׁבוֹת, כִּי לֹא תֹאבַד תּוֹרָה מִכֹּהֵן וְעֵצָה מֵחָכָם וְדָבָר מִנָּבִיא.

from them. You, Lord, know all their schemes against me to kill me. Forgive not their iniquity and do not blot out their sins from Your sight. Deal with them in the time of Your anger.

MAN OF CONTENTION

O Lord, You have enticed me and I
   was enticed, [18]
You have overpowered me and
   have prevailed; [19]
I have become the laughingstock
   all the day long,
Everyone mocks me.
As often as I speak, I cry out,
I cry: 'Violence and spoil';

Because the word of the Lord is
   made
A reproach and a derision all the day
   long.
If I say: 'I will not make mention of
   His name,
Nor speak any more in His name,'
Then it is in my heart as if it were a
   burning fire
Shut up in my bones.
I weary myself to hold it in,
But I cannot endure it. [20]
For I have heard the whispering of
   many,
Terror on every side: [21]
'Denounce, [22] and we will de-
   nounce him';

---

[18] I WAS ENTICED: If a man merits it, he will serve; if not, he will be lost.

[19] AND HAVE PREVAILED: *Though Jeremiah was reluctant, the Lord prevailed on him to accept his prophetic mission.*

[20] I CANNOT ENDURE IT: *The prophet would as soon leave the words of his prophecy unsaid, but they burn inside him until he must speak them out.*

[21] TERROR ON EVERY SIDE: Better to be with those who are persecuted than with those who are the persecutors.

[22] DENOUNCE: He who secretly informs against his fellowman has no share of the world to come.

וְאָמַרְתִּי: לֹא אֶזְכְּרֶנּוּ וְלֹא אֲדַבֵּר עוֹד בִּשְׁמוֹ – וְהָיָה בְלִבִּי כְּאֵשׁ בּוֹעֶרֶת, עָצֻר בְּעַצְמוֹתָי.

Even of all my familiar friends,
Them that watch for my halting: [23]
'Perhaps he will be enticed [24] and
we shall prevail against him,
And we shall take our revenge on
him.'

PROPHET OF STRIFE

Cursed be the day wherein I was
born;
The day wherein my mother bore
me,
Let it not be blessed.
Why did He not let me die in the
womb,
So that my mother would have
been my grave?
Why did I come forth from the
womb
To see trouble and sorrow,
That my days should be consumed
in shame?

Woe is me, my mother, that you
bore me,
A man of strife and a man of con-
tention to the whole earth!
Right would You be, O Lord,
Were I to contend with You,
Yet will I reason with You:
Why does the way of the wicked
prosper?
Why are all those secure who deal
very treacherously?
You have planted them, yes, they
have taken root;
They grow, yes, they bring forth
fruit;
You are near in their mouth,
And far from their reins. [25]

THE LORD'S REPLY

Am I a God near at hand, says the
Lord,
And not a God afar off?
Can any hide himself in secret places

◦§ [23] FOR MY HALTING: *Watching for Jeremiah to make a misstep.*

◦§ [24] HE WILL BE ENTICED: *Hoping that Jeremiah will be provoked into rash
acts or intemperate outbursts, so they can be revenged on him.*

◦§ [25] FROM THEIR REINS: God created the evil impluse *(yetzer hara)*, but
also provided the Torah as its antidote.

אָרוּר הַיּוֹם אֲשֶׁר יֻלַּדְתִּי בּוֹ, יוֹם אֲשֶׁר יְלָדַתְנִי אִמִּי אַל יְהִי בָרוּךְ.

That I shall not see him?

The heart is deceitful above all things,

And it is exceeding weak—who can know it?

I, the Lord, search the heart,

I try the reins,

Even to give every man according to his ways,

According to the fruits of his doings.

Blessed is the man that trusts in the Lord,

And whose trust the Lord is.

For he shall be as a tree planted by the waters,

And that spreads out its roots by the river,

And shall not see when heat comes,

But its foliage shall be luxuriant;

And shall not be anxious in the years of drought,

Neither shall cease from yielding fruit.

THE HEART REJOICES

O Lord, remember me and think of me,

And avenge me of my persecutors;

Know that for Your sake I have suffered reproach.

I sat not in the company of them that made merry and rejoiced;

I sat alone [26] because of Your hand;

For You have filled me with indignation.

Why is my pain perpetual,

And my wound incurable, so that it refuses to be healed?

But when Your words were found, I ate them; [27]

And Your words were to me a joy and the rejoicing of my heart;

Because Your name was called upon me, O Lord of hosts.

---

[26] I SAT ALONE: *The prophet's spirit and mission set him apart from other people.*

[27] I ATE THEM: The prophet Ezekiel (2:9–10; 3:1–3) recounts the same experience: "And He said to me: 'Son of man, eat this scroll and go and speak to the house of Israel.' So I opened my mouth and I ate it; and it was in my mouth sweet as honey."

Though the life of the prophet may be bitter and his efforts thwarted, the words of the Lord and the consciousness of his mission are sweet and joyous.

בָּרוּךְ הַגֶּבֶר אֲשֶׁר יִבְטַח בַּיְיָ וְהָיָה יְיָ מִבְטַחוֹ.

DROUGHT AND FAMINE

THE WORD OF THE LORD came to Jeremiah concerning the drought. Judah mourns and her cities are ruined. They sit in black upon the ground and the wail from Jerusalem goes up [to heaven]. Their nobles send their servants for water. They come to the cisterns and find no water. They return with their vessels empty. They are ashamed and confounded, and cover their heads.

The tillers of the soil are dismayed because there is no rain in the land. The plowmen are abashed and cover their heads. The hind in the field calved and abandoned her young because there was no grass. The wild asses stood upon the high hills and gasped for air like crocodiles; their eyes grew tired and glazed from looking for grass because there was none.

Are there any among the vanities of the nations that can bring rain? Or can the heavens of themselves give showers? Is it not You, O Lord, our God, on whom we set our hope? For You have made all these things. O Lord, though our iniquities testify against us, do it for Your name's sake. For our backslidings are many. We have sinned against You. O, the hope of Israel, its Savior in times of trouble, why should You be as a stranger in the land, and like a wayfarer who turns aside to lodge for a night? Why should You be as an astonished man, like a mighty man that cannot save? Yet, You, O Lord, are in the midst of us, and Your name is called upon us; leave us not. [28]

THEY LOVE TO STRAY

THUS SAID THE LORD to this people: "They love to stray, [29] they have not

---

[28] LEAVE US NOT: If Israel repents out of the love of God, then Israel needs no cure; if Israel repents out of fear, then it must first be healed.

[29] THEY LOVE TO STRAY: *Because men are prompted by the evil impulse, because the way of the Torah is difficult if rewarding, they are often led to stray after false gods which are the work of their own hands and which do not require of them the effort and restraint, the justice and mercy, necessary to approach the "image of God" within them.*

מִקְוֵה יִשְׂרָאֵל, מוֹשִׁיעוֹ בְּעֵת צָרָה, לָמָּה תִהְיֶה כְּגֵר בָּאָרֶץ וּכְאוֹרֵחַ נָטָה לָלוּן?

restrained their feet. Therefore the Lord does not accept them. This time He will remember their guilt and punish their sin. And the Lord said to me: 'Though Moses and Samuel stood before Me, I would show no favor toward this people. Send them out of My sight and let them go. And it shall come to pass when they say to you: Whither shall we go forth? then you shall tell them: Thus said the Lord: Such as are for death, to death; and such as are for the sword, to the sword; and such as are for famine, to the famine; and such as are for captivity, to captivity.'

"Who shall have pity upon you, Jerusalem? Who shall bemoan you? Who shall turn aside to ask of your welfare? You have rejected Me. You have gone backward; therefore I stretch out My hand against you and destroy you. I am weary of relenting."

JEREMIAH BUYS A FIELD

AND JEREMIAH SAID: The word of the Lord came to me, saying, 'Behold, Hanamel, the son of Shallum your uncle, shall come to you saying: Buy my field that is in Anathoth; for the right of redemption is yours to buy it.' So Hanamel, my uncle's son, came to me in the court of the guard according to the word of the Lord. And I bought the field that was in Anathoth of Hanamel and weighed him the money, even seventeen shekels of silver. And I subscribed the deed and sealed it, and called witnesses, and weighed him the money in the balances. So I took the deed of the purchase, both that which was sealed, containing the terms and the conditions, and that which was open; and I delivered the deed of the purchase to Baruch the son of Neriah in

כִּי מִי יַחְמֹל עָלַיִךְ, יְרוּשָׁלַיִם, וּמִי יָנוּד לָךְ, וּמִי יָסוּר לִשְׁאֹל לְשָׁלוֹם לָךְ?

the presence of Hanamel, my uncle's son, and in the presence of witnesses that subscribed the deed of the purchase, before all the Jews that sat in the court of the guard.

And I charged Baruch before them, saying: Thus said the Lord, God of Israel: 'Take these deeds, both that which is sealed and that which is open and put them in an earthen vessel that they may continue many days. For thus said the Lord of hosts: Houses and fields and vineyards [30] shall yet again be bought in this land.'

⋙ [30] FIELDS AND VINEYARDS: Long ago Rabban Gamaliel, Rabbi Elea-zar, Rabbi Joshua and Rabbi Akiba were coming up to Jerusalem after it had been conquered and destroyed by the Romans. As they arrived at Mt. Scopus, a fox ran out of the Holy of Holies and all fell to weeping except Rabbi Akiba, who was merry. The others said: "The place of which it was once written, 'The common man who comes near it shall be put to death' (Numbers 1:51) has now become a haunt of foxes. Should we not weep?"

Rabbi Akiba answered: "For that reason I am merry. In the days of the First Temple the prophets Jeremiah, Uriah and Micah prophesied that Zion would be plowed like a field and Jerusalem would become a ruin and the mountain of the house of the Lord like the high places of a forest (Micah 3:12; Jeremiah 26:6, 18, 20). Those prophecies came to pass. Now, in the time of the Second Temple, the prophet Zechariah foretold: "Thus said the Lord of the host: There shall be old men and old women in the streets of Jerusalem... the streets shall be full of boys and girls playing" (Zechariah 8:4-5). Now that the first prophecy has come to pass, I am certain the second one will also be fulfilled. There-fore was I merry."

Then the three Sages thanked him, saying: "Akiba, you have com-forted us."

וּבַלָשׁוֹן הַזֶּה אָמְרוּ לוֹ: עֲקִיבָא נִחַמְתָּנוּ, עֲקִיבָא נִחַמְתָּנוּ.

9. JEREMIAH [12–38] II KINGS [23, 24]

BABYLON WILL RULE

IN THE FOURTH YEAR of Jehoiakim, the son of Josiah, king of Judah, that was in the first year of Nebuchadnezzar, king of Babylon, the word came to Jeremiah concerning Judah. Jeremiah the prophet spoke to all the people of Judah and to all the inhabitants of Jerusalem, saying:

"From the thirteenth year of Josiah, the son of Amon, king of Judah, to this day, all these twenty-three years, the word of the Lord has come to me. I have spoken to you early and late, but you have not listened. The Lord has sent you all His servants, the prophets, early and late, and you did not incline your ears to hear. [1] [They urged you,] saying: 'Turn, I pray you, every one from his

---

[1] YOUR EARS TO HEAR. If you had not accepted My Law, says the Lord, I would not recognize you nor consider you more than any of the idolatrous peoples of the world.

וְשָׁלַח יְיָ אֲלֵיכֶם אֶת כָּל עֲבָדָיו הַנְּבִיאִים הַשְׁכֵּם וְשָׁלוֹחַ וְלֹא שְׁמַעְתֶּם, וְלֹא הִטִּיתֶם אֶת אָזְנְכֶם לִשְׁמֹעַ.

evil way and from his evil doings that you may dwell in the land that the Lord has given to you and to your fathers for ever and ever. Do not go after other gods to serve them and worship them and provoke Me not with the work of your hands, [2] and I will do you no hurt.'"

"But you did not listen to Me," said the Lord, "Therefore, because you have not listened to My words, [3] I will send and will bring all the families of the north, and Nebuchadnezzar, the king of Babylon, My servant, [4] and I will bring them against this land and against its inhabitants and all the nations round about. I will utterly destroy them and will make them a horror, a scorn and a perpetual devastation. I will banish from among them the voice of mirth and the voice of gladness, the voice of the bridegroom and the voice of the bride, the sound of the millstones and the light of the lamp. [5] And this whole land shall be a desolation and a waste; and these nations shall serve the king of Babylon seventy years. [6]

"And it shall come to pass when the

~§ [2] WORK OF YOUR HANDS: Idols and material things.

~§ [3] TO MY WORDS: If you have done God's will as your will, then you have not done God's will as His will. If you have done His will against your own will, only then have you done His will as His will.

Only when you have struggled against your own evil impulse (yetzer hara) *to do God's commandments, have you performed His will.*

~§ [4] MY SERVANT: *Nebuchadnezzar and Babylon will be God's instrument in punishing Israel for its transgressions.*

~§ [5] LIGHT OF THE LAMP: *The Lord will destroy all the domestic pleasures and routine: birth, marriage, laughter, the sound of corn being ground between the millstones for bread, the light of the lamp which holds back the darkness.*

~§ [6] SEVENTY YEARS: Even if Israel is in exile, if it studies Torah and walks in its ways, it is as if it were not in exile.

וְהַאֲבַדְתִּי מֵהֶם קוֹל שָׂשׂוֹן וְקוֹל שִׂמְחָה, קוֹל חָתָן וְקוֹל כַּלָּה, קוֹל רֵחַיִם וְאוֹר נֵר.

seventy years are accomplished, [then] will I punish [7] the king of Babylon and that nation for their guilt. I will make the land of the Chaldeans desolate for ever. I will bring upon the land all My words which I promised against it. They also shall serve mighty nations and great kings. I will repay them according to their deeds and the work of their hands."

THE OPPRESSORS JUDGED

THUS SAID TO ME the Lord, God of Israel: "Take this cup of the wine of fury [8] from My hand and make all the nations to whom I send you to drink it. They shall drink and reel and be like madmen because of the sword that I will send among them. You shall say to them: Thus said the Lord, the God of Israel: Drink until you are drunk and vomit

and fall to rise no more, because of the sword which I will send among you. If they refuse to take the cup from your hand to drink, you shall say to them: Thus said the Lord of the host: Drink you must, for I begin the destruction with the city which is called by My name and shall you go unpunished? You shall not go unpunished! I shall call a sword upon all the inhabitants of the earth."

JEHOIAKIM'S REIGN

JEHOIAKIM was twenty-five years old when he began to reign. He reigned eleven years in Jerusalem and he did evil [9] in the sight of the Lord. In his days Nebuchadnezzar, king of Babylon, came up and Jehoiakim became subject to him for three years. Then he rebelled against him. The Lord sent against him

---

◄§ [7] WILL I PUNISH: *Babylon, too, will be punished for its sins, and its down-fall will bring Judah's exile to an end.*

◄§ [8] THE WINE OF FURY: *Where you find wine you will also find stumbling.*
   The cup of wine is often used as a symbol of loss of control, madness and disaster in Scripture, but it is always wine taken in excess that is implied.

◄§ [9] HE DID EVIL: *When a man is appointed to office on earth, in heaven he becomes a man of evil.*

שָׁתוּ וְשִׁכְרוּ וּקְיוּ וְנִפְלוּ וְלֹא תָקוּמוּ, מִפְּנֵי הַחֶרֶב אֲשֶׁר אָנֹכִי שׁוֹלֵחַ בֵּינֵיכֶם.

bands of Chaldeans and Moabites and Ammonites. He sent them against Judah to destroy it. Then came up Nebuchadnezzar, king of Babylon, and shackled him in chains to carry him off to Babylon. But Jehoiakim died and his son Jehoiachin became king in his stead.

THE LORD'S LAMENT

I HAVE FORSAKEN My house [10]; I have abandoned My heritage. I have given the dearly beloved of My soul into the hands of her enemies. [11] My heritage has become to Me a lion in the forest; she has shouted [12] to Me; therefore have I hated her. My heritage is to me as a speckled bird of prey and all the birds of prey are circling around her. All the beasts of the field are gathered to devour her. Many shepherds [13] have destroyed My vineyard, they have trampled down My portion. They have made My pleasant portion a desolate wilderness. They have made it desolate and its desolation mourns upon Me. The whole land is made desolate because no man takes it to heart. [14] The spoilers came upon all the high places through the wilderness, for the sword of the Lord shall devour from one end of the land to the other, so no flesh shall have peace. They have sown wheat and reaped thorns. They have put themselves to pain, but shall not profit [15] from it. They shall be

---

    [10] MY HOUSE: *The Temple in Jerusalem.*

    [11] THE HANDS OF HER ENEMIES: Those who persecute Israel never weary.

    [12] SHE HAS SHOUTED: *Israel has been defiant in the face of the Lord's commandments.*

    [13] MANY SHEPHERDS: *Bedouin bands from the east, who joined in the invasion and despoiling of Judah.*

    [14] NO MAN TAKES IT TO HEART: *No one heeds God's warnings through the prophets, nor is moved about the calamity to come.*

    [15] BUT SHALL NOT PROFIT: *The scourge that smites Israel will meet an evil fate.*

עָזַבְתִּי אֶת בֵּיתִי, נָטַשְׁתִּי אֶת נַחֲלָתִי, נָתַתִּי אֶת יְדִידוּת נַפְשִׁי בְּכַף אֹיְבֶיהָ.

disappointed in their harvest because of the fierce anger of the Lord.

Hear you and give ear, be not haughty; for the Lord has spoken. Give glory to the Lord your God before it grows dark and before your feet stumble upon the mountains of twilight. While you hope for light, He turns it in the shadow of death and makes it thick darkness. If you will not listen, My soul shall weep in secret for your pride. [16] My eyes shall weep streaming with tears, because the Lord's flock was carried away captive.

JEHOIACHIN'S FATE

SAY TO THE KING and the queen-mother: [17] Sit down low, [18] for your beautiful crown fell down from your heads. The cities of the south are shut up and there is none to open them. All Judah is carried away captive, all of it is carried away in exile. Lift up your eyes and see who came from the north. Where is the flock I entrusted in your charge? Your beautiful flock? And if you say in your heart why have these things befallen me?—Because of the greatness of your iniquity, you were stripped and exposed. [19] Can the Ethiopian change his skin, or the leopard his spots? So you may also do good [20] who are accustomed to do evil. Woe to you, O Jerusalem, how long will it be till you cleanse yourself? Will it ever be?

As I live, said the Lord, though Coniah [Jehoiachin], the son of Jehoiakim, king

---

   [16] FOR YOUR PRIDE: God exalts him who jumbles himself and humbles him who exalts himself.

   [17] THE KING AND THE QUEEN MOTHER: *Jehoiachin and Nehushta.*

   [18] SIT DOWN LOW: *Descend from the throne.*

   [19] STRIPPED AND EXPOSED: Many come to the palace to see the splendor of the royal robes; others come to see the king's face; but the wise are those who come to observe the king's deeds.

   [20] YOU MAY ALSO DO GOOD: The evil impulse (the *yetzer hara*) is

הֲיַהֲפֹךְ כּוּשִׁי עוֹרוֹ וְנָמֵר חֲבַרְבֻּרוֹתָיו? גַּם אַתֶּם תּוּכְלוּ לְהֵיטִיב, לִמֻּדֵי הָרָע.

of Judah, were the signet ring upon My right hand, I would pluck you off, and I will give you into the hand of Nebuchadnezzar, king of Babylon, and into the hands of the Chaldeans. I will hurl you and your mother that bore you to another country where you were not born, and there shall you die. But to the land to which you long to return, there you shall not return.

Is this man Coniah a despised and broken image? Is he a vessel that no one cares for? Why was he hurled out into a land which he knows not? O land, land, land, hear the word of the Lord. Thus says the Lord: "Write this man down as childless, [21] for none of his children shall sit on the throne of David and rule again in Judah."

JEHOIACHIN EXILED

JEHOIACHIN was eighteen years old when he began to reign and he reigned three months in Jerusalem. He did evil in the sight of the Lord, as his father had done. At that time Nebuchadnezzar, king of Babylon, came up against the city while his army was besieging it. Jehoiachin went out to the king of Babylon, he and his mother and his servants, his princes and his officers. The king of Babylon took him captive. [22] He carried out all the treasures of the House of the Lord,

---

powerless against the Law. Over the man who has the Torah in his heart the evil impulse has no power.

Though preceded by the terrible pessimism of "Can the Ethiopian change his skin, or the leopard his spots?" the following line, "So you may also do good who are accustomed to do evil," declares, as always, the possibility of repentance and reform.

ᵛᶨ [21] WRITE THIS MAN DOWN AS CHILDLESS: A man without children is as one who is already dead.

ᵛᶨ [22] TOOK HIM CAPTIVE: Our Sages considered the first exile of Jehoiachin, before the greater exile of Zedekiah, to be a kindness of the Lord. Those taken in the first captivity were scholars, teachers and spiritual leaders. In Babylon they founded schools, organized communities and

הָעֶצֶב נִבְזֶה נָפוּץ הָאִישׁ הַזֶּה כָּנְיָהוּ, אִם כְּלִי אֵין חֵפֶץ בּוֹ?

and all the treasures of the king's house. He also cut to pieces all the vessels of gold which Solomon had made in the Temple of the Lord. He also carried into exile [23] the nobles and all the mighty warriors, all the craftsmen and smiths. None was left except the poorest of the people of the land. He exiled to Babylon Jehoiachin, his mother, his wives, his princes and his chief men of the land.

And the king of Babylon made Mattaniah, Jehoiachin's uncle, king in his stead; and changed his name to Zedekiah.

SURRENDER TO THE ENEMY

AND ZEDEKIAH, the son of Josiah, whom Nebuchadnezzar, king of Babylon had made king in the land of Judah, reigned as king instead of Coniah [Jehoiachin]. But neither he nor his servants, nor the people of the land listened to the word of the Lord which He spoke through the prophet Jeremiah. Then Zedekiah rebelled against the king of Babylon. So Nebuchadnezzar, king of Babylon, came, he and his army, and they besieged Jerusalem. Now Jeremiah was coming and going freely among the people, for they had not yet put him into prison. Zedekiah sent Pashhur and Zephaniah to Jeremiah, saying: "Pray in my behalf to the Lord; for Nebuchadnezzar, king of Babylon, makes war against us. Perhaps the Lord will make a miracle for us, as He has often done, and the Chaldeans will withdraw from us."

Then Jeremiah said to them: "Thus shall you say to Zedekiah: 'Thus said the

---

laid down the rules of conduct for Jews in a foreign and pagan land. By the time the exiles who came with Zedekiah, the poor and ignorant of Judah, arrived, the Jewish community in Babylon was thriving, and could provide religious and communal life to keep them intact as a people.

⤐ [23] CARRIED INTO EXILE: Why was a specific time given for the first exile, but not for the second? Though the generation of the First Temple practiced idolatry, they still retained good behavior (derech eretz). What was derech eretz? Dispensing charity and performing the mitzvot.

אוּלַי יַעֲשֶׂה יְיָ אוֹתָנוּ כְּכָל נִפְלְאוֹתָיו וְיַעֲלֶה מֵעָלֵינוּ.

Lord, God of Israel: I shall turn back on yourself the weapons of war which are in your hands, with which you fight against the king of Babylon and the Chaldeans who besiege you outside of this city. I, Myself, shall fight against you with an outstretched hand and with a strong arm.' And to this people you should say: 'Thus says the Lord: I set before you the way of life and the way of death. He who remains in this city shall die by the sword, famine and pestilence. But he who goes out and surrenders to the Chaldeans who besiege you, shall escape with his life.'"

THE BROKEN AGREEMENT

THIS IS THE WORD that came to Jeremiah from the Lord after King Zedekiah had made an agreement with all the people in Jerusalem to issue an edict of emancipation. Everyone was to set free his Hebrew slaves, male and female, so that no one should hold a man of Judah, his brother, in slavery. All the princes and the others agreed and freed them. Afterward they took back their slaves whom they had set free and again forced them into service. Then the word of the Lord came to Jeremiah: "Thus says the Lord, the God of Israel: The day I brought your fathers out of the land of Egypt, out of the place where they were slaves, I made this covenant with them: Every seventh year each of you shall set free his Hebrew brother who has sold himself to you; six years shall he serve you, but then you shall let him go free. [24] Your fathers, however, did not heed Me or obey Me. Today you indeed repented and did what is right in My eyes by proclaiming the emancipation of your brethren. But then you changed your mind and profaned My name by taking back your slaves to whom you had given freedom. Therefore, thus says the Lord, I now proclaim you free for the sword, famine and pestilence. The men who violated My covenant, I will make like the calf which they cut in two, between whose parts they passed. [25] I will hand

---

⇛ [24] LET HIM GO FREE: *According to the law of the Torah (Deut. 15:12–15), Hebrew slaves were to serve no longer than six years.*

⇛ [25] BETWEEN WHOSE PARTS THEY PASSED: *Covenants were sometimes ratified by walking between the divided pieces of slaughtered animals. Symbolically, the parties to the agreement invoked upon themselves the fate of the slaughtered animal if they should violate the pact.*

הִנְנִי קוֹרֵא לָכֶם דְּרוֹר, נְאֻם יְיָ, אֶל הַחֶרֶב, אֶל הַדֶּבֶר וְאֶל הָרָעָב.

over all of them to their enemies, to those who seek their lives. Zedekiah too, and his princes, I will hand over to the soldiers of the king of Babylon who have at present withdrawn from you. I will give the command, says the Lord, and bring them back to this city. [26] They shall attack and capture it, and destroy it with fire."

Then King Zedekiah said: "He is in your hands," because the king could not do anything [27] against them. So they took Jeremiah and cast him into the pit of Malchiah, the king's son, which was in the court of the guard. They let Jeremiah down with ropes. There was no water in the pit, only mud, and Jeremiah sank in the mud.

JEREMIAH IN THE PIT

WHEN THE PRINCES HEARD what Jeremiah spoke to the people, they said to the king: "This man must be put to death, for he weakens the hands of the men of war that remain in the city, and the hands of all the people, by speaking such words to them. This man seeks not the welfare of the people but their ruin."

THE KING SAVES THE PROPHET

WHEN EBED-MELECH the Ethiopian, [28] an officer in the king's palace, heard that they had put Jeremiah in the pit, he went [to the Benjamin Gate] and spoke to the king, saying: "My lord, the king, these men have done evil to Jeremiah the prophet whom they have cast into the pit. He is likely to die there."

&⸫ [26] BRING THEM BACK TO THIS CITY: *The siege of the city was temporarily lifted by the Babylonians when they heard that an Egyptian army was marching to the aid of the surrounded city.*

&⸫ [27] THE KING COULD NOT DO ANYTHING: *Clearly there were curbs to Zedekiah's power. He refused to authorize Jeremiah's death, but evidently could not save him from the princes.*

&⸫ [28] EBED-MELECH THE ETHIOPIAN: Why is Ebed-melech, which means the servant of the king, identified as an Ethiopian? Just as he could be recognized by the darkness of his skin, so too could he be recognized by his goodness and compassion.

כִּי הָאִישׁ הַזֶּה אֵינֶנּוּ דֹרֵשׁ לְשָׁלוֹם לָעָם הַזֶּה כִּי אִם לְרָעָה.

Then the king commanded Ebed-melech: "Take thirty men with you and draw Jeremiah the prophet up out of the pit before he dies." So Ebed-melech took the men with him and went to the wardrobe of the palace, and took from there torn cloths and tattered rags and let them down by ropes into the pit to Jeremiah, and said to him: "Put these rags under your armpits, under the ropes." And Jeremiah did so. So they drew up Jeremiah with the ropes and brought him out of the pit; and he was put in the guardhouse.

King Zedekiah sent for Jeremiah and received him at the entrance that was in the house of the Lord, and the king said to Jeremiah: "I will ask you a question; hide nothing from me." Then Jeremiah said to Zedekiah: "If I tell you the truth, you will surely put me to death, [29] and if I advise you, you will not heed me."

Zedekiah swore secretly to Jeremiah, saying: "As the Lord lives, I will neither put you to death, nor hand you over to the men who seek your life."

So Jeremiah said to Zedekiah: "Thus said the Lord, God of Israel: 'If you go out and surrender to the officers of the king of Babylon, your life will be spared and your household will be spared, and the city will not be put to the torch. But if you will not go out and surrender, this city shall be given into the hands of the Chaldeans, and they shall put it to the torch, and you will not escape from their hands.'" Zedekiah said to Jeremiah: "I am afraid of the Jews who have gone over to the Chaldeans, lest they deliver me into their hands and they shall humiliate me."

But Jeremiah said: "They will not deliver you. I beseech you, listen to the voice of the Lord in what I speak to you, so that your life may be spared and all may go well with you. But if you refuse to go out and surrender, this is what the Lord has revealed to me: You will not escape out of their hands, and your wives and your children will be captured by the king of Babylon, and the city shall be burned."

⋖ [29] YOU WILL SURELY PUT ME TO DEATH: He who has been bitten by a snake is frightened by a rope.

Having already been cast into the pit without Zedekiah's having defended him, Jeremiah was cautious about being candid with the king.

שְׁמַע נָא בְּקוֹל יְיָ לַאֲשֶׁר אֲנִי דוֹבֵר אֵלֶיךָ וְיִיטַב לְךָ וּתְחִי נַפְשֶׁךָ.

ZEDEKIAH'S SECRET

THEN ZEDEKIAH SAID to Jeremiah: "Let no man know [30] of these words between us, and you shall not die. If the princes hear that I have talked to you, and they come to you to ask: 'Tell us, what did you say to the king; hide nothing from us and tell us what he did say to you, and we will not put you to death,' then you shall say to them: 'I was presenting my petition before the king that he should not send me back to Jonathan's house to die there.'"

Then all the princes came to Jeremiah and questioned him; and he answered them accordingly, so they left off speaking with him. And Jeremiah dwelt in the guard court until the day Jerusalem was taken. [31]

⋙ [30] LET NO MAN KNOW: Do not tell secrets in a field where there are mounds.

Keeping a secret in the royal court was difficult then, as it is now.

⋙ [31] JERUSALEM WAS TAKEN: Why is Psalm 79, which laments the destruction of the Temple and the ruin of Jerusalem, called "A Song of Asaph" instead of a dirge? Our Rabbis say it is like the mighty king who built a magnificent palace for his son, but when the son committed a grave sin, came to destroy the palace. When the king had torn down the hangings and broken the rods on which they hung, the boy's tutor sat on a stool and played a joyous song on his flute.

"Why do you rejoice at the destruction of my son's household?" the king asked.

"Because," the tutor replied, "I am overjoyed that you vent your wrath on the house, and not on your son."

So it was with Jerusalem, and Asaph said to the Lord: "I sing because You have poured out Your wrath on wood and stone, and not on Israel."

וַיֹּאמֶר צִדְקִיָּהוּ אֶל יִרְמְיָהוּ: אִישׁ אַל יֵדַע בַּדְּבָרִים הָאֵלֶּה וְלֹא תָמוּת.

10. JEREMIAH [24–52]

TWO BASKETS OF FIGS

THE LORD showed me two baskets of figs [1] placed before the Temple of the Lord. It was after Nebuchadnezzar, king of Babylon, carried away captive Jeconiah, the son of Jehoiakim, king of Judah, and the princes of Judah, with the craftsmen and the smiths [2] from Jerusalem, and brought them to Babylon. One basket had very good figs. The other basket had very bad figs, so bad that they could not be eaten.

Then the Lord said to me: "What do

---

[1] TWO BASKETS OF FIGS: A pagan matron asked Rabbi Jose: "Can your God bring near to Him any one He wills?" Rabbi Jose brought the woman a basket of figs. She chose a good one and ate it. Then Rabbi Jose said to her: "If you know how to choose, should God not know how to choose? Whomever God sees performing deeds of loving-kindness He chooses and brings near to Him."

[2] CRAFTSMEN AND THE SMITHS: The skilled workmen.

הִרְאַנִי יְיָ, וְהִנֵּה שְׁנֵי דּוּדָאֵי תְאֵנִים מוּעָדִים לִפְנֵי הֵיכַל יְיָ.

you see, Jeremiah?" And I said: "Figs." The good figs are very good and the bad figs are so bad that they cannot be eaten." Then the word of the Lord came to me, saying: "Thus says the Lord, God of Israel: Like these good figs so will I regard for good [3] the captives of Judah whom I have sent out of this place to the land of the Chaldeans. I will look with friendly eyes upon them. I will bring them back [4] to this land and I will build them and not tear them down. I will plant them and not pluck them up. I will give them a heart to know Me, that I am the Lord, and they shall be My people and I will be their God, for they shall return to Me with all their heart."

"But like the bad figs which are so bad that they cannot be eaten," thus said the Lord: "So will I make Zedekiah, the king of Judah, his princes and the remnant of Jerusalem, which remained in this land, and those who live in the land of Egypt. I will make them a horror and an offence among all the kingdoms of the earth, a reproach and a byword, and a taunt and a curse wherever I drive them."

THE FALL OF JERUSALEM

AND IT CAME TO PASS in the ninth year of Zedekiah's reign, in the tenth day of the tenth month, that Nebuchadnezzar, king of Babylon, came, he and all his army, against Jerusalem, and encamped against it; and they built forts against it round about. So the city was besieged until the eleventh year of King Zedekiah. In the fourth month, in the ninth day of the month, the famine was so sore in the city that there was no bread for the people of the land. Then a breach was made in the wall of the city, and all the men of war fled, and went forth out of the city by night, by the way of the gate between the two walls which was by the king's garden—now the Chaldeans were against the city surrounding it—and they went by the way of the Arabah. [5]

ৰু§ [3] REGARD FOR GOOD: *The Lord will look with favor on the captives from Judah.*

ৰু§ [4] I WILL BRING THEM BACK: Rabbi Elazar said that Israel would be redeemed through five things only: calamity, prayer, the merits of the fathers, repentance and the end of days.

ৰু§ [5] THE ARABAH: *The deep valley of the Jordan north of the Dead Sea.*

כַּתְּאֵנִים הַטֹּבוֹת הָאֵלֶּה כֵּן אַכִּיר אֶת גָּלוּת יְהוּדָה אֲשֶׁר שִׁלַּחְתִּי מִן הַמָּקוֹם הַזֶּה אֶרֶץ כַּשְׂדִּים לְטוֹבָה.

But the army of the Chaldeans pursued after the king and overtook Zedekiah in the plains of Jericho; and all his army was scattered from him. Then they took the king and carried him up to the king of Babylon to Riblah in the land of Hamath; and he gave judgment upon him. [6] And the king of Babylon slew the sons of Zedekiah before his eyes. He also slew all the princes of Judah in Riblah. And he put out the eyes of Zedekiah; and the king of Babylon bound him in fetters and carried him to Babylon [7] and put him in prison till the day of his death.

JEREMIAH IS FREED

IN THE FIFTH MONTH, in the tenth day of the month, came Nebuzaradan, the captain of the guard of the king of Babylon, and burned the house of the Lord, [8] the king's house and all the houses of Jerusalem. And all the army of the Chaldeans that were with the captain of the guard broke down the walls of Jerusalem. [9]

Now Nebuchadnezzar, king of Babylon, gave orders concerning Jeremiah to Nebuzaradan, the captain of the guard, saying: "Take him and look after him

---

[6] GAVE JUDGMENT UPON HIM: *The king of Babylon punished Zedekiah for breaking his oath of alliance.*

[7] AND CARRIED HIM TO BABYLON: When the Temple was burned and Nebuzaradan had gathered the people to take them into exile, the Lord said to the people: "Whom shall you want as a leader, Abraham or Isaac, Jacob or Moses? Perhaps you would like King David at your head?" And the people of Judah replied: "None of them. We want only You." Then the Lord promised: "I will go with you into Babylon and I will bring you out of there."

[8] HOUSE OF THE LORD: The Temple was destroyed because of unfounded hatred.

[9] JERUSALEM: When will the Lord rebuild Jerusalem? When He assembles the dispersed.

וַיַּאַסְרֵהוּ בַּנְחֻשְׁתַּיִם וַיְבִיאֵהוּ מֶלֶךְ בָּבֶל בָּבֶלָה וַיִּתְּנֵהוּ בְּבֵית הַפְּקֻדוֹת עַד יוֹם מוֹתוֹ.

well. [10] Do him no harm. Treat him as he shall say to you."

It was when they brought Jeremiah [11] before Nebuzaradan in chains among the captives of Jerusalem, the captain of the guard said to the prophet: "Now see, I have released you this day from the chains which are upon your

---

&ε [10] LOOK AFTER HIM WELL: *Nebuchadnezzar's consideration for Jeremiah was probably due to the prophet's advice to Zedekiah to surrender to Babylon.*

&ε [11] THEY BROUGHT JEREMIAH: The king of Babylon had instructed the captain of his guard to take good care of Jeremiah but not of the people. He was not to harm Jeremiah but he could harm the people as much as he chose. He was also to fulfill whatever request the prophet made of him but to ignore the people's pleas.

When Jeremiah saw a group of young warriors chained together by their necks, he put his head in the chains and walked with them. Nebuzaradan saw him and removed the chains from the prophet's neck. Then Jeremiah saw a group of old men chained together and put his neck in their chains. Again Nebuzaradan removed the chains from the prophet's neck, and said: "Either you are a false prophet because you prophesied that this city would be destroyed, and now that your prophesy is fulfilled you are full of sorrow; or you like suffering and affliction, for you seek pain. And you love to shed blood, for if harm should come to you the king will kill me, and my blood will be on your head." Jeremiah made no reply.

Then Nebuzaradan declared: "If you wish, come with me to Babylon and we will take good care of you there. But if you want to remain here, you may go wherever you wish." Still Jeremiah was silent.

Then the word of the Lord came to Jeremiah: "Jeremiah, if you remain here with the remnant, I shall go with the captives into exile. If you go with the captives, then I shall remain here with the remnant."

Jeremiah promptly replied: "If I go with the captives, of what help

הָיָה רוֹאֶה כַּת שֶׁל בַּחוּרִים נְתוּנִים בְּקוֹלָרִין – וְנוֹתֵן אֶת רֹאשׁוֹ עִמָּהֶם.

hands. If it seem good to you to come with me to Babylon, come and I shall looks after you well. But if it seem ill to you to come with me to Babylon, the whole land is before you. Go wherever it seem good to you." Then the captain of the guard gave him provisions and sent him away. And Jeremiah went to Mizpah, to Gedaliah, whom the king of Babylon had made governor over the land.

THE MURDER OF GEDALIAH

WHEN THE CAPTAINS of the armies that were in the field together with their men heard that the king of Babylon had ap-pointed Gedaliah governor of the land and had entrusted to his charge the men, women and children of the poorest of the land that were not exiled to Babylon, they came and joined Gedaliah in Miz-pah.

But in the seventh month, Ishmael, a member of the royal family, and ten men with him came to Gedaliah in Mizpah. As they dined together there, Ishmael and the men who were with him arose and killed Gedaliah, [12] whom the king of Babylon had made governor over the land. Ishmael also killed all the Jews who were with Gedaliah and the Chaldean soldiers who were there. Then he carried away captive all the rest of the people

---

can I be to them? Let the Lord, who can help and succor, go with the afflicted; I shall remain with the remnant." So did the Lord go, bound in chains, with the captives to Babylon, and Jeremiah went to Mizpah and joined Gedaliah.

The midrash shows that Jeremiah was not a traitor to his people despite the fact that he had counseled surrender to the Babylonians. He saw Nebuchadnez-zar as "the rod of anger in the Lord's hand." But he refused to accept favors from the enemy or even talk to him. Later, through Seraiah (51:63–64), Jeremiah predicted Babylon's fall.

[12] AND KILLED GEDALIAH: The Day of Atonement brings forgiveness for sins against God; but the Day of Atonement brings no forgiveness for sins against one's neighbor until a man has become reconciled with his neighbor.

רְאֵה, כָּל הָאָרֶץ לְפָנֶיךָ, אֶל טוֹב וְאֶל הַיָּשָׁר בְּעֵינֶיךָ לָלֶכֶת – שָׁמָּה לֵךְ.

that were at Mizpah. When Johanan and all the captains of the armies who were with him heard of the evil Ishmael had done, he took all the men and went to fight Ishmael. He found him by the great waters that are in Gibeon. Now the captives saw Johanan and all the captains of the armies who were with him and they were filled with joy. So they turned around and went over to Johanan. But Ishmael with eight men escaped and went to the children of Ammon.

Then Johanan with all the people who were with him went and stayed in Geruth Chimham, which is near Bethlehem, to go on to Egypt, for they were afraid of the vengeance of the Chaldeans because Ishmael had killed Gedaliah whom the king of Babylon had made governor over the land.

JEREMIAH GOES TO EGYPT

THEN ALL THE CAPTAINS of the armies and Johanan and all the people, from the least to the greatest, approached Jeremiah and said to him: "Let the Lord, your God, show us the way we should go. Whatever He will say we shall do." After ten days the word of the Lord came to Jeremiah. He called Johanan, all the captains of the armies that were with him, and all the people, and said to them: "Thus said the Lord: If you stay on this land I will build you up and not tear you down; I will plant you and not uproot you; for I regret the evil I have done to you. Do not be afraid of the king of Babylon [13] for I am with you to save you and deliver you from his hand. But if you say: We will not stay on this land; we will go to Egypt where we shall see no war, nor hear the sound of the sound of the *shofar*, and we shall have no hunger for bread and there we will stay. Then, remnant of Judah, hear the word of the Lord: If you will go to Egypt to sojourn there, then the sword which you fear will overtake you there, and the famine which you dread shall follow hard after you there in Egypt; and there you shall die."

And it was when Jeremiah finished speaking the words of the Lord [14] to

---

◆§ [13] KING OF BABYLON: As a bee dies once it has stung, so Israel's enemy dies in disgrace once he has smitten Israel.

◆§ [14] THE WORDS OF THE LORD: He who counsels the just man well is as if he had observed all the Ten Commandments.

אִם שׁוֹב תֵּשְׁבוּ בָּאָרֶץ הַזֹּאת וּבָנִיתִי וּבְנִיתִי אֶתְכֶם וְלֹא אֶהֱרֹס, וְנָטַעְתִּי אֶתְכֶם וְלֹא אֶתּוֹשׁ.

all the people that all the proud men [15] said: "You speak falsely; the Lord did not send you to say to us that we should not go to Egypt to settle there." So Johanan and all the captains of the armies took all the remnant of Judah, men, women and children, and the king's daughters, and Jeremiah the prophet, and Baruch the son of Neriah, and they came to the land of Egypt and arrived at Tahpanhes. [16]

LETTERS TO THE EXILES:
DO NOT FOLLOW THE NATIONS

HEAR THE WORD which the Lord speaks to you, house of Israel. Thus said the Lord: "Do not learn to follow the way of the nations and be not dismayed at the signs of heaven, [17] though the nations are dismayed at them. The beliefs of the people are naught, because it is but a tree which one cuts out of the forest, the work of the hands of the workman with an ax. They deck it with silver and gold, with silver beaten into plates which are brought from Tarshish and gold from Uphaz. Blue and purple is their clothing, all work of skillful men. They fasten it with hammer and nails to keep it from falling, but they are like scarecrows in a garden of cucumbers. They speak not and they must be carried, because they cannot walk. [18] Do not be afraid of them, for they cannot do evil, neither have they the power to do good. But the Lord is a true God. He is a living God and the everlasting King.

Thus shall you say to them [the nations]: "The gods that have not made the heavens and the earth shall perish from the

---

~§ [15] THE PROUD MEN: *Presumptuous men.*

~§ [16] TAHPANHES: *A city on the frontier of Egypt.*

~§ [17] SIGNS OF HEAVEN: *Comets, meteors, eclipses and other astronomical occurrences which the pagans interpreted astrologically, usually as signs of impending disaster.*

~§ [18] THEY CANNOT WALK: *All of this is a description of how idols are made and decorated; work of skillful craftsmen but useless and powerless.*

אַל תִּירְאוּ מֵהֶם כִּי לֹא יָרֵעוּ, וְגַם הֵיטֵיב אֵין אוֹתָם.

earth and from under the heavens." Not like these is the portion of Jacob. [19] He is the Creator of all things. The Lord of the host is His name and Israel is the tribe of His inheritance.

AFTER SEVENTY YEARS

THESE ARE THE WORDS of the letter that Jeremiah the prophet sent from Jerusalem to the captivity in Babylon. Thus said the Lord of the host, God of Israel, to all the exiles whom I carried into exile from Jerusalem to Babylon: "Build houses and dwell in them, plant gardens and eat their fruit. Take wives and beget sons and daughters. Take wives for your sons and give your daughters to husbands that they may bear sons and daughters. Multiply there and be not diminished. Seek the peace of the city [20] to which I carried you into exile and pray to the Lord for it; for in its peace you shall have peace." For thus said the Lord: "Do not be deluded by the prophets in your midst and your diviners, nor listen to the dreams which you cause to be dreamed, for they prophesy falsely to you in My name. I have not sent them. After seventy years [21] in Babylon I will remember you and I will fulfill My good word toward you, to return you to this place. [22] You shall call upon Me and you will go in

---

ᵛᵍ [19] THE PORTION OF JACOB: As a lily dies only when its aroma dies, so Israel will not die so long as it obeys the commandments and performs the *mitzvot*.

Although the lily is plucked, it still retains its aroma; so too Israel, even in exile, will have the Torah and good deeds.

ᵛᵍ [20] PEACE OF THE CITY: Be sure that you pray for the well-being of the government, for it is only respect for authority that saves men from swallowing each other up alive.

ᵛᵍ [21] AFTER SEVENTY YEARS: *Babylon's downfall shall come.*

[22] RETURN YOU TO THIS PLACE: Israel proclaims: Lord, even Your anger which You have brought upon me is pleasant, because in that way You cause me to return and bring me back to virtue.

וְדִרְשׁוּ אֶת שְׁלוֹם הָעִיר אֲשֶׁר הִגְלֵיתִי אֶתְכֶם שָׁמָּה וְהִתְפַּלְלוּ בַעֲדָהּ אֶל יְיָ, כִּי בִשְׁלוֹמָהּ יִהְיֶה לָכֶם שָׁלוֹם.

My way, and you will pray to Me and I will listen to you. You shall seek Me [23] and you shall find Me when you search for Me with all your hearts, [24] and I will be found by you. I will return your captives and will gather you from all the nations and from all the places to which I have driven you," said the Lord, "and I will bring you back to the place from which I exiled you."

THE PROMISED RESTORATION

AGAIN I WILL BUILD YOU and you shall be built, maiden of Israel. Again you shall be adorned with your timbrels and shall go out dancing with them who make merry. Again you shall plant vineyards upon the mountains of Samaria. The planters that plant shall have the use of them. There shall be a day when the watchmen on the mountains of Samaria shall call out: "Arise and let us go to Zion, [25] to the Lord our God, for the Lord has ransomed Jacob and has redeemed him from the hand of him that is stronger than he." Then shall the maiden rejoice in the dance, and the old men and the young men shall make merry, for I will turn their mourning into joy and I will comfort them and make them rejoice from their sorrow.

Set up roadmarks, make yourselves guideposts; set your heart toward the highway, the way by which you are going. You will return to your cities.

Thus said the Lord of the host, God of Israel: "Once again they shall use this speech in the land of Judah and its cities, when I shall return their captivity: 'The Lord bless You, O home of righteousness, [26] O mountain of holiness.' They

---

[23] YOU SHALL SEEK ME: From wherever one seeks God, God will answer, be it from Judah or Babylon. When a man has the need and desire for God, he will find Him. Judah Halevi, in one of his poems, wrote: "I went in search of Him and I found that He came to meet me."

[24] WITH ALL YOUR HEARTS: God desires the heart.

[25] GO TO ZION: *The separation of Samaria and Judah will end.*

[26] O HOME OF RIGHTEOUSNESS: Was Israel created for the sake of the

עוֹד אֶבְנֵךְ וְנִבְנֵית, בְּתוּלַת יִשְׂרָאֵל, עוֹד תַּעְדִּי תֻפַּיִךְ וְיָצָאת בִּמְחוֹל מְשַׂחֲקִים.

will dwell in Judah. All the cities will be settled, the plowmen and those who wander with flocks shall be without fear."

JOY IN JERUSALEM

THUS SAID THE LORD: "In this place of which you say: 'It is a waste without men and without beasts,' even the cities of Judah and the streets of Jerusalem [27] are desolate; in all these places shall be heard again the voice of joy and gladness, the voice of the bridegroom and the voice of the bride, and the voice of them who bring offerings of thanksgiving in the house of the Lord and call out: 'Give thanks to the Lord of the host, for the Lord is good; His mercy endures forever.'"

Thus said the Lord: "In this place which is waste, there shall again be a habitation of shepherds, resting their flocks. In the cities of the hill-country, in the cities of the lowland, and in the cities of the south, in the land of Benjamin, and in the places about Jerusalem, and in the cities of Judah, shall the flocks again pass under the hands of those who count them. Days are coming," says the Lord, "that I will fulfill the good promise that I made to the house of Israel and the house of Judah."

MOTHER RACHEL COMFORTED

THUS SAYS THE LORD: "A voice is heard in Ramah, [28] lamentation and bitter weeping; Rachel, weeping for her children; she refuses to be comforted because they are gone." Thus says the Lord: "Cease your weeping and stay your eyes from tears, your effort for the children shall be rewarded. There is hope

---

Law, or the Law for the sake of Israel? Surely the Law for the sake of Israel. Then if the Law which was created for the sake of Israel shall endure forever, how much will Israel endure which was created by the merit of the Law.

◄§ [27] THE STREETS OF JERUSALEM: Any one may enter into the Jerusalem of the present, but only the invited may enter into the Jerusalem of the world to come.

◄§ [28] RAMAH: *Rachel's tomb is near the town of Ramah.*

קוֹל בְּרָמָה נִשְׁמָע, נְהִי בְּכִי תַמְרוּרִים, רָחֵל מְבַכָּה עַל בָּנֶיהָ.

for their future," says the Lord. "Your children shall return to their land."

I have surely heard Ephraim [29] bemoaning: "You have chastised me and I was chastised. [30] I was like an unbroken colt. [31] Bring me back. Let me return, for You are My God. After I was exiled, I became aware of my sins; I became ashamed, even confounded; [32] I bear the disgrace of my youth." "Is not Ephraim My precious son? Is he not My darling child? For as often as I speak of

him, I remember him with longing. My heart yearns for him. I will surely have compassion upon him," says the Lord.

A NEW COVENANT

THERE WILL COME A TIME [33] when you shall multiply and increase in the land. In those days, says the Lord, they shall say no more: The ark of the covenant of the Lord; neither shall it come to mind, neither shall they mention it, neither

---

&ᶹ [29] EPHRAIM: *The Northern Kingdom of Israel, already exiled into captivity.*

&ᶹ [30] I WAS CHASTISED: *The people accepted the exile as Divine judgment that they had sinned.*

&ᶹ [31] AN UNBROKEN COLT: *Ephraim was wild and undisciplined.*

&ᶹ [32] EVEN CONFOUNDED: The schools of Hillel and Shammai disputed for two and a half years about whether it would have been better if man had or had not been created. They finally agreed that it would have been better had man not been created; but since he had been, then man should investigate his past behavior, examine what he is about to do, and live a righteous life.

&ᶹ [33] THERE WILL COME A TIME: Rabbi Jochanan said: "All our prophets foretell only what will happen in the days of the Messiah. But no eye

הֲבֵן יַקִּיר לִי אֶפְרַיִם, אִם יֶלֶד שַׁעֲשׁוּעִים? כִּי מִדֵּי דַבְּרִי בּוֹ זָכֹר אֶזְכְּרֶנּוּ עוֹד.

shall they miss it, neither shall they make another one. [34] At that time they shall call Jerusalem the throne of the Lord. All the nations shall gather there to celebrate the name of the Lord in Jerusalem. They shall not walk any more after the stubbornness of their evil heart. In those days the house of Judah shall walk with the house of Israel, [35] and they shall come together from the land of the north to the land I have given for an inheritance to your fathers.

There will come a time, says the Lord, that I shall make a new covenant [36] with the house of Israel, and with the house of Judah: not like the covenant that I made with their fathers in the days when I took them by the hand to bring them out of Egypt. They broke the covenant though I remained their Lord. But this is the covenant that I shall make with the house of Israel after these days, says the Lord. I shall put My Torah within them and in their hearts I shall write it and I shall be their God and they shall be My people. No longer shall every man have to teach his neighbor and every man his brother, saying: "Know your God," because they all shall know Me, from the least to the greatest of them. I shall forgive them their iniquity and their sins shall I remember no more.

---

has seen and no ear has heard the world beyond the grave. Only God knows what He has prepared for those who wait for Him!"

⋙ [34] THEY MAKE ANOTHER ONE: *Because all Jerusalem will be filled with the Divine presence, the Ark will lose its special meaning and there will be no need to build another. No visible symbol of God will be needed.*

⋙ [35] THE HOUSE OF ISRAEL: *Israel and Judah will be joined together once more.*

⋙ [36] A NEW COVENANT: *The Lord will make a new covenant with Israel which, unlike the old one, will be permanent because it will be inscribed on the hearts of the people. Israel will remain faithful and the Lord will, therefore, never reject them.*

כִּי כוּלָּם יֵדְעוּ אוֹתִי לְמִקְטַנָּם וְעַד גְּדוֹלָם, כִּי אֶסְלַח לַעֲוֹנָם וּלְחַטָּאתָם לֹא אֶזְכָּר־עוֹד.

11. EZEKIEL [1–22]

VISION OF THE CHARIOT THRONE

THE WORD OF THE LORD came [1] to Ezekiel the priest, the son of Buzi, in the land of the Chaldeans by the river Chebar; [2] and the hand of the Lord was there upon him.

It came to pass in the fifth day of the fourth month in the fifth year of

---

[1] THE WORD OF THE LORD CAME: Whatever is said in the account of a vision—that the prophet heard, went forth, said, was told, stood, sat, went up, went down, journeyed, asked or was asked—even when there is a lengthy account whose details are logically connected in time, and where persons and places are referred to, the events described are to be understood figuratively. It must be assumed with certainty that the whole is a prophetic vision.

[2] THE RIVER CHEBAR: *Probably the Babylonian river Euphrates.*

הָיֹה הָיָה דְבַר יְיָ אֶל יְחֶזְקֵאל בֶּן בּוּזִי הַכֹּהֵן בְּאֶרֶץ כַּשְׂדִּים עַל נְהַר כְּבָר.

King Jehoiachin's captivity. I was among the captives by the river Chebar, the heavens were opened, and I saw visions of God. I looked up and I saw a stormy wind come out of the north, a great cloud shot through with fire, so that a radiance surrounded it. Out of the fire gleamed something like the luster of shining metal and out of the midst of all emerged the semblance of four living creatures.

This was their appearance: Every one of them had four faces, and every one four wings. And they had the hands of a man under their wings on their four sides. Their feet were straight and their soles were like the sole of a calf's foot; and they sparkled like the color of burnished brass. As for the likeness of their faces, the four of them had the face of a man in front, the face of a lion on the right, the face of an ox on the left and the face of an eagle behind. Thus were their faces and their wings stretched upward; the wings of every one were joined one to another and two covered their bodies. Every one went straight forward. Wher-

ever the spirit wished to go, they turned not when they went.

As for the likeness of the living creatures, their appearance was like burning fires of coal, burning like the appearance of torches; and there was brightness to the fire, and out of the fire flashed forth lightning. And the living creatures ran and returned as the appearance of a flash of lightning.

THE CHARIOT

NOW, as I saw the living creatures, there was one wheel at the bottom hard by the living creatures, at the four faces thereof. The appearance of the wheels and their work was like the color of beryl; and the four had one likeness; and their appearance and their work was as it were a wheel within a wheel. [3] When they went, they moved forward on their four sides; they turned not when they went. Their rings were high and dreadful; and the four had their rings full of eyes round about. And the spirit of the living creatures was in the wheels.

⊷§ [3] WHEEL WITHIN A WHEEL: *In his vision, Ezekiel sees the Divine Chariot (merkabah) leaving, thus symbolically explaining that the Divine spirit is leaving both Jerusalem and Judah. This is the ominous forecast of the fall of Jerusalem and the destruction of the Temple.*

וַאֲנִי בְּתוֹךְ הַגּוֹלָה עַל נְהַר כְּבָר, נִפְתְּחוּ הַשָּׁמַיִם וָאֶרְאֶה מַרְאוֹת אֱלֹהִים.

THE THRONE

OVER THE HEADS of the living creatures there was the likeness of a firmament, [4] like the color of terrible ice, stretched forth over their heads.

Above the firmament [5] was the likeness of a throne which had the color of sapphire stone. Upon it was the semblance of a man. From his loins upward I saw a luster like that of shining metal; from his loins downward something resembling fire with a radiance around it, resembling the rainbow that appears in the cloud on a rainy day. This was the appearance of the likeness of the glory of the Lord. When I saw it, I fell upon my face, [6] and I heard a voice of one that spoke.

❧ [4] THE LIKENESS OF A FIRMAMENT: Resh Lakish said that there are seven skies above us, each with its name and function. From the earth to the first sky is a journey of five hundred years and the same distance is between each sky above it. The thickness of each sky is also a journey of five hundred years. You can therefore imagine what a distance above the world the Lord is and what a distance from man. Yet if a man prays in a whisper the Lord hears his prayer, as if a man had spoken directly into his friend's ear. Is not the God who is so remote from the world yet so near to man?

❧ [5] ABOVE THE FIRMAMENT: Whoever speculates about four things, it would be better for him not to have come into the world. Do not ask what is above the heavens or underneath, what was before the world was created, and what will be hereafter. Search not and do not speculate about what is hidden from you; there is enough mystery for you in this world.

❧ [6] I FELL UPON MY FACE: *Ezekiel prostrated himself before the Lord.*

וָאֶרְאֶה וָאֶפֹּל עַל פָּנַי וָאֶשְׁמַע קוֹל מְדַבֵּר.

EZEKIEL'S MISSION

HE SAID TO ME: "Son of man, [7] stand up and I will speak to you." As He spoke to me, a spirit entered into me and set me on my feet and I heard Him that spoke to me:

"Son of man, I sent you to the children of Israel, [8] to a rebellious nation that has rebelled against Me; their fathers transgressed and their children to this very day are brazen-faced and stiff-hearted. [9] I sent you to them and you shall speak to them whether they listen

---

◆§ [7] SON OF MAN: Why was Ezekiel addressed as "son of man" when no other prophet was thus addressed? Our Sages give several explanations. The Lord addressed Ezekiel as *ben adam* as an expression of familiarity and love. In Hebrew *adam* means man, but so does *enosh* and *ish*. But *enosh* and *ish* have plurals, while *adam* has only a singular. In addressing Ezekiel as *adam*, the Lord was conveying the fact that Ezekiel was singular, a unique man.

In Hebrew Ezekiel's father's name, *Buzi*, means "degraded," so that the Lord was also demonstrating that even if the family name was degraded, it was a family which performed the *mitzvot* for the love of God and the honor of Israel.

Another explanation is that the Lord called Ezekiel son of man to remind him to be humble. Because the Lord had revealed Himself in all His glory to the prophet, Ezekiel might consider himself especially meritorious and grow proud or haughty; thus the Lord reminds him that he is only a son of man, a mortal.

◆§ [8] CHILDREN OF ISRAEL: *Ezekiel's mission is both to the exiles in Babylon and the remnant in Judah.*

◆§ [9] STIFF-HEARTED: Why is Israel like an olive? Just as the olive gives oil only when pressed, so Israel repents only when it is pressed.

בֶּן אָדָם, שׁוֹלֵחַ אֲנִי אוֹתְךָ אֶל בְּנֵי יִשְׂרָאֵל, אֶל גּוֹיִם הַמּוֹרְדִים אֲשֶׁר מָרְדוּ בִי.

or refuse to listen, because they are a rebellious people, yet they shall know that there has been a prophet among them. [10]

"But the house of Israel will not consent to listen to you; for they will not listen to Me, because all of them are of a hard forehead and a stiff heart. But I will make your face as hard as theirs and your forehead hard as theirs. I will make you as adamant, [11] harder than flint; fear them not, nor be dismayed at their jeering for they are a rebellious house."

THE BITTER SCROLL

"AND YOU, son of man, listen to what I say to you. Do not be rebellious like that rebellious house. Open your mouth and eat what I give you." I looked and I saw a hand stretched out to me and in it there was a scroll. He unrolled it before me and it was written on both sides, lamentations, moaning and woe. He said to me: "Eat this scroll!" [12] I opened my mouth and He made me eat the scroll, and He said to me: "Son of man, swallow and digest this scroll which I give you." Then I ate it and it was as sweet as honey in my mouth. He said to me: "Son of man, go to the house of Israel and speak what I say to them, for you are not sent to a people of a foreign tongue, but you are sent to Israel."

Then a spirit lifted me up [13] and took me away. I went in bitterness and

---

⇒ [10] A PROPHET AMONG THEM: *Though the people may not heed his words, at least they will know that a prophet has brought God's message to them; and they will have been forewarned of the calamity which is impending.*

⇒ [11] I WILL MAKE YOU AS ADAMANT: *A man should be pliable as a reed, not stiff as a cedar.*

⇒ [12] EAT THIS SCROLL: *This symbolic action describes Ezekiel's taking in God's message and digesting it, so that he can then speak the Lord's words to the people of Israel.*

⇒ [13] A SPIRIT LIFTED ME UP: *In his vision Ezekiel is carried away to the exiles living in Babylon.*

כִּי לֹא אֶל עַם עִמְקֵי שָׂפָה וְכִבְדֵי לָשׁוֹן אַתָּה שָׁלוּחַ – אֶל בֵּית יִשְׂרָאֵל.

in raging spirit. [14] The hand of the Lord [15] was strong upon me. I came to the captivity at Tel-abib, [16] by the river Chebar, and remained there for seven days in a state of stupor.

THE PROPHET WATCHMAN

AT THE END of seven days the word of the Lord came to me, saying: "Son of man, I appoint you a watchman [17] to the house of Israel, and when you shall hear a word from My mouth, you shall give them a warning [18] from Me. If I say to the wicked: 'You shall die,' and you say nothing to warn the wicked man from his wicked way, to save his life, the wicked man shall die for his iniquity; but his blood will I require at your hand. If, however, you warn the wicked man

---

    [14] IN RAGING SPIRIT: *Ezekiel was both pained and angry to have to deliver so bitter a message to the exiles.*

    [15] THE HAND OF THE LORD: *The compelling spirit of his prophetic mission.*

    [16] TEL-ABIB: *Very likely the chief settlement in Babylon of the exiled Jews.*

    [17] I APPOINT YOU A WATCHMAN: If there is no vineyard, why a fence? If there is no herd, what need for a shepherd? If there is no people of Israel, what need for the prophets? Our Rabbis say that the Lord speaks to the prophets only because of the merits of the people of Israel. The people choose and appoint their leaders, but the Lord declares that leaders remain leaders only if they rule justly and righteously and educate the people. To the rulers, the Lord says: "I too have a share in your office. If the rulers do not do their duty, then punishment for the people's sins falls on their heads. But if the leaders warn and educate the people, and the people sin of their own accord, then each sinner is punished for his own sins."

    [18] GIVE THEM A WARNING: How long and to what extent should one go on warning another? Until he is decisively and peremptorily forbidden the act.

צוֹפֶה נְתַתִּיךָ לְבֵית יִשְׂרָאֵל, וְשָׁמַעְתָּ מִפִּי דָבָר וְהִזְהַרְתָּ אוֹתָם מִמֶּנִּי.

and he does not turn from his wickedness, he shall die for his iniquity; but
you have saved your soul. Or, if a righteous man turns from his righteousness
and you did not warn him, he shall die
for his sin, but his blood will I require [19]
at your hand. If, however, you warned
the righteous man not to sin, and he did
not sin, you have saved your soul." [20]

And the hand of the Lord came there
upon me, and He said to me: "Arise and
go to the valley [21] and there will I
speak to you." I arose and went to the
valley and the glory of God stood there,
like the glory which I saw by the river
Chebar. I fell upon my face. Then the
spirit entered into me and set me upon
my feet and spoke to me and said:

THE SIEGE OF JERUSALEM

"SON OF MAN, take a brick [22] and en-
grave upon it a city, Jerusalem; and lay
siege against it. [23] Throw up a mound
against it, set camps against it and put
battering rams around it. Then take an
iron plate and place it as an iron wall between you and the city. Set your face

---

[19] HIS BLOOD WILL I REQUIRE: *He who can and does not save a soul is akin
to a murderer. Ezekiel, therefore, may not keep silent; he must speak out in
the hope that he can avert the disaster which threatens Judah, however bitter
his message.*

[20] YOU HAVE SAVED YOUR SOUL: *Rabbi Assi said: If one merely thinks
of performing a good deed, but is forcibly prevented from doing it, it
is as if he had performed it; but an evil intention which does not result
in an evil deed is not punished.*

[21] GO TO THE VALLEY: *Ezekiel is sent to a more private place where the
Lord may speak to him.*

[22] TAKE A BRICK: *In Assyria and Babylonia slabs of clay were used for
writing.*

[23] LAY SIEGE AGAINST IT: *God commands the prophet to draw on the clay
slab the plan of a siege of Jerusalem with all the various elements of battle:
soldiers, battering rams, observation posts.*

קַח לְךָ לְבֵנָה וְחַקּוֹתָ עָלֶיהָ עִיר, אֶת יְרוּשָׁלַיִם, וְנָתַתָּה עָלֶיהָ מָצוֹר.

toward it [24] and it shall be besieged. This shall be a sign for the house of Israel.

"Then lie upon your left side three hundred and ninety days, each day for a year, to bear the punishment for the sins of Israel. When you have done this, you shall lie on your right side forty days, a day for a year, to bear the punishment for the house of Judah. As for the siege of Jerusalem, fix your gaze upon the city, while your arm is bared, and you shall prophesy against it. I will place upon you cords [25] that you may not turn from one side to another.

"Then take wheat, barley, beans, lentils, millet and spelt, put them in one pot and make them into bread for yourself. The food that you shall eat shall be by weight, twenty shekels a day. You shall eat it at a fixed time each day. The water you shall drink, also by measure, a sixth of a *hin* a day, also at a fixed time." The Lord said to me: "I shall break the staff of bread in Jerusalem and they shall eat bread by weight and with anxiety, and they shall drink water by measure in horror because there will be a want of bread and water. [26] They shall fall in a stupor and pine away in their iniquity."

THE PEOPLE'S FATE

"SON OF MAN, take a sharp sword and as a barber's razor pass it over your head and beard. Then take a scale and divide the hair in three portions. Burn a third of it in the midst of the city when the days of your siege are over. Take another third and strike it with the sword all around the city. The last third you shall scatter to the wind. From them take a few and wrap them in the skirts of your robe, then take some of these and cast them into the fire. As I live," said the Lord, "because you have defiled My

---

◄§ [24] SET YOUR FACE TOWARD IT: *Ezekiel is symbolically to play the role of besieger of the city.*

◄§ [25] UPON YOU CORDS: *To symbolize the rigors of the siege in which Jerusalem will be hemmed in and unable to move, Ezekiel will be bound so that he too cannot move.*

◄§ [26] WANT OF BREAD AND WATER: *Famine will afflict the besieged.*

קַח לְךָ חֶרֶב חַדָּה, תַּעַר הַגַּלָּבִים תִּקָּחֶנָּה לָּךְ, וְהַעֲבַרְתָּ עַל רֹאשְׁךָ וְעַל זְקָנֶךָ.

Sanctuary with all your abominations, [27] I also will diminish you; neither shall Mine eye spare you. I also will have no pity. A third part of you shall die of pestilence, and consumed by famine; a third part shall fall by the sword; and a third part will I scatter to the winds. I the Lord have spoken it."

THE EXILE

THE WORD OF THE LORD came to me, saying: "Son of man, you live in the midst of a rebellious people that have eyes to see [28] and see not, that have ears to hear and hear not, for they are a rebellious house. Now, son of man, prepare yourself for exile, [29] in daytime, before their eyes. Then go yourself out in the evening as though you were really going into exile. Dig a hole through the wall before their eyes and go out by it, carrying your baggage upon your shoulders in the darkness, and you shall cover your face not to be seen, for I have set you for a sign to the house of Israel."

I did as I had been commanded. I brought out my baggage in the daytime, as though it were real baggage for exile. Then in the evening I dug a hole through the wall with my hand and went out in the dark, carrying my baggage upon my shoulders before their eyes.

In the morning came the word of the Lord to me, saying: "Son of man, has not the house of Israel, the rebellious house, said to you: 'What are doing?' Say to them: 'Thus said the Lord God: This prophecy applies to the prince in Jerusalem [30] and the whole house of Israel.' Tell them: 'I am your sign.' As I have done, so shall be done to them—

⋙ [27] ABOMINATIONS: *The Temple had been defiled by idolatry and unrighteous practices. Manasseh was even said to have put an idol in the sanctuary itself (II Kings 21:7).*

⋙ [28] HAVE EYES TO SEE: *The people of Judah have not learned either from the fall of Samaria or from the first exile of Judah. They do not see what has happened or will happen, and they do not listen to the Prophet's message.*

⋙ [29] PREPARE YOURSELF FOR EXILE: *Symbolically, Ezekiel enacts the exile which will shortly be inflicted on all Jerusalem.*

⋙ [30] PRINCE IN JERUSALEM: *King Zedekiah.*

אֲשֶׁר עֵינַיִם לָהֶם לִרְאוֹת וְלֹא רָאוּ, אָזְנַיִם לָהֶם לִשְׁמֹעַ וְלֹא שָׁמֵעוּ.

they shall go into exile, into captivity. The prince shall carry his baggage upon his shoulders and go out in the dark. They shall dig a hole in the wall to go out through it. The prince shall cover his face so that he should not be recognized. I shall spread My net upon him and he shall be caught by My snare. I will bring him into Babylon, to the land of the Chaldeans, though he shall not see it, [31] and he will die there. I will disperse to every wind all those who are around him to help him, and all his troops. I will pursue them with the sword. But I will spare a few of them from the sword, from the famine and from the pestilence, that they may tell of all their abominations among the nations where they come, and they shall know I am the Lord."

vine-tree which grows in the woods [32] better than any other tree of the forest? Is wood taken from it to make anything? Can even a peg be made of its wood to hang a utensil on? It is usually flung into fire for fuel. Now, when the fire consumed both ends and the very core became scorched, is it good for anything?"

Therefore, thus said the Lord God: "As the wood of the vine-tree of the forest which I have given to the fire for fuel, so do I give the inhabitants of Jerusalem. I have set My face against them. They were saved from fire, but now fire shall consume them; and you shall know that I am the Lord when I set My face against them. I will make the land desolate because they have acted treacherously," said the Lord.

A WILD VINE

THE WORD OF THE LORD came to me, saying: "Son of man, in what respect is the

THE LAND IS DEFILED

THE WORD OF THE LORD came to me, saying: "Set your face toward the mountains

---

⭊ [31] THOUGH HE SHALL NOT SEE IT: *Nebuchadnezzar blinded Zedekiah at Riblah before taking him captive to Babylon. (II Kings 25:7; Jeremiah 39:7)*

⭊ [32] VINE-TREE WHICH GROWS IN THE WOODS: *The parable of the vine and vineyard is common in Scripture. Here, God's special vine, Israel, has become a wild vine, good neither for fruit nor any other useful purpose other than to be consigned to the fire of God's punishment.*

כַּאֲשֶׁר עֵץ הַגֶּפֶן בְּעֵץ הַיַּעַר אֲשֶׁר נְתַתִּיו לָאֵשׁ לְאָכְלָה, כֵּן נָתַתִּי אֶת יוֹשְׁבֵי יְרוּשָׁלָיִם.

of Israel and prophesy against them. Say: You mountains of Israel, hear the word of the Lord God: Thus said the Lord to the mountains and the hills, [33] the ravines and the valleys: I will bring a sword upon you and I will destroy the high places. Your altars shall become desolate, your sun-pillars [34] shall be broken and I will throw your slain before your idols and scatter their bones around the altars. In all your settlements, the cities shall be laid waste, the high places shall be desolate, so that your altars may be laid waste and your idols shattered and your sun-pillars cut down and all your work blotted out.

"Yet will I leave a remnant, [35] those who escape the sword, among the nations scattered through the countries.

Those who escape among the nations, where they shall be carried away captives, will remember that I have been anguished [36] by their straying hearts which have departed from Me, and their eyes which have gone astray after idols. They shall loathe themselves in their own eyes, for the evil which they have committed in all their abominations. They shall know that I am the Lord, that it was not in vain that I said I would bring this evil upon them."

SOCIAL CORRUPTION

THE WORD OF THE LORD came to me, saying: "Son of man, say to her: You are a land that is not being cleansed nor rained upon because of my indignation. Her

---

[33] THE MOUNTAINS AND THE HILLS: *Ezekiel inveighs against the places where idols were worshiped, the high places and valleys, and warns the people that their bones will lie among the bones of the animal carcasses sacrificed to those pagan idols.*

[34] SUN-PILLARS: *Obelisks built to the sun god.*

[35] WILL I LEAVE A REMNANT: *If Jews were to disappear, the Torah would disappear, and God Himself would lose the most effective witnesses of His presence.*

[36] I HAVE BEEN ANGUISHED: *Israel's sins have deeply grieved the Lord.*

וְיָדְעוּ כִּי אֲנִי יְיָ, לֹא אֶל חִנָּם דִּבַּרְתִּי לַעֲשׂוֹת לָהֶם הָרָעָה הַזֹּאת.

princes are like a ravening lion tearing his prey; they have devoured souls. They seize treasures and precious things. They multiply widows in her midst. Her priests have done violence to My law and have profaned My holy things. They have made no distinction between the holy and the common, neither have they taught the differences between the clean and the unclean. They have hidden their eyes from the Sabbaths and I am profaned among them.

"Her princes in her midst are like wolves tearing the prey, to shed blood and destroy for dishonest gain. Their prophets have daubed for them with whitewash, with visions, divining lies to them, saying: 'Thus said the Lord God,' when the Lord God has not spoken. The people of the land have practiced oppression and committed robbery. They have wronged the poor and the needy and have oppressed the stranger unlawfully. I sought for a man among them that should put up a fence and stand in the breach before Me for the land, that I should not destroy it; but I found none. Therefore have I poured out My indignation; I have consumed them with the fire of My wrath. Their own way have I brought upon their heads."

וָאֶשְׁפֹּךְ עֲלֵיהֶם זַעְמִי, בְּאֵשׁ עֶבְרָתִי כִּלִּיתִים, דַּרְכָּם בְּרֹאשָׁם נָתַתִּי.

12. EZEKIEL [11–33]

THE SINS OF THE PAST

IT CAME TO PASS in the seventh year [1] in the fifth month in the tenth day [2] that some of the elders of Israel came to inquire of the Lord and they sat before me.

Then the word of the Lord came to me, saying: "Son of man, speak to the elders of Israel and say to them: Thus said the Lord God: Did you come to inquire of Me? As I live, you are not worthy that I should answer your query. Son of man, judge them, judge them! Acquaint them

---

[1] THE SEVENTH YEAR: *The year 590 B.C.E., the seventh year of Jehoiachin's captivity. This was four years before the Temple in Jerusalem was to be destroyed.*

[2] THE TENTH DAY: *The tenth of Ab, the day when, four years later, Jerusalem was to be conquered.*

הַלְדְרֹשׁ אוֹתִי אַתֶּם בָּאִים? חַי אָנִי, אִם אִדָּרֵשׁ לָכֶם.

with the abominations of their fathers!" [3]

"Say to them: Thus said the Lord
God: On the day I chose Israel and made
Myself known to them in the land of
Egypt, I lifted My hand and swore to the
descendants of the house of Jacob, saying: 'I am the Lord and I will bring you
forth out of the land of Egypt into the
land which I have selected for you, [a
land] flowing with milk and honey
which is the glory of all lands.'

"So I brought them out of the land of
Egypt and led them into the wilderness.
I gave them [there] My statutes and taught
them My ordinances which, if a man
observe them, he shall live by them. I
also gave them My Sabbath to be a sign
between Me and them that they might
know that I am the Lord that sanctifies
them. But the house of Israel rebelled
against Me in the wilderness. They walked not in My statutes, they rejected My
ordinances and they profaned My Sabbaths. So I said I would pour out My
fury upon them in the wilderness and
destroy them.

"But I withdrew My hand [and spared
them]. I did it for My Name's sake that
My Name should not be profaned in
the eyes of the nations in whose sight
I brought them out. [4]

"I brought them to the land which I
lifted My hand to give it to them. Then
they saw every high hill and every thick
tree, and they offered their sacrifices
there, and they presented their sweet
offerings and poured out their drink-
offerings.

"Now, say to the house of Israel: Thus
said the Lord: Do you [want to] pollute
yourself in the manner of your fathers

---

[3] ABOMINATIONS OF THEIR FATHERS: *God commands the prophet to tell
the elders of Israel that because they and their ancestors have committed
abominations, the Temple will be destroyed and the state will fall.*

[4] I BROUGHT THEM OUT: *Rabbi Simeon ben Lakish taught that God's
attachment to Israel could be likened to a king who fastened a chain to
the key of a valuable jewel box, so that if it were lost or misplaced he
could easily find it again. So did the Lord attach His name "El" to
"Israel" to prevent the Israelites from being swallowed up among the
nations.*

וָאֶתֵּן לָהֶם אֶת חֻקּוֹתַי וְאֶת מִשְׁפָּטַי הוֹדַעְתִּי אוֹתָם, אֲשֶׁר יַעֲשֶׂה אוֹתָם הָאָדָם
וָחַי בָּהֶם.

and go astray after their abominations? And shall I answer your inquiry, O house of Israel? [5]

"That which comes to your mind shall not come to pass at all in what you say: We will become like other nations, as other peoples of the land, to worship wood and stone. [6] As I live, says the Lord God, with a mighty hand and an outstretched arm, and with an outpouring of rage will I reign over you. I will bring you out from among the peoples and I will gather you from the countries where you are scattered, with a mighty hand and an outstretched arm and with an outpouring of rage; and I

will bring you into the wilderness of the peoples and there will I invoke proceedings against you face to face.

"I will pluck out from among you the rebels and those that transgress against Me. I will bring them out from the land of their exile, but they shall not enter the land of Israel so that you shall know that I am the Lord.

"As for the rest of you, O house of Israel, thus said the Lord God: Because you do not hearken to Me, go each one of you and worship your idols and do not profane My holy Name with your gifts. [7] Only on My holy mountain, and on the mountain of the height of

---

⇜ [5] O HOUSE OF ISRAEL: Isaiah says (64:7), "We are the clay and Thou art our Father." So Israel declares, "Even if we sin and You are angry, O Lord, do not forsake us. For if the potter makes a jug and leaves a pebble in it and the jug drips where the pebble is until all the fluid is lost, who is at fault? The potter who left the pebble in the jug." Therefore, the children of Israel say to the Lord, "In us you left the *yetzer hara*, the evil inclination, which causes us to sin. Now we pray that You take it from us so that we can do Your will."

⇜ [6] WORSHIP WOOD AND STONE: "Though there is nothing real in idols," the Lord said, "no sooner does a man separate himself from them when it is as if he had drawn nearer to Me."

⇜ [7] WITH YOUR GIFTS: It was Rachel who pleaded for the children of Israel with the Lord. The Lord knew, she said, that Jacob had worked seven years for her and that Laban had given him Leah instead. When

וְהֵבֵאתִי אֶתְכֶם אֶל מִדְבַּר הָעַמִּים וְנִשְׁפַּטְתִּי אִתְּכֶם שָׁם פָּנִים אֶל פָּנִים.

Israel, there shall you serve Me and there shall I accept and require your heave-offerings and the first fruits of your presentations in all your holy things."

THE LAND WILL NOT PROTECT

THE WORD OF THE LORD came to me, saying: "Son of man, say to them who inhabit the place that shall become waste land in the land of Israel, saying: Abraham was one and he inherited the land; but we are many and the land shall surely be given us as an inheritance.

Therefore, say to them: Thus said the Lord God, you eat flesh with the blood and you lift up your eyes to your idols and you shed innocent blood: shall you possess the land? You depend on your sword, you commit abominations: shall you possess the land? Thus said the Lord God: As I live, they who are in this waste place, they shall surely fall by the sword, [8] and he who is in the open field will I give to the beasts to be devoured, and they who are in the strongholds and in the caves shall die of pestilence."

Rachel learned of this and told Jacob, she gave Jacob a sign so that Jacob would be able to tell her and her sister apart. But then she pitied Leah and in the night, when they had substituted Leah for her, Rachel gave her sister all the signs which she had earlier given to Jacob. "I was not jealous," Rachel declared before God, "and I did not put my sister to shame. If I, who am only flesh and blood and dust, did not expose Leah to shame and reproach, why should You, O loving and merciful One, be jealous of idols who have no reality in them? Why should You, because of them, send my children into exile, let them be slain by the sword, and our enemies oppress them at their will?"

Then the Lord was stirred and He said, "For your sake, Rachel, will I restore Israel to its land."

&ε§ [8] FALL BY THE SWORD: If a ruler commands you to disobey all the commandments of the Torah on penalty of death, you may disobey them all except the commandments which forbid idolatry, incest and the shedding of blood.

מִיָּד נִתְגַּלְגְּלוּ רַחֲמָיו שֶׁל הַקָּדוֹשׁ־בָּרוּךְ־הוּא וְאָמַר: בִּשְׁבִילֵךְ, רָחֵל, אֲנִי מַחֲזִיר אֶת יִשְׂרָאֵל לִמְקוֹמָם.

THE CAPTIVES SHALL NOT DESPAIR

THE WORD OF THE LORD came to me, saying: "Son of man, the inhabitants of Jerusalem say to your brethren in the exile, to all the house of Israel: 'You are far from the Lord so that the land is given us as a possession,' Therefore, say thus," said the Lord, "Although I have removed them far off among the nations and have scattered them among the countries, yet I shall be to them as a little sanctuary [9] in the countries where they have gone. I will also gather you from the peoples and assemble you out of the countries where you have been scattered, and I shall give you the land of Israel. [10] You shall return there and remove all detestable things and all abominations there. I will give you one heart and I will put a new spirit within you. I will remove the heart of stone from you and give you a heart of flesh so that you shall walk in My statutes and keep My ordinances; [11] and you shall be My people and I shall be your God."

⋅⋛ [9] A LITTLE SANCTUARY: *The little sanctuary means the synagogues and houses of study which arose in Babylon where the Israelites studied and prayed.*
    The Lord said, "Though I exiled My people and scattered them among the nations, I did not reject them and My Divine Presence remains among them. I will cause My Presence to be in their synagogues and houses of study; though they are far from My Temple in Jerusalem, they are near Me, because their synagogues and houses of study take its place.

⋅⋛ [10] THE LAND OF ISRAEL: Rabbi Hisde asked what the verse in Jeremiah, "I gave you a pleasant land, the heritage of the deer," meant. The prophet Ezekiel also uses those terms in speaking of the land of Israel. Rabbi Hanina answered that just as when a deer is slain and flayed, its skin shrinks and can no longer cover the animal's body, so too, when the land of Israel is inhabited by Jews, there is room for all, but when it is not inhabited, the land contracts.

⋅⋛ [11] KEEP MY ORDINANCES: Our Sages say that the word *basar* here does not mean flesh. The word is rather *boser*, which means to despise,

וַהֲסִירוֹתִי לֵב הָאֶבֶן מִבְּשָׂרָם וְנָתַתִּי לָהֶם לֵב בָּשָׂר.

THE AVENGING SWORD

THE WORD OF THE LORD came to me, saying: "Son of man, set your face toward Jerusalem and preach against its Sanctuary and prophesy against the land of Israel. Say to the land of Israel: Thus said the Lord: Behold I am against you and I will draw My sword out of its sheath and I will cut off from you the righteous and the wicked alike, and all flesh shall know that I the Lord have drawn My sword from its sheath and shall not return [it] any more. [12] Sigh,

so that the line says, "I will give you a heart that will despise your neighbor's possessions." Rabbi Aba said that in the world to come, the Lord will change man's heart so that it will not covet or envy his neighbor's possessions; he will value only what he himself owns.

Our Sages tell the tale of the man who was taken on a guided tour of Hell. There, in the dining hall, he saw people seated at tables before the most tempting delicacies, but in each person's hand there was a spoon or a fork with such a long handle that he could not convey the food from the dishes to his mouth. And each of them was emaciated and trembling with hunger, straining with all his might to put the food into his mouth, and failing.

"What kind of punishment is this?" the visitor asked. "Why don't they just feed each other? The long-handled spoons and forks are perfect for putting food into the mouth of the person who sits opposite."

The visitor was told, "These are evil people who would rather starve to death than feed their fellowmen."

❧ [12] SHALL NOT RETURN [IT] ANY MORE: Our rabbis daringly declare that only through the awareness of the children of Israel does the Lord exist in and for the world. It is written, "You are My witnesses, said the Lord, and I am God" (Isaiah 43:10). That means that if the people of Israel testify to God's existence, He exists; if they do not, He does not exist. It is also written, "To You I raise my eyes, to You who dwells in heaven" (Psalms 123:1). If not for the people of Israel raising their eyes to God, He would not be in heaven.

בֶּן אָדָם, שִׂים פָּנֶיךָ אֶל יְרוּשָׁלַיִם וְהַטֵּף אֶל מִקְדָּשִׁים.

son of man, sigh before them, with heartbreaking, with bitterness, shall you sigh before their eyes. And if they shall ask you, 'Why do you sigh?' you shall answer them: Because of the tidings that came. Every heart shall melt and the hands shall be limp, every spirit shall grow faint and all knees shall become weak as water. It came and it shall be done says the Lord."

The word of the Lord came to me, saying: "Son of man, prophesy and say: Thus said the Lord: A sword, a sword is sharpened and polished for slaughter. The sword is sharpened and polished to give into the hand of the slayer. Cry and wail, son of man; for it has fallen upon My people, upon all the princes of Israel. Therefore, smite your thigh. You, son of man, prophesy; smite your hands together and let the sword come down a second time, let it come down a third time, the sword of those to be slain, the sword of the great slaughter that will pierce them. Sword, show your sharpness! Turn to the right, turn to the left,

turn to wherever your face is set. I shall also strike My hands together, and I will satisfy My fury. I, the Lord, have spoken it."

THE GREAT EAGLES

THE WORD OF THE LORD came to me, saying: "Son of man, intrigue them with a riddle, speak in a parable to the house of Israel and say: Thus said the Lord: The great eagle with broad wings, [13] and long pinions, full of plumage of diverse colors, came to Lebanon, plucked the topmost of its twigs and carried them into the land of the traders.

"He also took some seed of the cedar and planted it in fertile soil beside the many waters and set it as a willow that it might grow and whose branches might turn toward him and its roots under his eye. So it became a spreading vine that put forth branches and sent out roots sprawling on the ground.

"But there was another great eagle [14] with great wings and many feathers,

[13] EAGLE WITH BROAD WINGS: *Nebuchadnezzar is the first eagle, a bird of prey, which carried off king Jehoiachin (the topmost of its twigs) to Babylon.*

[14] ANOTHER GREAT EAGLE: *The second great eagle is the Egyptian Pharaoh Hophra, to whom Zedekiah turned for help.*

בֶּן אָדָם, חוּד חִידָה וּמְשֹׁל מָשָׁל אֶל בֵּית יִשְׂרָאֵל.

and the vine bent its roots toward him and stretched its branches toward him from the soil in which it was planted that it might grow branches and yield fruit and become a glorious vine. Say to them: Thus said the Lord: Can such a vine flourish? Shall he not pluck up its roots and strip off its fruit and all its sprouting leaves shall wither? It will not require much strength and many people to pluck it from its roots. Indeed, it is planted, but can it flourish? As soon as the east wind touches it, shall it not wither away? [15] It shall wither away on the bed in which it grows."

THE PARABLE EXPLAINED

THE WORD OF THE LORD came to me, saying: "Say to the rebellious house: You know what these things mean: The king of Babylon came to Jerusalem and took its king and princes and brought them to him in Babylon. He took one of the royal family and made a covenant with him and put him under oath. He took away the mighty of the land so that the kingdom might be kept lowly, that it might not lift itself up, so that it would be forced to keep the covenant. But the king rebelled against him and sent his ambassadors to Egypt asking for horses and many soldiers. Will he succeed?

"Shall he break the covenant and yet escape? As I live, says the Lord God: He shall die in Babylon, in the land of the king who made him king, whose oath he scorned [16] and whose covenant he broke. I will spread My net upon him, he shall be caught in My snare, and I will bring him to Babylon. There will I judge him for his treachery against Me. All the mighty men in all his bands shall fall by the sword, and those that remain shall be scattered to the winds. You shall know that I, the Lord, have spoken."

৩ৎ [15] SHALL IT NOT WITHER AWAY: *Babylonia, which is northeast of Palestine, is the east wind which will wither the vine that is Zedekiah and his kingdom; its fruit and leaves—its princes and mighty men—will be destroyed.*

৩ৎ [16] WHOSE OATH HE SCORNED: Rabbi Eliezer said, "Yes is an oath, and no is an oath."

וּפָרַשְׂתִּי עָלָיו רִשְׁתִּי וְנִתְפַּשׂ בִּמְצוּדָתִי וַהֲבִיאוֹתִיהוּ בָבֶלָה.

LAMENTATION FOR THE KINGS OF JUDAH

NOW YOU TAKE UP a lamentation over the princes of Israel [17] and say: What was your mother? A lioness among lions. She crouched in the midst of young lions and reared her whelps. She brought up one of her whelps and he became a young lion. He learned to rend his prey and devour men. Then nations raised a clamor against him and he was taken in their pit and they dragged him with hooks to the land of Egypt.

She saw that she was undone and her hopes perished, she took another of her whelps and made him a young lion. He stalked among lions and learned to rend his prey and devoured men, he ravaged palaces and laid cities waste. Then the nations cried out against him and placed their snares around him. They spread their net over him and he was taken in their pit. With hooks they put him in a cage and brought him to the king of Babylon. Then they put him into a stronghold so that his voice might not be heard upon the mountains of Israel again.

JUDAH THE WRETCHED MOTHER

YOUR MOTHER was like a vine in a vineyard planted by the waters. [18] She was fruitful and full of branches because of the many waters. She had a strong branch for a royal scepter. She rose in her height among thick branches and was seen in her stateliness among the mass of boughs.

---

    [17] THE PRINCES OF ISRAEL: *Jehoahaz, Jehoiakim and Zedekiah, all of whom came to disastrous ends. Jehoahaz was taken to Egypt in chains after ruling for only three months and died there in 608 B.C.E. Jehoiakim, his brother, who succeeded him, was taken to Babylon by Nebuchadnezzar and died en route in 597 B.C.E. Jehoiachin, his son and successor, was exiled to Babylon by Nebuchadnezzar after being on the throne for only three months. Zedekiah, the son of Josiah, who replaced Jehoiachin, revolted against Babylon and was dethroned by Nebuchadnezzar and blinded and taken captive to Babylon in 586 B.C.E.*

    [18] A VINEYARD PLANTED BY THE WATERS: *The kingdom of Judah which was flourishing and powerful.*

וַיִּתְהַלֵּךְ בְּתוֹךְ אֲרָיוֹת כְּפִיר הָיָה, וַיִּלְמַד לִטְרָף־טֶרֶף אָדָם אָכָל.

But she was plucked up in a fury. She was cast down to the ground and the east wind dried up her fruit. [19] Her strong branches withered away and the fire consumed her. Now she is planted in the wilderness in a dry and thirsty land. A fire has gone out of her branches and has devoured her boughs and now she has no strong rod to be a royal scepter. [20]

This is a dirge and became [forever] a dirge.

NEBUCHADNEZZAR INVADES JERUSALEM

THE WORD OF THE LORD came to me, saying: "You, son of man, visualize two roads set for the sword of the king of Babylon to take. Both shall come forth from one land. A sign post is set at the head of the road which clearly marks the way to the city. At the crossroads, one road leads to Rabbah, the other to fortified Jerusalem. The king of Babylon stood at the fork in the roads to use divination. He shook the arrows, he consulted the teraphim, and he looked into a beast's liver. [21] In his right hand was the lot Jerusalem, to open the mouth for slaughter, to lift up voices for the shout of battle, to set battering rams against the gates, to throw up mounds and to build a siege wall. It will look to them [in Jerusalem] like a false divination because they remember the oath that the Chaldeans swore to them when they made a covenant with Zedekiah. But this makes Me to remember their guilt and they shall be taken with the hand. A ruin, a ruin, a ruin will I make it."

THE FALL OF JERUSALEM

THE WORD OF THE LORD came to me, saying: "Son of man, I am taking away from you the delight of your eyes [22]

⁙ [19] THE EAST WIND DRIED UP HER FRUIT: *Until Babylon overcame her.*

⁙ [20] ROYAL SCEPTER: *The royal house has been destroyed, and no heir is left.*

⁙ [21] A BEAST'S LIVER: *These are the primitive superstitions connected with divination.*

⁙ [22] THE DELIGHT OF YOUR EYES: *This was meant to be Ezekiel's wife.*
   God creates new worlds constantly. In what way? By causing marriages to take place.

יַעַן הִזָּכֶרְכֶם, בַּכַּף תִּתָּפֵשׂוּ. עַוָּה עַוָּה עַוָּה אֲשִׂימֶנָּה.

by a stroke. Yet you shall neither lament nor weep nor let a tear fall. Sigh in silence. Make no mourning for the dead. Wind your headdress upon you and put shoes upon your feet. Cover not your upper lip and eat not the bread of mourning." [23]

I did in the morning as I was commanded and in the evening my wife died. [24] The people said to me: "Will you not tell us what the things you do mean?" I said to them: "The word of the Lord came to me, saying: Speak to the house of Israel. Thus said the Lord: I am about to profane My Sanctuary; the pride of your strength, your sons and your daughters, the delight of your eyes, that you left behind, shall fall to the

sword. And you shall do as I have done: You shall not cover your upper lip nor eat the bread of mourning. [25] Your headdress shall remain on your head and your shoes on your feet. You shall pine away in your iniquities and moan one toward the other. Thus Ezekiel shall be to you as an omen; just as he has done you shall do. When this comes to pass, then shall you know that I am the Lord God."

"And you, son of man, on the day when I take from them their stronghold, the joy of their glory, the delight of their eyes and the yearning of their souls, their sons and daughters, [26] on that day, he that escapes shall come to you with the news. On the day that the fugi-

---

⋙ [23] EAT NOT THE BREAD OF MOURNING: *The calamity will be so great that the ordinary methods of mourning and lament will be both inadequate and impossible.*

⋙ [24] MY WIFE DIED: If a man merits it, his wife gladdens his life. If he does not merit it, she desolates it.

⋙ [25] EAT THE BREAD OF MOURNING: *This is the meal of comfort brought by neighbors to the mourner after returning from the cemetery. In Hebrew this is called* seudath habraah.

⋙ [26] THEIR SONS AND DAUGHTERS: The old have no taste and the young no power of counsel.

וְהָיָה יְחֶזְקֵאל לָכֶם לְמוֹפֵת, כְּכֹל אֲשֶׁר עָשָׂה – תַּעֲשׂוּ.

tive shall come to you, your mouth shall be opened and you shall speak and not be mute any longer. Then they shall know that I am the Lord."

THE FUGITIVE CAME

IN THE TWELFTH YEAR [27] of our captivity, in the tenth month, on the fifth day of the month, a fugitive from Jerusalem came to me, saying: "The city has fallen."

Now the hand of the Lord had been upon me in the evening before the fugitive came. He opened my mouth when the fugitive came to me in the morning, and I was no longer mute. [28]

&ampersand; [27] THE TWELFTH YEAR: *The twelfth year of Jehoiachin's captivity, which began in 597 B.C.E. Jerusalem was conquered in the eleventh year of Zedekiah's reign, or 586 B.C.E.*

&ampersand; [28] I WAS NO LONGER MUTE: *On the same day that Nebuchadnezzar besieged Jerusalem, Ezekiel's wife died in the epidemic which broke out among the captive exiles in Babylon. In his grief the prophet remained aware of the calamity which had befallen the nation, but none around him thought of the impending national disaster. In the death of his beloved wife—"He whose first wife dies it is to him as if the Temple in Jerusalem had happened in his time; the world darkens for him" (Sanhedrin 22a and b)— Ezekiel saw a symbol of the coming calamity. Ezekiel remained mute until the first fugitive came to report that Jerusalem had been destroyed. That was three years later, because it took Nebuchadnezzar two-and-a-half years to breach the walls of Jerusalem and six months for the fugitive to travel from Jerusalem to Babylon. After the news of the destruction of the Temple, Ezekiel began to prophesy words of comfort, and devoted his efforts to building a new community in Babylon.*

יִפָּתַח פִּיךָ וְלֹא תֵאָלֵם עוֹד, וְיָדְעוּ כִּי אֲנִי יְיָ׃

13. EZEKIEL [18–48]

INDIVIDUAL RESPONSIBILITY

"YOU, SON OF MAN, say to the house of Israel: You speak thus, saying: Our transgressions and our sins are upon us, we waste away. How can we live? [1] Say to them: As I live, says the Lord God, I have no delight in the death of the wicked, but that the wicked turn from his way and live. [2] Turn, turn

---

[1] HOW CAN WE LIVE: Every man should see himself as half good and half evil. By performing one more good act, he becomes a righteous man; by performing one more evil act, he becomes a wicked man.

[2] TURN FROM HIS WAY AND LIVE: Though everything is foreseen by God yet man is granted free will.

חַי אָנִי, אִם אֶחְפֹּץ בְּמוֹת הָרָשָׁע, כִּי אִם בְּשׁוּב רָשָׁע מִדַּרְכּוֹ וְחָיָה.

from your evil ways. [3] Why should you die, O house of Israel?"

The word of the Lord came to me, saying: "What do you mean by using this proverb in the land of Israel, saying: 'The fathers have eaten sour grapes and the children's teeth are set on edge'? As I live, says the Lord God, you shall have no more occasion to use this proverb in Israel. All souls are Mine: the soul of the father as well as the soul of the son is Mine. The soul that sins, that soul shall die. [4]

"The soul that sins shall die. The son shall not bear the iniquity of the father, nor shall the father bear the iniquity of the son; the righteousness of the righteous shall be on him, and the wickedness of the wicked shall be on him. [5] But if the wicked turn from all the sins he has committed and keep all My statutes he shall surely live, he shall not die. None of his transgressions that he has committed shall be held against him; for his righteousness that he has performed he shall live. [6] Have I any pleasure at

---

 [3] TURN FROM YOUR EVIL WAYS: Just as the Creator willed that fire and air should ascend and water and earth should fall, so He willed that man should have freedom to act and have all his actions within his power, and hence be judged according to his deeds.

 [4] THAT SOUL SHALL DIE: *In the captivity the exiles blamed their fathers' sins for their punishment, and Ezekiel spoke out sharply against this. A man's fate is determined by his own actions, not by those of his father or his children. The righteous will be judged righteous and the wicked will be punished. No generation will be punished for the sins of its forebears or for its descendants.*

 [5] THE WICKEDNESS OF THE WICKED SHALL BE ON HIM: Only if the children are like their fathers and sin against the Almighty will they suffer for their fathers' sins as well as for their own.

 [6] HE SHALL LIVE: Woe will come to me from my Creator if I obey my impulses. And woe to me from my impulses if I obey my Creator.

אָבוֹת יֹאכְלוּ בֹסֶר וְשִׁנֵּי הַבָּנִים תִּקְהֶינָה.

all that the wicked should die? says the Lord; and not rather that he should return from his ways and live? [7]

"You, son of man, say to your people, the righteousness of the righteous man shall not deliver him on the day of his transgression; and the wickedness of the wicked man shall not bring his downfall in the day of his turning away from his wickedness. When I say to the righteous man that he shall surely live, if then he relies upon his righteousness and commits iniquity, none of his righteous deeds shall be remembered; but for the iniquity that he committed shall he die. [8] Again, when I say to the wicked: 'You shall surely die,' and he turn from his sin and does justice and righteousness, if the wicked returns the pledge, [9] gives back what he had taken by robbery, [10] follows the statutes which lead to life, commits no iniquity, he shall

---

[7] RETURN FROM HIS WAYS AND LIVE: It is written, "Good and upright is the Lord, therefore He will instruct sinners in the way" (Psalms 25:8). They asked Wisdom, "What shall be the punishment of the sinner?" Wisdom answered. "Evil pursues sinners" (Proverbs 13:21). They asked Prophecy. It replied, "The soul that sins shall die" (Ezekiel 18:4). They asked the Law. It replied, "Let him bring a sacrifice" (Leviticus 1:4). They asked God, and He replied, "Let him repent, and obtain his atonement. My children, what do I ask of you? Seek Me and live."

[8] SHALL HE DIE: If one sins, saying, I shall sin and repent, sin and repent, then no opportunity will be given to him to repent.

[9] RETURNS THE PLEDGE: When repentance is derived from fear, premeditated sins are counted as errors; when repentance is so great because it is derived from the love of God, premeditated sins are counted as though they were merits.

[10] WHAT HE HAS TAKEN BY ROBBERY: He who robs the public cannot win full forgiveness through repentance, because he does not know to whom he must make restitution.

צִדְקַת הַצַּדִּיק לֹא תַצִּילֶנּוּ בְּיוֹם פִּשְׁעוֹ, וְרִשְׁעַת הָרָשָׁע לֹא יִכָּשֶׁל בָּהּ בְּיוֹם שׁוּבוֹ מֵרִשְׁעוֹ.

surely live; he shall not die. [11] None of the sins that he has committed shall be remembered against him, because he has done that which is just and right; therefore, he shall surely live.

"Yet your people say: The way of the Lord is not fair. O house of Israel, your way is not fair. I judge each according to his ways." [12]

comes from the Lord. They come to you in a crowd and sit before you as My people, and hear your words but heed them not. [13] You are to them as a love song, as one that has a beautiful voice and can play well on an instrument. They hear your words, but they do them not. When this comes to pass, they shall know that a prophet was among them."

THEY HEAR BUT DO NOT OBEY

"AS FOR YOU, son of man, your people who talk about you by the walls and in the doors of the houses, they speak to one another: Come and hear the word that

THE VISION OF THE DRY BONES

THE HAND of the Lord was upon me and the Lord carried me by the spirit and set me down in the midst of a valley, and it was full of bones. [14] He led me all

---

⳩ [11] HE SHALL NOT DIE: Rabbi Alexander said that if a mortal man uses broken vessels it is a disgrace. But for God it is otherwise, because all His servants are broken vessels, as it is said, "The Lord is near to the broken-hearted, and the contrite of spirit will He save."

⳩ [12] EACH ACCORDING TO HIS WAYS: All the judgments of the Holy One, blessed be He, are on the basis of measure for measure.

⳩ [13] BUT HEED THEM NOT: He whose deeds exceed his wisdom is like a man who rides a horse with a bridle and reins; he can direct the horse as he wills. But he whose wisdom exceeds his deeds is like a man who rides a horse without either rein or bridle.

⳩ [14] FULL OF BONES: Rabbi Judah said that the story that Ezekiel brought the dead to life is true, but a parable. Then Rabbi Nehemiah asked, "If it is true, then it cannot be a parable; and if it is a parable, then it cannot be true." Then Rabbi Judah answered, "Truly, it is a parable; and truly it happened and is the fate of Israel."

הָיְתָה עָלַי יַד יְיָ וַיּוֹצִיאֵנִי בְרוּחַ יְיָ וַיְנִיחֵנִי בְּתוֹךְ הַבִּקְעָה, וְהִיא מְלֵאָה עֲצָמוֹת.

around them and I saw that there were many of them in the open valley and they were very dry. And He said to me: "Son of man, can these bones live?" I answered: "Lord, only You know." He said to me: "Prophesy over these bones and say to them: O you dry bones, hear the word of the Lord. Thus said the Lord God to these bones: I will put sinews upon you and will bring up flesh upon you. I will cover you with skin and put breath in you, and you shall live, that you shall know that I am the Lord."

I prophesied as I was commanded, and as I prophesied there was a noise and a commotion and the bones came together, bone to bone. I looked and there was sinew upon them and flesh came up and skin covered them above but there was no breath in them. Then He said to me: "Prophesy to the breath. Prophesy,

son of man, and say to the breath: Thus said the Lord God: <u>Come from the four ends of the earth. Come breath and breathe life into these corpses that they may live.</u>"

So I prophesied as He commanded and breath came into them and they lived and stood up upon their feet, a great host. Then He said to me: "Son of man, these bones are the whole house of Israel. They say: We are dried up bones, and our hope is lost. We are completely cut off. Therefore prophesy to them and say: Thus said the Lord God: I will open your graves and raise you up out of your graves and bring you to the land of Israel. [15] I will put My spirit in you and you shall live, and I will settle you in your own land; [16] and you shall know that I the Lord have spoken and performed it, says the Lord."

---

    [15] THE LAND OF ISRAEL: Rabbi Eliezer said that whoever dies outside of the land of Israel will be brought to Israel and resurrected when the time comes. It was customary to put a clod of earth from the land of Israel on the coffin of all those who died outside of the land of Israel, and later to put a little bag of earth from the soil of Israel under the dead man's head.

    [16] IN YOUR OWN LAND: *Ezekiel's prophecy that Israel would be restored was the most heartening prophecy he could bring to the exiles. The vision of the dry bones brought to life was a forecast of the resurrection of the children of Israel and the kingdoms of Israel and Judah.*

מֵאַרְבַּע רוּחוֹת בֹּאִי הָרוּחַ וּפְחִי בַּהֲרוּגִים הָאֵלֶּה – וְיִחְיוּ.

RESTORATION OF THE LAND

YOU MOUNTAINS of Israel, hear the word of the Lord. Thus said the Lord God to the mountains and the hills, to the streams and the valleys, to the desolate wastes and the abandoned cities which have become a prey and a derision to the nations that are round about. Therefore, thus said the Lord God: "I have lifted up My hand that the nations round about you shall bear their shame. But you mountains of Israel put forth your branches and yield your fruit to My people Israel, because soon they will come back. I am with you. I shall look to you and shall see that you shall be tilled and sown. The cities shall be inhabited and the waste places shall be rebuilt. [17] I will multiply men and beasts upon you and they shall increase and be fruitful. I will settle you, as in former days, and I will do better to you than at your be-ginnings; and you will know that I am the Lord."

THE PEOPLE REGENERATED

THE WORD OF THE LORD came to me, saying: "Son of man, when the house of Israel dwelt in their own land they defiled it by their doings. So I poured out My fury upon them for the blood which they shed upon the land and because they had defiled it with their idols. I scattered them among the nations and dispersed them through the countries. According to their ways and their doings I judged them.

"When they came among the nations, wherever they came, they profaned My holy Name in that men said to them: 'These are the people of the Lord and yet they were driven out of their land.' I had concern for My holy Name which the house of Israel had profaned among the nations [18] where they came. Therefore,

---

ᏋᏅ [17] THE WASTE PLACES SHALL BE REBUILT: *The first steps in Israel's re-generation will be the regeneration of the despoiled land and the desolate cities.*

ᏋᏅ [18] PROFANED AMONG THE NATIONS: The pagan neighbors of Jews never returned anything they found which belonged to a Jew, and so it was decided that legally a Jew might also keep the possessions of pagans

וְהוֹשַׁבְתִּי אֶתְכֶם כְּקַדְמוֹתֵיכֶם וְהֵיטִבֹתִי מֵרֵאשֹׁתֵיכֶם וִידַעְתֶּם כִּי אֲנִי יְיָ.

say to the house of Israel: Thus said the Lord: It is not for your sake that I am doing this, O house of Israel, but for My holy Name, which you have profaned among the nations to which you came. I will sanctify My great Name [19] that has been profaned among the nations; and the nations shall know that I am the Lord, when I will be sanctified in you before their eyes.

"I will take you out of the nations and gather you out of all the countries, and will bring you into your own land. I will give you a new heart, and a new spirit [20] will I put within you. I will remove the heart of stone out of your flesh and will give you a heart of flesh. I will put My spirit within you and make you follow My statutes and you shall keep My ordinances and do them. And you shall dwell in the land which I gave to your fathers. Then you shall be My people and I shall be your God."

THE KINGDOMS REUNITED

THE WORD OF THE LORD came to me, saying: "You, son of man, take a piece of

---

which he found. Some rabbis, however, declared that it glorified God's Name to return such things nonetheless.

Simeon ben Shetah bought a donkey and under its saddle discovered a pearl. He returned the pearl to the Arab from whom he had bought it and the Arab exclaimed, "Blessed be the God of Israel." The rabbi's students asked why he had not kept the pearl, in accordance with the law. And the rabbi replied, "Am I then a pagan? His blessing is worth more to me than all the money the pearl might have brought."

[19] MY GREAT NAME: Rabbi Johanan ben Berokah said, "If a man profanes the Name of God secretly, he will be repaid openly. In the profanation of the Name, there is no distinction between the inadvertent and the presumptuous."

[20] A NEW SPIRIT: Our Sages say that when the children of Israel will live peacefully among themselves and become as brothers to one another, they will then be worthy to be redeemed.

וִישַׁבְתֶּם בָּאָרֶץ אֲשֶׁר נָתַתִּי לַאֲבוֹתֵיכֶם וִהְיִיתֶם לִי לְעָם וְאָנֹכִי אֶהְיֶה לָכֶם לֵאלֹהִים.

wood [21] and write upon it: 'Judah and all that belongs to it.' Then take another piece of wood and write upon it: 'Israel and all that belongs to it.' Then join them together so as to form a single plank in your hand. When your people shall ask you, saying, 'Will you tell us what you mean by this?' say to them: Thus said the Lord God: I will take the children of Israel out from among the nations where they have gone. I will gather them from every side and bring them into their own land. I will make them one nation in the land on the mountains of Israel and one king shall be king over them. <u>My servant David shall be king over them. Neither shall they be divided into two kingdoms any longer.</u> I will make a covenant of peace with them and it shall be an everlasting covenant. I will establish them and multiply them and will set My sanctuary in their midst forever. I will be their God and they shall be My people. When My sanctuary shall be in their midst forever, then shall the nations know that I am the Lord that sanctifies Israel."

REBUKE TO SELFISH LEADERS

THE WORD OF THE LORD came to me, saying: "Son of man, prophesy against the shepherds of Israel. [22] Prophesy and say to them: Woe to the shepherds of Israel who have fed none but themselves. Should not the shepherds feed the sheep? You have fed on the milk and have clothed yourself with the wool. You have killed the fatlings, but you have not tended the flock. You have not strengthened the weak, neither have you healed the sick, neither have you bound up the wounded, neither have you brought back the strayed, neither have you sought out the lost. You ruled over them with force and rigor. So they scattered because there was no shepherd; and they became food to all the beasts of the field. My sheep wandered through all the mountains and upon every high

---

⋙ [21] A PIECE OF WOOD: *A symbolic scepter representing the kingdoms of Israel and Judah.*

⋙ [22] SHEPHERDS OF ISRAEL: *For Israel to be revived and restored, it must have virtuous and responsible leaders. Ezekiel here condemns Israel's past rulers and promises better ones in the future.*

וְעַבְדִּי דָוִד מֶלֶךְ עֲלֵיהֶם וְרוֹעֶה אֶחָד יִהְיֶה לְכֻלָּם.

hill. My flock was scattered over all the earth and there was none to seek and search for them. [23]

"Therefore, you shepherds, hear the word of the Lord: Thus said the Lord God: I am against the shepherds. I will require My sheep at their hands and I will stop them from feeding the sheep. I will deliver My sheep from their mouths that they may not be food for them."

Thus said the Lord: "Here I am and I will search for My sheep and seek them out. As a shepherd searches for his flock in the day when they are scattered, so will I seek out My sheep. I will deliver them out from all the nations and gather them from all the countries and bring them into their own land. I will feed My sheep. I Myself will lead them to their pasture," says the Lord. "I will seek out the lost, I will bring back those who are strayed, I will bind up the wounded, I will strengthen the sick, I will watch over the fat and the strong ones. I will feed them with justice. [24]

"As for you, My flock," thus said the Lord God: "I will judge between the sheep and the rams and the he-goats. Is it not enough for you to have fed on good pasture but must you trample down with your feet the rest of the pasture? You drink clear waters, but must you foul the rest with your feet? My sheep have to eat that which you have trampled with your feet and drink that which you have fouled." [25]

THE IDEAL SHEPHERD

THEREFORE says the Lord God: "I will judge between the fat and lean sheep. Because you push with side and shoulder and huff all the weak with your horns, therefore will I help My flock and they

---

[23] NONE TO SEEK AND SEARCH FOR THEM: A shepherd protects his flock from lions, wolves and other enemies; so too must a leader protect his people from all enemies and lead them to obey the law.

[24] I WILL FEED THEM WITH JUSTICE: How unique is the lamb that can survive among seventy wolves!

[25] WHICH YOU HAVE FOULED: God revealed the earth in His wisdom, and He prepared the world for His congregation.

כְּבַקָּרַת רוֹעֶה עֶדְרוֹ בְּיוֹם הֱיוֹתוֹ בְתוֹךְ צֹאנוֹ נִפְרָשׁוֹת, כֵּן אֲבַקֵּר אֶת צֹאנִי.

shall no longer be a prey. [26] I will judge between sheep and sheep. [27] I will set up one shepherd over them to tend them, that is My servant David. [28] He shall tend them and be their shepherd. I will make a covenant of peace with them and I will banish the wild beast out of the land so they may live safely in the wilderness and sleep in the woods. I will send down the rain in its season. The tree of the field shall yield its fruit and the earth shall yield its produce; and they shall be safe in their land. And they shall know that I am the Lord when I have broken the bars of their yoke and have delivered them out of the hand of those who enslaved them.

"You, My sheep, the sheep of My pasture, are man and I am your God," said the Lord God.

THE LAND OF MAGOG

THE WORD OF THE LORD came to me, saying: "Son of man, set your face toward Gog, of the land of Magog, [29] the chief prince of Meshech and Tubal, and prophesy against him." Thus said the Lord God: "It shall come to pass in that day that thoughts shall come into your mind and you shall devise an evil design. You shall say: I will go up against the land of unwalled villages. [30] I will come upon them who are peaceful peo-

---

⇛ [26] SHALL NO LONGER BE A PREY: The life of a man is not true life if he does not help his fellowman.

⇛ [27] SHEEP AND SHEEP: *The Lord will judge between the poor oppressed (the lean sheep) and the rich oppressors (the fat sheep), between good and evil.*

⇛ [28] MY SERVANT DAVID: *When the Messiah comes, a leader, like David, will rule justly and wisely.*

⇛ [29] THE LAND OF MAGOG: *But before the end of days arrives, there will be one great invasion by Gog, of the land of Magog. Gog has been variously interpreted as Babylon, Crete, and the Scythians; but most likely Gog was an apocalyptic and symbolic figure rather than a historical one.*

⇛ [30] UNWALLED VILLAGES: *This defenselessness will prompt Gog to war.*

וְנָתַן עֵץ הַשָּׂדֶה אֶת פִּרְיוֹ וְהָאָרֶץ תִּתֵּן יְבוּלָהּ וְהָיוּ עַל אַדְמָתָם לָבֶטַח.

ple who all live in villages without walls, having neither bars nor gates, to take the spoil and to take the prey; to turn your hand against the waste places that are now reinhabited, against the people that are gathered from the nations, who dwell in the hilly country and who peacefully raise cattle. The traffickers of Sheba and Dedan, the merchants of Tarshish shall say to you: Have you come to despoil them? Have you assembled your army to take prey? To carry away the gold and silver, to take away cattle and goods, to take great spoil? [31]

You bestirred yourself and came from the uttermost part of the north with a great host, all of them riding upon horses, a mighty array. You came against My people Israel as a cloud covering the land. Thus said the Lord God: You are the one of whom I spoke in olden times through My servants, the prophets of Israel that prophesied in those days that I will bring you against them. But it shall come to pass in that day when Gog shall come up against the land of Israel, My fury shall be roused. In My indignation and the fire of My wrath I swear that on that day there shall be a great earth-quake in the land of Israel, so that the fishes in the sea, the birds in the air, the beasts in the field and all things that creep on the ground, and all men that are on the face of the earth shall shake at My presence. The mountains shall be thrown down, the towers shall fall, and every wall shall tumble to the ground. I will call a sword against him throughout all My mountains, said the Lord God, every man's sword shall be against his

---

&ε [31] TO TAKE GREAT SPOIL: When Alexander the Great asked to enter the gates of Paradise, he was told that only the righteous could enter. He then asked for a gift, and a piece of a human skull with one eye open was thrown to him. Alexander wished to weigh it on his scales and placed it on a balance with gold and silver, but no matter how much gold he added, the skull was always heavier. Then the Sages advised him to put a clod of earth on the eye, and at once the gold in the balances became heavier than the skull. "This teaches," the Sages told Alexander, "that a human eye is not satisfied with all the gold that exists until it is covered with the earth of the grave."

וְרָעֲשׁוּ מִפָּנַי דְּגֵי הַיָּם וְעוֹף הַשָּׁמַיִם וְחַיַּת הַשָּׂדֶה וְכָל הָרֶמֶשׂ הָרוֹמֵשׂ עַל הָאֲדָמָה
וְכֹל הָאָדָם אֲשֶׁר עַל פְּנֵי הָאֲדָמָה.

brother. [32] I will punish him with pestilence and with blood. I will rain upon him and his bands, and upon the many peoples that are with him, a lashing rain, fire and brimstone. Thus will I magnify Myself and sanctify Myself and make Myself known in the eyes of the many nations; and they shall know that I am the Lord.

AFTER THE DEFEAT OF GOG

YOU SHALL FALL on the mountains of Israel, you and all your bands, and the peoples who are with you. I will give you to be devoured by ravenous birds of every sort and the beasts of the field. Then it shall come and it shall be in the day I have predicted that they who live in the cities of Israel shall go out and make firewood of their weapons and use them as fuel. [33] They shall collect the shields and the bucklers, the bows and the arrows, the handpikes and the spears, and for seven years they shall make firewood of them. For seven years they shall not need to take wood from the fields, neither cut down any out of

---

ᴈ [32] EVERY MAN'S SWORD SHALL BE AGAINST HIS BROTHER: Two men are traveling in the desert but only one of them has a waterskin. If only one of them drinks, he will reach civilization. The son of Petura taught that it is better that both should die and neither live to see his brother's death. But then Rabbi Akiba came and taught: Your life takes precedence over his.

ᴈ [33] USE THEM AS FUEL: A rabbi stood in the marketplace when Elijah the prophet appeared to him. The rabbi asked, "Is there anyone here in this marketplace who will have a share in the world-to-come?" Elijah replied that there was not. Just then two men came into the square, and Elijah remarked that those two would have a share in the world-to-come. The rabbi turned to the two men and asked them, "What is your occupation?" They answered, "We are merrymakers. When we see men troubled we cheer them. And when we see men quarreling we make peace between them."

וּבְעֲרוּ וְהִשִּׂיקוּ בְּנֶשֶׁק וּמָגֵן וְצִנָּה, בְּקֶשֶׁת וּבְחִצִּים וּבְמַקֵּל יָד וּבְרֹמַח, וּבִעֲרוּ בָהֶם אֵשׁ שֶׁבַע שָׁנִים.

the forests, for they shall make fires of the weapons. [34] Thus will I set My glory among the nations, and all nations shall see My judgment that I have executed and My hand that I have laid upon them. From that day forward the house of Israel shall know that I am the Lord their God.

THE LIFEGIVING STREAM

IN THE FIVE AND TWENTIETH YEAR of our captivity, in the beginning of the year, in the tenth day of the month, in the fourteenth year after the city had fallen, [35] in the selfsame day, the hand of the Lord was upon me and He brought me in a vision to the land of Israel. He set me down upon a very high mountain, and in front of me was the outline of a city. He brought me there, and there was a man whose appearance was like the appearance of shining bronze, with a measuring line of flax and a measuring rod in his hand. [36] He stood at the gate and said to me: "Son of man, look with your eyes and hear with your ears and set your heart upon what I know. You were brought here in order that I might show them to you; and then for you to declare what you see to the house of Israel."

I saw a wall on the outside of the house. He brought me to the gate which looked toward the east. Then he brought me to the porch of the house and measured each post of the porch. Then he brought me to the Temple and measured the posts. He went inward and measured each post of the entrance. He measured its length, it was twenty cubits, and the

---

[34] MAKE FIRES OF THE WEAPONS: For seven full years after the defeat of Gog, the people of Israel will need no wood from the forests for making fires. Instead, they will build their fires from the handles of the knives, spears and swords of the enemy. Those seven years will be joyous as a wedding feast, a feast of joy to the righteous.

[35] THE CITY HAD FALLEN: *Jehoiachin was captured in 597 B.C.E., so that the time now is 572.*

[36] A MEASURING ROD IN HIS HAND: *Prophecy is given in either a dream or a vision. When a prophet is inspired, he may perceive an allegory, or he may in a prophetic vision perceive that God speaks to him, or he hears an angel addressing him, and sees him also.*

בֶּן אָדָם, רְאֵה בְעֵינֶיךָ וּבְאָזְנֶיךָ שְׁמָע, וְשִׂים לִבְּךָ לְכֹל אֲשֶׁר אֲנִי מַרְאֶה אוֹתְךָ.

width twenty cubits before the Temple. He said: "This is the most holy place."

He returned me to the door of the Temple and I saw water flowing from under the threshold of the house eastward, for the forefront of the house looked toward the east. He brought me out by the way of the gate that looked east. When the man went out eastward with the line in his hand he measured a thousand cubits and made me pass through the waters. The waters came up to my ankles. Again he measured a thousand cubits and made me pass through the waters. The waters came up to my knees. Again he measured a thousand cubits and made me cross the waters. The waters came up to my loins. Again he measured a thousand cubits and it was a river that I could not pass through. Then he said to me: "Have you seen this, son of man?" Then he led me and brought me to the bank of the river and I saw many trees growing on both sides.

He said to me: "These waters go forth to the eastern region and they shall reach to the Arabah and when they fall into the sea, into the sea of bitter waters, the waters shall be healed. Then every living creature shall live in it. Fishermen shall stand on its shore. There shall be a place for the spreading of nets. Fish of all sorts will be plentiful, like those of the Great Sea. But the [water in the] marshes and swamps shall not become fresh. It shall be left for the supply of salt. On both banks of the river shall grow every kind of tree for food. The leaves on the trees shall never wither, neither shall the fruit of the trees ever fail. Every month the trees shall bear fresh fruit because the water that feeds them flows from the Sanctuary. Their fruit shall be for food and their leaves for healing.

"The circumference of the city shall be eighteen thousand cubits [37] and from that day the name of the city shall be 'The Lord is There.'"

✑ [37] EIGHTEEN THOUSAND CUBITS: Abaye said: The world must contain no fewer than thirty-six righteous men in each generation, who are vouchsafed the sight of the *shechinah*. Rabba said: The righteous standing immediately before the Holy One, blessed be He, consist of 18,000, for it is written: "It shall be eighteen thousand round about." The thirty-six refer to those who see the Lord in a bright mirror; the 18,000 those who contemplate Him in a dim one.

לְחָדָשָׁיו יְבַכֵּר כִּי מֵימָיו מִן הַמִּקְדָּשׁ הֵמָּה יוֹצְאִים, וְהָיָה פִרְיוֹ לְמַאֲכָל וְעָלֵהוּ לִתְרוּפָה.

14. HOSEA [1–14]

THE WORD OF THE LORD that came to Hosea, son of Beeri, [1] in the days of Uzziah, Jotham, Ahaz and Hezekiah, kings of Judah, and in the days of Jeroboam, the son of Joash, king of Israel.

THE MARRIAGE OF HOSEA

WHEN THE LORD FIRST SPOKE to Hosea, the Lord said to him: "Go and take a wife who will become a harlot [2] and

[1] SON OF BEERI: Hosea's father was a prophet who prophesied only two verses (Isaiah 8 : 19–20): "When they will say to you: Consult the ghosts and the spirits that chirp and gibber: should not a people consult their God? But, on behalf of the living, they consult the dead." The children of Israel should turn to the Torah for instruction, and if they will not, then there is no light of dawn.

[2] WHO WILL BECOME A HARLOT: *Some of the rabbis believe the command to be allegorical, and others believe it to be a command which Hosea did in*

דְּבַר יְיָ, אֲשֶׁר הָיָה אֶל הוֹשֵׁעַ בֶּן בְּאֵרִי.

have the children of a harlot, for the land has committed great harlotry in turning away from the Lord." [3]

So Hosea went and took Gomer, the daughter of Diblaim. She conceived and bore him a son. And the Lord said to him: "Call his name Jezreel; [4] for yet a little while and I will demand the blood of Jezreel from the house of Jehu, and I will bring to an end the house of Israel. On that day will I break the power of Israel in the valley of Jezreel."

Then Gomer conceived again and bore a daughter. And the Lord said to Hosea:

---

fact obey, so that the people would see their waywardness and infidelity in his action. This was to be the symbol of Israel's apostasy.

[3] FROM THE LORD: When the Lord said to Hosea: "Your children have sinned. What shall I do to them?" Hosea should have replied, "They are Your children, the children of Abraham, Isaac and Jacob. Show them Your mercy." But instead Hosea said, "Sovereign of the universe, the whole world is Yours. Exchange them for a different nation."

Then the Lord said, "I shall order him to marry a wonam of harlotry and beget three children by her. Then will I command him to send her away from his presence, so that he will understand."

After two sons and a daughter were born to Hosea, the Lord commanded Hosea to part with Gomer. Hosea pleaded that she had borne him children and that he could neither cast her out nor divorce her. Then the Lord said, "If you, whose wife is a harlot so that you cannot know whether your children are your own or belong to others, cannot exchange your wife for another, how can you tell Me to exchange Israel, who are My children, for another people?"

Hosea saw that he had sinned and begged for mercy, but the Lord rebuked him again, saying, "Instead of pleading for mercy for yourself, plead for mercy for Israel." So Hosea began to bless Israel and to speak his prophecies of comfort.

[4] JEZREEL: *This means "God sows."*

וְהָיָה בַּיּוֹם הַהוּא, וְשָׁבַרְתִּי אֶת קֶשֶׁת יִשְׂרָאֵל בְּעֵמֶק יִזְרְעֶאל.

"Call her name Lo-ruhamah; [5] for I will not again have compassion upon the house of Israel that I should ever forgive them."

When she had weaned Lo-ruhamah she conceived and bore a son. And He said to him: "Call his name Lo-ammi, [6] for you are not My people and I am not your God."

ISRAEL: THE FAITHLESS WIFE

Plead with your mother, plead;
Let her put away her harlotry from her face,
And her adultery from between her breasts; [7]
Lest I strip her naked,
And set her naked as the day she was born,

And make her like a desert,
And set her in a dry land,
And leave her to die of thirst.
I will have no compassion on her children;
For they are the children of harlotry
Because their mother played the harlot;
She bore them and has acted shamefully. [8]
She said: "I will follow my lovers,
Who give me my bread and my water,
My wool and my flax, my oil and my wine."
But she did not know that it was I that gave her
The corn and the wine and the oil;
And the silver and gold which I multiplied for her,

&ε [5] LO-RUHAMAH: *The name means "the unpitied one," and very likely this child was illegitimate.*

&ε [6] LO-AMMI: *The name means "not My people."*

&ε [7] FROM BETWEEN HER BREASTS: *In those days harlots painted their faces and carried a talisman on a chain around their necks, which fell between their breasts and identified them as harlots.*

&ε [8] HAS ACTED SHAMEFULLY: Rabbi Johanan said in the name of Rabbi Jose: "Better one self-reproach in the heart of a man than a thousand lashes."

קְרָא שְׁמוֹ לֹא עַמִּי, כִּי אַתֶּם לֹא עַמִּי וְאָנֹכִי לֹא אֶהְיֶה לָכֶם.

Which they used for Baal.
Therefore will I take back My corn
in its harvest time,
And My wine in its season,
And I will reclaim My wool and
My flax
Given to cover her nakedness.
Now I will uncover her shame in
the sight of her lovers
And none shall save her out of My
hand.
I will lay waste her vines and her
fig-trees
Which she said, "They are mine,
My lovers have given them to me."
I will turn them into a forest,
And beasts of the field shall devour
them.
I will bring all her joy to an end,
Her feasts, her new moons and her
sabbaths,
And all her festivals.
I will punish her for her days of the
Baalim,
To whom she offered sacrifices,
And decked herself with earrings
and jewels

And went after her lovers,
And forgot Me, said the Lord.

HOSEA TAKES HIS WIFE BACK

AGAIN the Lord said to me: "Go and love the woman beloved of a paramour, who is an adulteress, even as the Lord loves the children of Israel, though they turn to other gods and love their raisin cakes." [9]

So I bought her for myself for fifteen pieces of silver and a homer and a half of barley. And I said to her: "For many days you shall live a secluded life. You shall not be any man's wife, nor will I myself come near you. [10] For the children of Israel shall abide many days without a king, without a prince, without sacrifices, without a sacred pillar, *ephod* or *teraphim*."

THE SINS OF ISRAEL

HEAR THE WORDS of the Lord, you children of Israel. The Lord has a quarrel with the inhabitants of the land, because

---

ᴇᵍ [9] RAISIN CAKES: *These were part of the pagan offerings to Baal.*

ᴇᵍ [10] I MYSELF COME NEAR YOU: *God commands Hosea to give his erring wife another chance, just as the Lord has given the children of Israel another chance after their betrayal. But first there must be a period of seclusion.*

כִּי יָמִים רַבִּים יֵשְׁבוּ בְּנֵי יִשְׂרָאֵל אֵין מֶלֶךְ וְאֵין שָׂר וְאֵין זֶבַח וְאֵין מַצֵּבָה וְאֵין אֵפוֹד וּתְרָפִים.

there is no truth, nor kindness, nor knowledge of God in the land. Cursing and lying, stealing and killing; they break all bounds and blood touches blood. [11] My people inquire of a block of wood to guide them, and their staff instructs them. A whoring spirit caused them to err and they have abandoned their God.

There is no man to bring charges, no one to reprove; [12] the people reproach the priest. Therefore the land mourns and everything that dwells therein languishes; even the beasts of the earth, the birds in the air and the fish in the sea perish.

I will not punish your daughters when they commit harlotry, nor your daughters-in-law when they commit adultery; when you yourselves consort with harlots and sacrifice with temple-prostitutes; [13] and a people that is without understanding must come to ruin.

GUILT AND PUNISHMENT

Blow the shofar in Gibeah,
And the trumpet in Ramah;
Sound the alarm in Beth-aven: [14]
"Look behind you, O Benjamin!"
Ephraim shall be desolate in the day
    of punishment;

⋑ [11] BLOOD TOUCHES BLOOD: *Everywhere there is violence and murder.*

⋑ [12] NO ONE TO REPROVE: Our Sages say that when the scholar, rabbi or leader sees evils done and does not point them out to the people and reprove them, he shares the punishment.

Abba Saul ben Nannas said: There are four types of scholars. One is the man who learns, but does not teach others. The second is the man who teaches others but does not learn. The third is he who neither learns nor teaches. And there is the man who both teaches and learns.

⋑ [13] TEMPLE PROSTITUTES: If parents commit transgressions, the example they set will be copied by their children.

⋑ [14] BETH-AVEN: *The prophet derisively calls Beth-el, which means the house of God, Beth-aven, which means the house of sin, because Jeroboam had set up a golden calf to be worshiped there.*

עַמִּי בְּעֵצוֹ יִשְׁאָל, וּמַקְלוֹ יַגִּיד לוֹ.

Among the tribes of Israel do I make
known that which will surely
occur.
The princes of Judah are like those
who remove the landmark;
I will pour out My wrath upon
them like water.
Ephraim is oppressed, justly
crushed;
Because he willingly walked after
filth.
Therefore I am to Ephraim like a
moth,
To the house of Judah like a
rottenness.
When Ephraim saw his sickness,
And Judah his wound,
Ephraim went to Assyria
And sent to the great king.
But he is not able to heal you,
Neither can he cure your wound.
For I will be to Ephraim like a lion,

And like a young lion to the house
of Judah.
I will tear and depart,
I will take away, and there shall be
none to rescue.

FEIGNED REPENTANCE

I WILL GO and return to My place until
they acknowledge their guilt and seek
My face. [15] In their distress they will
seek me earnestly.

[They will say,] "Come, let us return
to the Lord, for He has torn but will heal
us. He has wounded us, but He will bind
us up, that we may live in His presence.
Let us know Him, let us strive to know
the Lord. His coming is sure as the coming of dawn. He shall be to us as the rain,
as the spring rain that waters the
earth." [16]

❧ [15] SEEK MY FACE: When Israel sinned, the Temple was deprived of
the presence of God until the people should repent. The Lord withdrew His presence so that the enemy might enter the Temple. But
once the children of Israel acknowledged their guilt and sought Him
in earnest, He would return.

❧ [16] THAT WATERS THE EARTH: A pious father visited his older daughter
who was married to a potter. Before he left her house, his daughter
said, "Father, please pray for dry, sunny weather so that my husband's
pots will dry well. Because you are pious, the Lord will answer you."

לְכוּ וְנָשׁוּבָה אֶל יְיָ כִּי הוּא טָרָף וְיִרְפָּאֵנוּ, יַךְ וְיַחְבְּשֵׁנוּ.

O Ephraim, what shall I do with you? O Israel, what shall I do with you? Your goodness is like the morning cloud, like the dew that passes away early. <u>I desire goodness and not sacrifices, and the knowledge of God rather than burnt offerings.</u> [17] But like Adam they have transgressed the covenant. They have dealt treacherously against Me. Gilead is a city of evildoers, tracked with bloody footprints. The priests hide themselves on the road and murder those going to Shechem. In the house of Beth-el I have seen horrible things; harlotry is found in Ephraim, Israel is defiled. [18]

KINGS AND PRINCES FALLEN

WHEN I WOULD RESTORE the fortunes of My people; when I would heal Israel, then the iniquity of Ephraim and the wickedness of Samaria is uncovered.

The next day the father visited his younger daughter who was the wife of a farmer, and she asked him to pray for rain. "We need rain badly for the crops, for the corn and the wheat to grow."

The father raised his eyes to heaven and prayed, "O Lord, blessed be Thy Name. In Your compassion, I leave it to You to know when to send rain and when sunshine, to arrange the blessings of the world so that none are hurt and all are satisfied."

⁌ [17] BURNT OFFERINGS: When Johanan ben Zakkai and Rabbi Joshua passed the ruins of the Temple in Jerusalem, Rabbi Joshua lamented, "Woe unto us. The Temple where we made offerings to atone for our sins is destroyed. How shall we atone for our sins now?"

"We have other means of atonement," Rabbi Johanan ben Zakkai replied. "Benevolence to our fellowmen. Charity. Loans without interest to the poor. And other deeds of lovingkindness. For it is written: 'I desire mercy and not sacrifice.'"

⁌ [18] ISRAEL IS DEFILED: *No place, not the Temple or Gilead or Shechem or Beth-el are intrinsically holy. Holiness and sacredness depend on men's deeds. When the spirit of God departs from a place it is defiled; when the Lord's presence is removed from the Temple, it can be destroyed by the pagans.*

כִּי חֶסֶד חָפַצְתִּי וְלֹא זָבַח, וְדַעַת אֱלֹהִים מֵעוֹלוֹת.

They commit falsehood, the thief enters into the house, the robbers roam the streets, no one says even in his heart that I remember all their wickedness. Now their sins have encompassed them and they are before My sight. They make the king glad with their wickedness and their princes with their lies. [19] On the day of coronation the princes make him sick with the heat of the wine and the king revels with worthless men. For they have made ready their heart like an oven, in the morning it burns like a flaming fire. They are all as heated as an oven and devour their rulers. All their kings are fallen and there is none that calls to Me.

WORTHLESS FOREIGN ENTANGLEMENTS

Ephraim mingles among the nations;

Ephraim has become a cake not turned.
Strangers have devoured his strength,
And he is not aware of it.
Yes, gray hairs are sprinkled upon him,
And he knows it not.
The arrogance of Israel testifies against him;
Still they have not returned to the Lord their God,
Nor sought Him in spite of all this.
Ephraim has become like a silly dove, without understanding. [20]
They call to Egypt, they go to Assyria.
Even as they go, I will spread My net over them.

&ও [19] WITH THEIR LIES: Four types of people are unworthy of receiving the presence of God: scoffers, flatterers, liars and slanderers.

&ও [20] WITHOUT UNDERSTANDING: The Roman Emperor Hadrian installed three garrisons in Israel, and sent his couriers to announce that any Jews who came out of hiding and presented themselves to the Emperor would be granted their wishes about where they would live. Many of the Jews believed those announcements, so "Ephraim became like a silly dove, without understanding," and came out of hiding. All gathered in the valley of Remmon. There, Hadrian said to the commander of his legions: "By the time I finish eating this loaf of bread and capon's drumstick, I do not want to see a single Jew alive." The Roman soldiers surrounded the refugees and slaughtered them.

וַיְהִי אֶפְרַיִם כְּיוֹנָה פוֹתָה אֵין לֵב, מִצְרַיִם קָרָאוּ, אַשּׁוּר הָלָכוּ.

I will bring them down as the fowls
    from heaven.

I will bind them because of their
    wickedness,

I will chastise them as their congre-
    gation has heard before.

Woe to them, for they have strayed
    from Me!

Destruction will overtake them, for
    they have transgressed against
    Me!

How can I redeem them,

When they speak lies to Me?

They did not cry to Me with their
    heart;

Though they wail upon their beds,

They bestir themselves for corn and
    wine, they rebel against Me.

Though I have trained and strength-
    ened their arms,

Yet they devise wickedness against
    Me.

FALSE GODS

Put a *shofar* to your lips!

A vulture swoops upon the house
    of the Lord,

Because they have broken My
    covenant

And sinned against the law.

Israel cast off that which is good;

[Therefore] an enemy shall pursue
    him.

They have set up kings, but not with
    My consent;

They deposed them, but not with
    My approval.

Because they sowed the wind, they
    shall reap the whirlwind;

There will be no stalks, the sprout
    shall yield no meal;

If it should yield fruit, foreigners
    shall devour it.

Israel is swallowed up;

Now they are become among the
    nations

A worthless vessel.

Ephraim had enough altars to sin,

But it has multiplied altars to sin
    more.

As for the burnt offerings that they
    sacrifice to Me,

Let them eat the flesh,

For the Lord does not desire them.

Israel has forgotten its Maker and
    built palaces, [21]

And Judah has multiplied fortified
    cities.

℞ [21] FORGOTTEN ITS MAKER AND BUILT PALACES: After Rabbi Abum had
built two large gates before the great synagogue, he showed them
proudly to Rabbi Mana. Rabbi Mana then quoted Hosea's verse
and asked if there were no poor scholars to support instead.

כִּי רוּחַ יִזְרָעוּ וְסוּפָתָה יִקְצֹרוּ, קָמָה אֵין לוֹ צֶמַח בְּלִי יַעֲשֶׂה קֶּמַח.

But I will send a fire upon the cities,
And it shall devour their palaces.

THE HORROR OF EXILE

EPHRAIM surrounded Me with lies and the house of Israel with deceit. Ephraim herds the wind and hunts the east wind; he multiplies lies and destruction all the time. They make a covenant with Assyria and carry oil to Egypt. The Lord has a quarrel with Israel and will punish Jacob according to his deeds.

They shall not dwell in the Lord's land. Ephraim shall return to Egypt and in Assyria they shall eat unclean food. They shall not pour wine offerings to the Lord nor prepare His sacrifices. Their bread shall be mourner's bread; all who eat of it shall defile themselves because the food for their eating shall not come into the house of the Lord.

And what will you do on the festival day, on the day of the feast of the Lord?

ISRAEL'S FAITHLESSNESS

IN THE WOMB he seized his brother's heel and in his full vigor he strove with a godlike being. He fought with the angel and prevailed. He wept and entreated him for mercy. At Beth-el he would find him and there he would talk to him. Then Jacob fled to the field of Aram, Israel served for a wife, for a wife he guarded sheep. By a prophet the Lord brought Israel up out of Egypt and by a prophet Israel was guarded.

Like grapes in the wilderness I found Israel. [22] Like the first fruit of a fig tree I saw your fathers. But as soon as they came to Baal-peor, they separated themselves [from Me and clung] to that shameful thing, and they became an abomination like that which they loved. But I am the Lord, your God [who brought you up] from the land of Egypt, and you know no God but Me. There is no savior but Me. I knew you in the wilderness, in the land of great drought. But when they were fed and they filled themselves, they became arrogant and forgot me.

When Israel was a child I came to love him, and out of Egypt I called him to be My son. But the more I called them, the further they went away from Me. They sacrificed to the Baalim and made offer-

---

ᵛᖕ [22] I FOUND ISRAEL: When the children of Israel received the Law at Mount Sinai, the Lord found them like grapes in the desert, a refreshment and delight, a joy to the world.

כַּעֲנָבִים בַּמִּדְבָּר מָצָאתִי יִשְׂרָאֵל, כְּבִכּוּרָה בִתְאֵנָה בְּרֵאשִׁיתָהּ רָאִיתִי אֲבוֹתֵיכֶם.

ings to graven images. Yet it was I who taught Ephraim to walk, taking them by the arms, and I bent down and fed them gently. But from the days of Gibeah, you have sinned, Israel. There they stand [in their defiance] now. Will the war against the sons of iniquity [23] not overtake them?

Where is your king now, that he may save you in all your cities, and where are your princes, of whom you said: Give me a king and princes. I gave you a king in My anger and took him away in My wrath.

REAP AS YOU PLOW

SOW RIGHTEOUSNESS for yourselves, reap the fruit of mercy. [24] Break up your fallow ground, for it is time to seek the Lord, till He comes and rains righteousness upon you. But you have plowed wickedness and reaped iniquity, you have eaten the fruit of lies; you have trusted in your chariots and in the multitude of your mighty men. Therefore shall confusion arise among your people; all your fortresses shall be destroyed, as Shalman destroyed Beth-arbel on the day of battle; the mother was dashed in pieces with the children. Beth-el has done all this to you because of your great wickedness. At daybreak the king of Israel was utterly destroyed.

GOD'S COMFORT

How can I give you up, Ephraim?
How can I surrender you, Israel?
How can I treat you like Admah?
How can I make you like Zeboim?
My heart turns within Me,
My compassion is kindled within Me.

◆§ [23] THE SONS OF INIQUITY: A father had a son whom he bathed and anointed, gave plenty to eat and drink, and dressed in rich garments. He then put a purse of gold around his neck and set him down before a house of ill-repute. How, then, could the son help but sin?

◆§ [24] THE FRUIT OF MERCY: "Benevolence (*gemilat hesed*) and kindness are greater and more important then charity," Rabbi Eleazar said. "If a man sows, it is doubtful whether he will enjoy the harvest or not. But when a man reaps he will surely eat. So the rewards of charity depend entirely upon the kindness of it."

אֵיךְ אֶתֶּנְךָ אֶפְרַיִם, אֲמַגֶּנְךָ יִשְׂרָאֵל?

I will not carry out My fierce anger.
I will not return to destroy Eph-
raim;
For I am God and not man,
The Holy One in the midst of you,
And I will not come in fury.

THE PLEA AND THE PROMISE

RETURN, O ISRAEL, [25] to the Lord your God, for in your iniquity you have stumbled. Prepare yourselves with words and return to the Lord. Say to Him: "Forgive all iniquities, count only the good and instead of oxen we will render offerings with our lips. [26] Assyria shall not save us, nor will we ride on horses, neither will we call any more the work of our hands our gods. For in You the fatherless find mercy."

I will heal their rebellion, I shall love them as a gift, for My anger shall be turned away from them. I will be as dew to Israel. He shall blossom as the lily [27] and strike his roots as Lebanon. His branches shall spread and his beauty shall be like an olive-tree and his fragrance like Lebanon. Again there will be dwellers in His shadow who will make corn to grow and shall blossom as the vine; and he will be known as the wine of Lebanon. Ephraim [shall say]: "What have I to do with idols?" As for Me, I respond to him and watch over him. I am like a leafy cypress-tree; from Me your fruit is found.

Now I will hedge up her way with thorns and I will put a fence about her that she shall not find her path. She will run after her lovers, but she shall not

---

ᳱ [25] RETURN, O ISRAEL: "Return to Me," says the Lord, "and I will return to you" (Malachi 3:7). When a man goes out to seek God, he meets the Lord who has gone out to meet him halfway.

ᳱ [26] OFFERINGS WITH OUR LIPS: If penitence is motivated by the love of God, then it is complete; no trace of taint remains. But if it is motivated by the fear of punishment alone, a taint remains.

ᳱ [27] BLOSSOM AS THE LILY: Hosea was one of the harshest of the Lord's prophets. In his anger, he said at the beginning, "O Lord, give them whatsoever You will give; give them a miscarrying womb and a dry breast" (9:14). But at the last he was able to prophesy, "They will blossom like a lily."

שׁוּבָה יִשְׂרָאֵל עַד יְיָ אֱלֹהֶיךָ, כִּי כָשַׁלְתָּ בַּעֲוֹנֶךָ.

overtake them; she shall seek them, but shall not find them. Then she shall say: "I will go and return to my first husband, for then it was better with me than now."

Now I shall entice her and lead her into the wilderness and speak to her heart, and I will give her back her vineyards, and the waste valley will I turn into the door of hope. And she shall respond there as in the days when she came up out of the land of Egypt. That day shall you call Me: "My husband," and shall no longer call Me: "My Baal." For I shall take away the names of the Baalim from her mouth and they shall never again be mentioned.

On that day I will make a covenant for them with the beasts of the field and the fowls of the heaven and the creeping things on the ground. I will break the bow and the sword and I will abolish war from the land and let you lie down safely. I will betroth you to Me forever, I will betroth you to Me in righteousness and in justice, and in lovingkindness and in compassion. I will betroth you to Me

in faithfulness and you shall know that I am the Lord.

On that day, said the Lord, I will respond [to the petition] of the heavens and they shall respond to the earth; and the earth shall respond to the corn and the wine and the oil; and they shall respond to Israel. I will increase her to Me in the land and I will have compassion on her that has no compassion, and I will say to them that were not My people, "You are My people," and she will say, "You are My God."

THE INGATHERING OF EXILES

AND IT SHALL COME TO PASS that, instead of that which was said to them, "You are not My people," it shall be said to them, "You are the children of the living God." And the children of Judah and the children of Israel shall be gathered together and they shall appoint themselves one head and shall go up out of the land. For great shall be the day of their ingathering. [28]

◄§ [28] THE DAY OF THEIR INGATHERING: "The ingathering of the exiles," Rabbi Johanan said, "is as important as the day when heaven and earth were created."

וְהָיָה, בִּמְקוֹם אֲשֶׁר יֵאָמֵר לָהֶם לֹא עַמִּי אַתֶּם, יֵאָמֵר לָהֶם בְּנֵי אֵל חָי.

15. JOEL [1-4]

THE LOCUST PLAGUE

THE WORD OF THE LORD that came to Joel, [1] the son of Pethuel.

Hear this, you old men,
And give ear all who dwell in the
    land:
Has the like of this happened in your
    days,
Or in the days of your fathers?
Tell it to your children,
And let your children tell their
    children,
And their children the following
    generations.
That which the shearer left, the
    swarmer has eaten;
That which the swarmer has left,
    the lapper has eaten;

---

[1] JOEL: *The name means "The Lord is God." It is the same name as Elijah, but with the two halves of the name reversed.*

עֲלֵיהָ לִבְנֵיכֶם סַפֵּרוּ, וּבְנֵיכֶם לִבְנֵיהֶם וּבְנֵיהֶם לְדוֹר אַחֵר.

That which the lapper has left, the
    finisher has eaten. [2]
A nation has invaded my land,
Mighty and without number;
His teeth are the teeth of a lion,
And his jaw-teeth those of a lioness.
He has turned my vine to waste,
And splintered my fig trees,
He has stripped them clean and
    thrown down the shreds,
And made the branches gleam white.
The field is devastated,
The earth mourns;
For the corn is laid waste,
The new wine is dried up,
And the oil has failed.
Be abashed, you farmers,
Lament, you vinedressers,
For the wheat and the barley,
And the harvest of the field have
    perished.
The vine is withered,
The fig-tree wilts;
The pomegranate-tree, the palm-
    tree also, and the apple-tree,
All the trees of the field are wither-
    ed;
And joy has fled from the sons of
    men.

THE INVASION

BLOW THE SHOFAR in Zion, sound the alarm in the holy mountain; let all the inhabitants of the land tremble; for the day of the Lord comes, it is near. A day of darkness and gloom, a day of clouds and thick darkness, as blackness spread on the mountains; a great and mighty people, the like of them has never been seen, neither shall be seen again after them, throughout the years of generations upon generations. Before them a fire devours and behind them a flame blazes. The land before them was a garden of Eden, behind them a desolate wilderness; nothing escapes them.

They look like horses, and like war-horses they run. They sound like the clatter of chariots as they leap on the top of the mountains, like the crackling of a flame that eats up the stubble. They are like mighty people arrayed in battle. In their presence nations are anguished, all faces darken. They run like mighty men; they climb the wall like men of war. Every one moves in his own way and their paths are not entangled. They break through the weapons and are not held

---

❦   [2] THE FINISHER HAS EATEN: *Four kinds of locust have made a wasteland of what was once a fertile country.*

לְפָנָיו אָכְלָה אֵשׁ וְאַחֲרָיו תְּלַהֵט לֶהָבָה, כְּגַן־עֵדֶן הָאָרֶץ לְפָנָיו וְאַחֲרָיו מִדְבַּר שְׁמָמָה.

back. They rush upon the city, they run upon the wall, they climb into the houses; through the windows, they enter like a thief.

CALL FOR REPENTANCE

YET, EVEN NOW, said the Lord, return to Me with all your heart, with fasting, with weeping and lamentation. Rend your heart and not your garment. [3] Turn to the Lord your God, for He is gracious and compassionate, long-suffering and abundant in mercy. Who knows but what He will again relent and leave a blessing behind Him, a meal offering and a libation to the Lord your God?

THE LORD'S BLESSING

THEN THE LORD became solicitous for His land and had pity on His people. And the Lord answered and said to His people: I will send you corn, wine and oil, and you shall be satisfied therewith; and I will no longer make you a reproach among nations; and the northern one I will remove from you. [4] I will drive him into a barren and desolate land, and his face toward the eastern sea and his hind parts toward the western sea till he rots and the stench of him rises.

I will restore to you the years that the locust has devoured. [5] And you shall eat in plenty and be satisfied, and you

---

◦§ [3] NOT YOUR GARMENT: Scripture does not say that the people of Nineveh were saved by sackcloth and fasting, but that God saw their deeds, that they had turned away from their evil ways. So, in Joel, it is said, "And rend your hearts not your garments," because neither sackcloth nor fasting will help, only penitence and good deeds.

◦§ [4] I WILL REMOVE FROM YOU: The "northern" or "hidden one," the Rabbis say, refers to the evil inclination embedded in the hearts of men. When the Messiah comes, the Lord will isolate the evil propensity in a desolate and barren place so that it can no longer tempt or prompt men.

◦§ [5] THE LOCUST HAS DEVOURED: As did all the prophets, Joel begins his prophecy with words of rebuke and ends it with words of comfort: "I will restore to you the years that the locust has devoured."

וְקִרְעוּ לְבַבְכֶם וְאַל בִּגְדֵיכֶם, וְשׁוּבוּ אֶל יְיָ אֱלֹהֵיכֶם.

shall praise the name of the Lord your God. My people shall nevermore be put to shame. [6] And you shall know that I am in the midst of Israel, and I am the Lord your God, and there is none else.

And it shall come to pass afterward,
That I will pour My spirit on all flesh; [7]
And your sons and your daughters shall prophesy.
Your old men shall dream dreams,
And your young men shall see visions.
And also upon male-slaves and female-slaves
Will I pour out My spirit.

In those days I will show wonders in the heaven and on earth.
Blood and fire and pillars of smoke.
The sun shall be turned into darkness,
And the moon into blood,
Before the great and terrible day of the Lord comes.
But whosoever shall call on the name of the Lord shall be delivered.
For in Mount Zion in Jerusalem there shall be those that escape,
As the Lord has promised;
And among the remnant those whom the Lord shall call.

&ε [6] BE PUT TO SHAME: Once, when Rabbi Simeon ben Halafta took leave of a colleague, the colleague sent his son along for Rabbi Simeon's blessing. And Rabbi Simeon blessed the youth, saying, "May it be heaven's pleasure that you never be put to shame nor be ashamed yourself." The young man returned to his father and told him that what Rabbi Simeon had said was unimportant, and then repeated his words. Then the father told his son that he was twice blessed. "Rabbi Simeon blessed you with the same blessing with which the Holy One, blessed be He, blessed Israel twice over."

&ε [7] MY SPIRIT ON ALL FLESH: At the end of days the Lord will pour out His Divine Presence on all humanity. Before then, only chosen individuals were prophets; but in the time of the Messiah all men will be prophets, living at peace and studying the Law. In that day all mysteries will be revealed and all men will have the knowledge of God, each according to his human capacity.

כִּי בְּהַר־צִיּוֹן וּבִירוּשָׁלַיִם תִּהְיֶה פְלֵיטָה כַּאֲשֶׁר אָמַר יְיָ.

JUDGMENT DAY

IN THOSE DAYS and in that time, when I shall bring back the captivity of Judah and Jerusalem, I will gather all the nations and bring them down into the valley of Jehoshaphat; [8] and I will enter into judgment with them there, because of My people and for My heritage Israel, whom they have scattered among the nations, and divided My land. They have cast lots over My people and have given a boy for a harlot and sold a girl for a drink of wine.

Proclaim this among the nations: Consecrate war! Stir up the mighty men; let all the men of war draw near, let them come up. Beat your plowshares into swords and your pruning hooks into spears. [9] Let the weak say: "I am strong!" For the nations shall be stirred up and come up to the valley of Jehoshaphat, and there I will sit [10] to judge all the nations from every quarter.

ᨇ [8] THE VALLEY OF JEHOSHAPHAT: *This means "Valley of God the Judge," and it is here that Joel sees his vision of Judgment Day.*

ᨇ [9] PRUNING HOOKS INTO SPEARS: There is a time when it is necessary to do battle, to beat plowshares into swords and pruning hooks into spears. Such a time was that of Antiochus who ordered the end of Jewish religious practices on the pain of death. Pious Jews fled to the desert or hid in mountain caves, but none resisted, so that the tyrant ruled until Mattathias and his sons resorted to arms and freed Judea from tyranny.

ᨇ [10] THERE I WILL SIT: In the time of Hadrian, when the persecution of Jews was severe, two disciples of Rabbi Joshua who were disguised in pagan clothes were discovered by a Roman officer learned in Jewish law. "Are you not required by Jewish law to sanctify the name of your God by readiness to die for your faith? Since you are alive, you must not be believers, and if you don't believe, why not convert?"

The two answered together, "It is unnatural for men to commit suicide."

The Roman officer then said: "If you interpret these two verses

וְנִשְׁפַּטְתִּי עִמָּם שָׁם עַל עַמִּי וְנַחֲלָתִי יִשְׂרָאֵל אֲשֶׁר פִּזְּרוּ בַגּוֹיִם וְאֶת אַרְצִי חִלֵּקוּ.

Multitudes, in the valley of decision, for the day of the Lord is near in the valley of decision. The sun and the moon have grown dark and the stars have withdrawn their splendor. [11] The Lord shall roar from Zion and from Jerusalem He will thunder, and heaven and earth shall quake. But the Lord will be a refuge to His people and a stronghold for the children of Israel. Then you shall know that I am the Lord your God, dwelling in Zion, My holy mountain. Then shall Jerusalem be holy and there shall be no invaders to pass through her any more.

And it shall come to pass in that day that the mountains shall drip sweet wine, and the hills shall flow with milk; and all the riverbeds of Judah shall flow with water. A spring shall come forth of the house of the Lord and shall water the valley of Shittim. Egypt shall be a desolation and Edom shall be a desolate wilderness, for the violence against the children of Israel, and because they have shed innocent blood in their land. I will avenge the innocent blood. But Judah shall be forever inhabited and Jerusalem for generations to come. For the Lord dwells in Zion.

---

correctly, I'll let you go. If you don't, I'll kill you." One verse (Isaiah 3:13) says, 'The Lord stands to judge the people'; the other (Joel 4:12) declares, 'For there will I sit to judge all the nations round about.' Why does the Lord stand in Isaiah and sit in Joel?"

The disciples of Rabbi Joshua answered tauntingly, "When the Lord judges our people, He stands, judging us briefly and with compassion. But when He judges you pagans, He sits so that He can minutely and at His leisure examine all your transgressions."

[11] WITHDRAWN THEIR SPLENDOR: The Roman philosophers asked the Sages, "If your God has such aversion to idolatry, why doesn't He destroy all idols?"

The Rabbis replied: "People worship sun, moon and stars, and other useful things. Should the Lord destroy the universe because of the ignorance of fools?" And they said again, "Suppose that a man stole a measure of wheat and than sowed it. Should the wheat not grow?"

וִיהוּדָה לְעוֹלָם תֵּשֵׁב, וִירוּשָׁלַיִם לְדוֹר וָדוֹר, וַיְיָ שֹׁכֵן בְּצִיּוֹן.

16. AMOS [1–9]

THE WORDS OF AMOS [1] who was among the shepherds [2] of Tekoa [3] and his visions concerning Israel. [He prophe-sied] in the days of Uzziah king of Judah,

---

[1] THE WORDS OF AMOS: The three prophets—Amos, Jeremiah and Koheleth—whose words were chiefly rebuke and reproach have their prophecies attributed not to the Lord but to themselves.

In Hebrew the word *amos* means heavy or burdened. The people of his generation jeered saying, "Of all God's creatures, the Almighty has rested His holy inspiration on that crippled tongue."

[2] SHEPHERDS: Amos herded sheep and goats and was a dresser of sycamore trees. This was a very humble occupation in which each sycamore fig was punctured while still on the tree so that its bitterness would escape and the fig would be palatable when ripened. Sycamore figs were then ground into flour for the coarse bread of the poor.

[3] TEKOA: *A village south of Jerusalem on the edge of the Judean desert.*

לָמָה נִקְרָא שְׁמוֹ עָמוֹס? – שֶׁהָיָה עָמוֹס בִּלְשׁוֹנוֹ.

and of Jeroboam son of Joash king of Israel, two years before the earthquake.

THE MOTTO

HE SAID: The Lord roars from Zion and raises His voice from Jerusalem; the pastures of the shepherds mourn and the top of Carmel withers.

For the three transgressions of Damascus [4] and for the fourth I will not forgive them, because they have threshed Gilead with threshes of iron. So I will send a fire upon the house of Hazael, and it shall devour the palaces of Ben-hadad. I will break the defenses of Damascus and cut off the inhabitants from the valley of the idols [5] and the holder of the scepter from Beth-eden and the people of Aram shall go into captivity, said the Lord.

Thus said the Lord: For the three transgressions of Gaza [6] and for the fourth I will not forgive them, because they carried away into exile the whole people, to sell them as slaves to Edom. And I shall send a fire on the wall of Gaza which shall devour its palaces. And I will cut off the inhabitants from Ashdod, and the holder of the scepter of Ashkelon, so I will turn My hand against Ekron that the remnant of the Philistines shall perish.

Thus said the Lord: For the three transgressions of Tyre [7] and the fourth I will not forgive them, because they handed over a whole people as captives to Edom, and remembered not the covenant of brotherhood. I will send a fire

---

[4] DAMASCUS: *The capital city of Syria, long the enemy of Israel. Hazael and his son Ben-hadad were its rulers.*

[5] THE VALLEY OF THE IDOLS: *The Hebrew is* bikath-aven, *the valley of vanity, where the Syrians worshiped the sun.*

[6] GAZA: *Capital city of the Philistines.*

[7] TYRE: *Capital city of Phoenicia.*

יְיָ מִצִּיּוֹן יִשְׁאָג וּמִירוּשָׁלַיִם יִתֵּן קוֹלוֹ, וְאָבְלוּ נְאוֹת הָרוֹעִים וְיָבֵשׁ רֹאשׁ הַכַּרְמֶל.

on the wall of Tyre which shall devour it.

Thus said the Lord: For the three transgressions of Edom [8] and for the fourth I will not forgive them, because he pursued his brother with the sword and cast off all pity and kept his rage forever. Therefore will I send a fire upon Teman and it shall devour the palaces of Bozrah.

Thus said the Lord: For the three transgressions of the Ammonites, and for the fourth I will not forgive them, for they have ripped open the pregnant women of Gilead that they might enlarge their borders. So I will set fire to the wall of Rabbah and it shall devour her palaces with shouting on the day of battle, with a tempest on the day of the whirlwind, and the king shall go into captivity, he and his princes together.

Thus said the Lord: For the three transgressions of Moab and the fourth I will not forgive him, because he burned the bones of the king of Edom for lime.

So will I send a fire upon Moab and it shall devour the palaces of Kerioh. [9] Moab shall die with tumult, amidst the shouting and the blare of trumpets. I will cut off her king from the midst of her and all her princes will I slay with him.

ISRAEL'S TRANSGRESSIONS

THUS SAID THE LORD: For the three transgressions of Israel and for the fourth I will not forgive them, because they sell the righteous for silver and the needy for a pair of shoes. They trample down the poor like dust, and make the humble turn aside from the way; and a man and his father go to the same maid to profane My holy name. They stretch themselves beside every altar, on garments seized in pledge, and the wine of those who have been fined they drink in the house of their God.

It was I who brought you out of Egypt and led you forty years in the wilderness to possess the land of the Amorites.

⁍ [8] EDOM: *Capital of the Edomites.*

⁍ [9] KERIOTH: *One of the major cities of Moab where the Moabite god was worshiped.*

עַל שְׁלֹשָׁה פִּשְׁעֵי יִשְׂרָאֵל וְעַל אַרְבָּעָה לֹא אֲשִׁיבֶנּוּ – עַל מִכְרָם בַּכֶּסֶף צַדִּיק וְאֶבְיוֹן בַּעֲבוּר נַעֲלָיִם.

And it was I who destroyed the Amorite before you, whose height was like the height of cedars, and he was strong as the oaks. Yet I destroyed his fruit above and his roots below.

I raised up some of your sons [for] prophets and some of your young men for Nazirites. [10] But you made the Nazirites drink wine and commanded the prophets not to prophesy. Is it not so, O children of Israel? Therefore I will make you groan in your places as the cart filled with sheaves makes the threshing floor groan. Flight shall fail the swift, strength shall not encourage the strong; and the warrior shall not save himself. He who holds the bow shall not stand, and he who is swift of foot shall not save himself; neither shall he who rides the horse save himself. The most courageous among the mighty shall flee away naked on that day, said the Lord.

⤳ [10] NAZIRITES: *Nazirites were men consecrated to God for a definite time during which they strove to break a bad habit or improve their ways. A glutton or a drunkard might vow to abstain for a given period, or for his whole life. Yet even in such matters our Sages opposed the making of vows; man should abstain from things harmful to him without a vow.*

"Whoever takes a vow," the Rabbis said, "it is as if he had built a high place for idols; and he who fulfills his vow, it is as if he had sacrificed thereon."

Judaism believes a man is made to enjoy the legitimate pleasures of the world, and asceticism is to be avoided. "A man is destined to give an account of all that his eye sees, and to taste all that his mouth might taste." Rabbi Lazar, concerned about this injunction, saved pennies to buy all kinds of fruit that ripen in different seasons, making the blessing *shehecheyanu* and giving thanks to God for all the good things that He had created in the world.

Rabbi Abaye said: Simeon the Just, Rabbi Simeon and Rabbi Eleazar ha-Kappar all agree that a Nazirite is a sinner, because it is taught, 'And he shall make atonement for him, for that he sinned against a soul' (Numbers 6:11). Against what soul did the Nazirite sin? His own, because he afflicted himself by refraining from everything. Hence, he who fasts is called a sinner.

וְאָבַד מָנוֹס מִקָּל, וְחָזָק לֹא יְאַמֵּץ כֹּחוֹ, וְגִבּוֹר לֹא יְמַלֵּט נַפְשׁוֹ.

ISRAEL THE CHOSEN

HEAR THIS WORD that the Lord has spoken against the whole family which I brought up out of the land of Egypt. Are you not to Me like the Ethiopians, O children of Israel? said the Lord. I have brought Israel up out of the land of Egypt, but did not I bring up the Philistines out of Caphtor and Aram from Kir? But only you alone have I known [11] of all the families of the earth. Therefore will I punish you for all your iniquities.

Behold, the eyes of the Lord God are upon this sinful kingdom. I will destroy it from off the face of the earth; except that I will not utterly destroy the house of Jacob, said the Lord. For I will give a command and I will sift the house of Israel which is scattered among all the nations, as one sifts corn in a sieve. Not the least grain shall fall upon the earth. All the sinners of My people shall die by the sword, those that say: Disaster shall not overtake us [12] nor confront us.

NOTHING BY CHANCE

Will two walk together unless they
   met in a place?
Will a lion roar in the forest
When it has no prey?
Will a young lion raise his voice out
   of his lair
Unless he has seized something?
Will a bird fall in a snare
If there is no hunter?

---

[11] YOU ALONE HAVE I KNOWN: *The children of Israel are chosen by God not for special privilege, nor to rule over others. They are chosen to carry a special yoke, the yoke of the commandments. "Blessed art Thou, O Lord our God, King of the universe," the festival Kiddush says, "who has chosen us among all peoples and singled us out among all the nations by sanctifying us with Thy commandments."*

[12] DISASTER SHALL NOT OVERTAKE US: *No man shall say that I am only me, an insignificant one among many; so no matter how evil the thing I do, it will not cause a calamity. The prophet says, "They shall die by the sword, all those who say that evil shall not come because of our doing."*

הֲיֵלְכוּ שְׁנַיִם יַחְדָּו, בִּלְתִּי אִם נוֹעָדוּ?

Will a snare spring up from the
ground
And have caught nothing at all?
If a shofar be sounded in the city,
Shall the people not tremble?
If disaster befalls a city,
Has not the Lord caused it?
But the Lord God will do nothing
Unless He reveals His purpose to
His servants the prophets. [13]
The lion has roared,
Who will not fear?
The Lord God has spoken,
Who can but prophesy?
Proclaim over the palaces of Assyria,
And over the palaces in the land of
Egypt,
And say: Assemble yourselves upon
the mountains of Samaria,
And see the great confusion and op-
pression within her.
They know not to do the right, says
the Lord.
They store up violence and robbery
in their palaces.
Therefore, thus said the Lord God:
An enemy shall surround the
land,
And he shall strip the strength from
you,
And your palaces shall be plundered.
I will smite the winter-house with
the summer-house;
And the houses of ivory shall perish,
And the great houses shall come to
an end.

---

   [13] HIS SERVANTS THE PROPHETS: Rabbi Simeon says that this refers to
the time when there were prophets. But when they were no more, the
Sages took their place and in one sense even excelled the prophets, for
the Holy Spirit had visited the prophets only intermittently, but it
rested steadily on the wise.

    A voice from heaven once promised the Gaon of Vilna that he was
worthy of having Elijah the Prophet come to him to explain the difficult passages and mysteries in the Torah and the Talmud. But the
Vilna Gaon would not have it. "I want no knowledge given me as a
gift," he said. "I want to earn it by my own labor."

אַרְיֵה שָׁאָג, מִי לֹא יִירָא? אֲדֹנָי אֱלֹהִים דִּבֶּר – מִי לֹא יִנָּבֵא?

DIRGE FOR ISRAEL

HEAR YOU the words of lamentation that I take up against you, O house of Israel:

> The virgin of Israel has fallen,
> Never to rise again;
> Cast down upon her own land,
> There is none to raise her up.

For thus said the Lord God: the city that sent forth a thousand shall have a hundred left; and the city that sent forth a hundred shall have ten left.

You turn justice to wormwood and cast down righteousness to the earth. They hate him who reproves in the gate and they abhor him that speaks uprightly. I know your transgressions, how many and mighty are your sins. You oppress the just, you take bribes and turn aside the needy who come to seek justice.

Woe to them that are at ease in Zion and are confident in the mountain of Samaria, the notable men of the nation to whom the house of Israel come. You think that the evil day is far off and you cause the seat of violence to come near. They lie upon beds of ivory and stretch themselves upon couches. They eat fat lambs out of the flock and the calves from the midst of the stall. They improvise songs to the sound of the harp and consider themselves like David in the making of a song.

They drink wine from bowls, anoint themselves with the choicest of oils and they grieve not over the woe of Joseph.

The Lord God has sworn by Himself: I abhor the pride of Jacob and hate his palaces, and I will deliver up the city with all that is in it. For behold, I will raise up against you a nation, O house of Israel, said the Lord, the God of the host, and they shall crush you from the entrance of Hamath to the brook of Arabah.

THE KING OF SAMARIA

HEAR THIS WORD, you king of Bashan, who are in the mountain of Samaria, that oppress the poor, that crush the needy, that say to their husbands: "Bring, that we may feast." The Lord God has sworn by His holiness that days shall come upon you, that they will drag you with hooks, and the last of you with fishhooks, and then you shall be cast into the harems.

Therefore, because you trample upon the poor and take from him exactions of

הַפּוֹרְטִים עַל פִּי הַנָּבֶל, כְּדָוִיד חָשְׁבוּ לָהֶם כְּלֵי שִׁיר.

wheat, [14] you have built houses of hewn stones and you shall not dwell in them. You have planted pleasant vineyards, but shall not drink their wine.

Therefore, thus said the Lord: In all the squares shall be [heard] lamentations, and a cry of woe shall be heard in all the streets. They shall call all the farmers to mourning and all who know how to wail to lamentation. [15] In the vineyards shall there be lamentation, for I will pass through the midst of you.

Hear this, O you who would swallow the needy and destroy the poor of the land, saying: When will the [day of the] new moon be gone that we may sell grain, and the Sabbath, that we may offer corn? Make the measure small and the price great and tamper with the scales. To buy the poor for silver and the needy for a pair of shoes, and sell the refuse of the corn.

The Lord has sworn by the pride of Jacob: I will never forget any of their deeds. Shall not the earth tremble on this account and shall not every inhabitant in it mourn? Yes, the whole of it shall rise like the Nile and heave and sink like that river in Egypt.

And it shall come to pass on that day, says the Lord, that I will cause the sun to go down at noon, and I will darken the earth in the clear day. I will turn your feasts into mourning, and your songs into dirges. I will put a sackcloth on all loins and baldness on every head. I will make it as the mourning for an only son and its end like a bitter day.

THE GREAT FAMINE

BEHOLD, days are coming, said the Lord God, that I will send a famine upon the land, not a famine of bread, nor a thirst

---

ᕔᔤ [14] EXACTIONS OF WHEAT: Rabbi Johanan said that a person who held produce until prices rose, then sold it to the poor, was a speculator and a wrongdoer. Samuel's father sold fruit at the prices prevailing immediately after the harvest, but his son held the fruit. Then when the prices were high, Samuel's son sold his fruit at the earlier, cheaper harvest prices, thus enabling the poor to buy fruit when otherwise the prices would have been beyond their means. Therefore the son's action was better than the father's.

ᕔᔤ [15] TO LAMENTATION: As it is forbidden to work during a festival, so is it forbidden to work during a time of mourning.

הִנֵּה יָמִים בָּאִים, נְאֻם אֲדֹנָי אֱלֹהִים, וְהִשְׁלַחְתִּי רָעָב בָּאָרֶץ, לֹא רָעָב לַלֶּחֶם...

for water, but of hearing the words of the Lord. And they shall wander from sea to sea, and from north to the east; they shall seek for the word of the Lord and shall not find it. [16] And that day shall the fairest of maidens and the youths faint.

Woe to you who crave the day of the Lord. Wherefore would you have the day of the Lord? It is darkness, not light. As if a man were fleeing from a lion and a bear met him. He entered the house to hide himself and leaned his hand on the wall, and a serpent bit him. [17] Shall not the day of the Lord be darkness, not light? Blackness with no brightness in it?

I hate, I despise your feasts. I take no delight in your solemn assemblies. Though you offer me burnt offerings and meal-offerings, I will not accept them. Take away from Me the noise of your songs, and the melody of your

---

    ↊ [16] AND SHALL NOT FIND IT: Heaven forfend that the Torah be forgotten in Israel! Rabbi Simeon ben Yohai asked how to interpret the verse "They shall seek the word of the Lord ansd shall not find it." The answer: They shall find no clear and definitive ruling in any of the places where they seek.

    ↊ [17] A SERPENT BIT HIM: Ulla said, "Let the Messiah come, but because of the birth pangs preceding his arrival, let me not see him." Rabba said likewise, and also Rabbi Jochanan. But Resh Lakish said, "Why so? This is how it is in the world. When one goes into the field and meets a bailiff who contests his title to the field, it is as if he met a lion. When he enters the town and is accosted by a tax collector, it is as if he met a bear. When he enters his house. and finds his sons and daughters in the throes of hunger, it is as if he were bitten by a serpent. So we experience the same succession of troubles even now, without the coming of the Messiah. Why then should we be afraid? Our unwillingness to see the Messiah is because God Himself will then bewail the fate of the Gentiles whom He will have to punish for persecuting His children. But the Almighty will say: "The Gentiles are also My handiwork, as are the children of Israel, so how shall I destroy the former on account of the latter?"

וְלֹא צָמָא לַמַּיִם, כִּי אִם לִשְׁמֹעַ אֶת דִּבְרֵי יְיָ. . . .

lyres: I will not hear them. But let just-ice well up like waters and righteousness like a mighty stream.

Did you bring to Me sacrifices and offerings in the wilderness for forty years, O house of Israel? Therefore I will exile you beyond Damascus.

FIVE VISIONS: THE LOCUST

THE LORD showed me; Behold He was forming a locust, at the start of the later growing. This was the growing after the king's mowings. As they devoured the grass of the land, I said: "O, Lord God, forgive, I pray You. How can Jacob rise up? He is so small."

The Lord relented concerning this and said: "It shall not be."

DESTRUCTION BY FIRE

THUS THE LORD GOD showed me: Behold, the Lord God called down fire to de-vour. It devoured the great deep and it

began to devour the land. Then I said: "O, Lord God, cease, I pray You. How can Jacob rise up? He is so small!"

The Lord relented of this and said: "This also shall not be."

THE WALL AND THE PLUMBLINE

THUS HE SHOWED ME: Behold, God stood upon a wall with a plumbline in His hand. And the Lord said: "What do you see, Amos?" I said: "A plumbline." [18] God said: "I am setting a plumbline in the midst of my people Israel. I will not forgive them. [19] The high places of Isaac shall become desolate and the sanc-tuaries of Israel shall be laid waste; and I will rise against the house of Jeroboam with the sword."

AMAZIAH THE INFORMER

THEN AMAZIAH, the priest of Beth-el, sent to Jeroboam king of Israel, saying: "Amos has conspired against you in the

---

[18] A PLUMBLINE: In Hebrew a plumbline is *onach*, and the word also means to deceive, cheat or wrong someone.

[19] I WILL NOT FORGIVE THEM: Rabbi Hisda said: "All gates are locked except those through which the cries of the wronged echo. As it is written: Behold the Lord stood at the wall of the wronged and in His hand were the wronged. God is always ready to plead the case of one who has been wronged."

וְיִגַּל כַּמַּיִם מִשְׁפָּט, וּצְדָקָה כְּנַחַל אֵיתָן.

midst of the house of Israel. The land cannot endure all his words, for this is what Amos said: 'Jeroboam shall die by the sword and Israel shall surely be carried into captivity out of this land.'"

Then Amaziah said to Amos: "Seer, go, flee the land of Judah and earn your bread by prophesying there. But do not prophesy again in Beth-el, for it is the king's sanctuary and the kingdom's house."

Then Amos answered and said to Amaziah: "I am no prophet, neither am I a prophet's son; but I am a herdsman and a trimmer of sycamores. The Lord took me from behind the sheep and said to me: 'Go, prophesy to My people Israel.' You tell me I am not to prophesy against Israel and not to preach against the house of Isaac. Now hear the word of the Lord: Your wife shall whore [with the enemy] in the city, your sons and daughters shall fall by sword. Your land shall be divided up, and you yourself shall die in an unclean land, and Israel shall be driven into captivity out of the land."

A BASKET OF SUMMER FRUIT

THE LORD showed me a basket of summer fruit. And He said: "What do you see, Amos?" And I said: "A basket of summer fruit."

Then the Lord said to me: "The end comes upon My people Israel. I will not forgive them any longer. [20] The songs of the palace shall become lamentations, said the Lord. There will be many dead bodies and then a hush [will envelop] the whole place."

NONE WILL ESCAPE

I SAW THE LORD standing beside the altar, and He said: Smite the capitals [on the columns], that the foundations may shake. Break them in pieces on the heads of all of them. And those who are left I will slay with the sword. None of them shall escape when he flees. Though they dig themselves into the netherworld, from there My hand shall take them. Though they climb up into heaven, I will bring them down. Though they

---

᪥ [20] I WILL NOT FORGIVE THEM ANY LONGER: Our Sages taught that if a man repents, do not ask him to recall his former evil deeds. If he is a convert, do not taunt him with remembering the deeds of his ancestors. If he is a proselyte and comes to study Torah, it is forbidden to say to him: "Shall the mouth which ate forbidden food study Torah written from the mouth of the Omnipotent?"

לֹא נָבִיא אָנֹכִי וְלֹא בֶן נָבִיא אָנֹכִי, כִּי בוֹקֵר אָנֹכִי וּבוֹלֵס שִׁקְמִים.

hide themselves on the top of Carmel, I will search them out and take them down from there. Though they hide themselves from My sight at the bottom of the sea, I will command the serpent and he shall bite them. Though they are driven into captivity before their enemies, there will I command the sword to slay them. I will set My eye upon them for evil and not for good.

A CALL TO REPENT

THUS SAID THE LORD to the house of Israel: Seek Me and live. [21] But seek not Beth-el, go not to Gilgal, and visit not Beer-sheba, for Gilgal shall go into captivity and Beth-el shall come to naught. Seek the Lord and live, lest He set the house of Joseph on fire and it shall devour, and there will be none to quench it in Beth-el. Seek good and not evil, that you may live, and so the Lord, the God of hosts, will be with you as you have implored. Hate evil and love good and establish justice in the gate. It may be that the Lord, the God of hosts, will be gracious to the remnant of Joseph.

On that day I will raise up the fallen tabernacle of David and close up its

---

[21] SEEK ME AND LIVE: Rabbi Simlai preached that 613 precepts were given to Moses, of which 365 were negative and 248 positive. King David came and reduced them to 11 principles (Psalm 15), as it is written, "Lord, who shall sojourn in Thy tabernacle? Who shall dwell in Thy holy mountain? 1. He who walks uprightly, and 2. walks in righteousness, and 3. speaks truth in his heart, 4. who has no slander upon his tongue, 5. nor does evil to his fellow, 6. nor takes up reproach against his neighbor, 7. in whose eyes a vile person is despised, but 8. he honors them that fear the Lord, 9. he swears to his neighbor and does not change, 10. he does not give his money for interest, 11. nor take bribes against the innocent.

The prophet Isaiah came and reduced them to six principles (Isaiah 33:15–16): 1. He who walks righteously, and 2. speaks uprightly; 3. he who despises the gain of oppression; 4. he who shakes his hand

כִּי כֹה אָמַר יְיָ לְבֵית יִשְׂרָאֵל: דִּרְשׁוּנִי וִחְיוּ.

breaches, repair its ruins and rebuild it as in the days of old. The days come, said the Lord, that the plowman shall overtake the reaper, and the treader of grapes the sower of seeds. The mountains shall drip sweet wine and all the hills shall melt. I will return the captivity of My people, and they shall rebuild the ruined cities and inhabit them. They shall plant vineyards and drink their wine; make gardens and eat their fruit. I will plant them on their own land and they shall never again be plucked up out of their land which I have given them.

---

from holding bribes, 5. he who stops his ear from hearing of blood; and 6. shuts his eyes from looking on evil.

Then Micah came and reduced them to three (Micah 6:8), as has been told, "O man, what is good and what does the Lord require of thee? 1. Only to do justly, and 2. to love mercy, and 3. to walk humbly before your God."

Then came Isaiah and reduced them to two (Isaiah 56:1). "Thus said the Lord: 1. Keep justice, 2. do righteousness."

Then Amos came and reduced them all to one principle (Amos 5:4): "For thus says the Lord to the house of Israel: Seek Me and live."

The Maharsha rightly remarks that the Talmud does not mean that if one performs the enumerated precepts—six, sixteen or any number— he is a perfect man. Those are holy guides, principles, by which men may live.

וּנְטַעְתִּים עַל אַדְמָתָם וְלֹא יִנָּתְשׁוּ עוֹד מֵעַל אַדְמָתָם אֲשֶׁר נָתַתִּי לָהֶם.

17. OBADIAH [1]

EDOM'S DESTRUCTION

THE VISION of Obadiah: [1] Thus said the Lord God concerning Edom. [2] I have heard a message from the Lord and a messenger has been sent among the

---

[1] OBADIAH: *A name meaning "one who serves God."*

Our Sages say that Obadiah the prophet is the same Obadiah who was governor of King Ahab's household. Rabbi Isaac said, "Let Obadiah, who lived with two evil people—Ahab and Jezebel—and yet did not take example from their deeds, come to prophesy against the wicked Esau who lived with two righteous people—Isaac and Rebecca—and still did not learn from their good deeds."

[2] EDOM: *Edomites were said to be the descendants of Esau, the brother of Jacob. Later they were known as Idumeans. Because they were blood brothers, their hostility and treachery to Israel over the centuries was doubly resented.*

שְׁמוּעָה שָׁמַעְנוּ מֵאֵת יְיָ וְצִיר בַּגּוֹיִם שֻׁלָּח.

nations: [3] "Gather yourself together and come against her, rise up for war."

I made you small among nations, greatly despised among men. But the pride of your heart deceived you because you dwell in the cleft of the rock, on the height of the mountain. You say in your heart: "Who can bring me down to the ground?"

But though you mount high as an eagle and set your nest among the stars, I shall bring you down from there.

How you are cut off. If thieves came to you at night, they would steal only till they had enough. If grape-gatherers came to you, they would have left some gleaning grapes. But these robbers searched out Esau and sought out the most hidden places. The men who had a covenant with you conducted you to the border, then prevailed over you. The men who ate your bread set a snare for you.

THE DAY OF JUDGMENT

FOR THE VIOLENCE you have done to your brother, shame shall cover you,
And you shall be cut off forever.
On that day that you stood aloof [4]
When strangers plundered his substance,
And foreigners entered his gates
And cast lots on Jerusalem,
You were as one of them.
You should not have gloated on the day of your brother's disaster,
Neither should you have rejoiced over the children of Judah
In the day of their destruction.
Neither should you have magnified yourself with your mouth
In the day of their trouble.
You should not have entered into My people's gate
In the day of their calamity,

⋙ [3] A MESSENGER AMONG THE NATIONS: Rabbi Meir taught that Obadiah was himself an Edomite convert, and therefore, "From the very forest itself came the handle of the axe that felled the trees." The descendant of Edom was the most fit person to reprimand the people of Edom for their evil deeds.

⋙ [4] YOU STOOD ALOOF: When Nebuchadnezzar besieged Jerusalem, the Edomites stood aloof and watched from a distance. When any of the people of Israel escaped the city and the besieging Babylonian soldiers, the Edomites caught and killed them.

וְאַל תֵּרֶא בְיוֹם אָחִיךָ בְּיוֹם נָכְרוֹ, וְאַל תִּשְׂמַח לִבְנֵי יְהוּדָה בְּיוֹם אָבְדָם.

Nor should you have stood at the crossroads [5]
To cut off those who escaped;
Neither should you have delivered up to the enemy
Those who remained in the day of distress.
The day of the Lord is near upon all the nations;
As you have done, it shall be done to you;
Your deeds shall return upon your own head. [6]
On that day, said the Lord, I shall destroy the wise men of Edom
And wisdom out of the mount of Esau.
The mighty men of Teman shall be dismayed,
So that every man may be cut off from the mount of Esau by slaughter.
As you have drunk upon My holy mountain,
So shall all the nations continually drink the cup of fury;
They shall drink and gulp down
And become as if they had not been.

ISRAEL WILL BE RESTORED

BUT MOUNT ZION shall be a refuge and it shall be holy. The house of Jacob shall possess its own possessions. And the house of Jacob shall be fire, and the house of Joseph a flame, and the house of Esau shall be stubble. They shall kindle them and devour them, and none shall remain of the house of Esau. Then they shall possess the Negev, the mount of Esau, and the

---

⋙ [5] AT THE CROSSROADS: The Edomites waited to see who would have the upper hand in the battle. If the Babylonians, then they would join them; if the people of Israel, they would join them.

⋙ [6] UPON YOUR OWN HEAD: King Antonius asked Rabbi Jehudah, "Shall I enter the world to come?"

"Yes," the rabbi answered.

"But," the king asked again, "is it not written, 'There shall be no remnant of the house of Esau'?"

Rabbi Yehudah nodded. "It applies only to those whose evil deeds are like those of Esau."

וּבְהַר צִיּוֹן תִּהְיֶה פְלֵיטָה וְהָיָה קֹדֶשׁ, וְיָרְשׁוּ בֵּית יַעֲקֹב אֵת מוֹרָשֵׁיהֶם.

lowlands of the Philistines. They shall possess the field of Ephraim and the field of Samaria, and the people of Ammon in Gilead; and the captivity of the host of the children of Israel shall possess that which belonged to the Canaanites, even to Zarephath, and the captivity of Jerusalem that is in Sepharad shall possess the cities of the Negev.

Saviors shall come out of the mount Zion to judge the mount of Esau; and the kingdom shall be the Lord's.

וְעָלוּ מוֹשִׁיעִים בְּהַר צִיּוֹן לִשְׁפֹּט אֶת הַר עֵשָׂו, וְהָיְתָה לַיְיָ הַמְּלוּכָה.

18. JONAH [1-4]

FLIGHT FROM THE LORD

THE WORD OF THE LORD came to Jonah the son of Amittai, saying: "Arise, go to Nineveh, that great city, and proclaim to it that its wickedness has come up before Me." But Jonah rose up to flee to Tarshish [1] from the presence of the

---

[1] FLEE TO TARSHISH: How could Jonah believe that he could flee the presence of God? Is it not written, "The eyes of the Lord see through the whole world" (Zechariah 4:10). Our Sages explain that Jonah thought he could flee to a country outside of the land of Israel, where the Divine Presence did not rest on prophets. Then the Lord spoke to Jonah, saying, "You are like the unruly servant of the *kohen* who runs to the cemetery where his master's hand cannot reach him. But the stupid servant forgets that his master has many servants at his disposal who can be sent to fetch him from the burial ground. So will I send one of My messengers for you—a storm—and it will bring you back."

קוּם לֵךְ אֶל נִינְוֵה הָעִיר הַגְּדוֹלָה וּקְרָא עָלֶיהָ, כִּי עָלְתָה רָעָתָם לְפָנָי.

Lord. He went down to Joppa and found a ship going to Tarshish. He paid his fare [2] and went down into it to go with them to Tarshish from the presence of the Lord.

But the Lord hurled a great wind into the sea, and it became a mighty tempest and it was feared that the ship would be broken. The sailors were frightened and each cried to his god. Then they threw into the sea the wares that were in the ship to lighten it. But Jonah had gone down into the innermost part of the ship; he lay there and fell asleep. The shipmaster came to him and said to him: "Why are you sleeping? Arise and call to your God. Perhaps God will think of us and we will not perish. [3] [And Jonah did not answer.]

INTO THE SEA

THEN THE SAILORS said to one another:

"Come, let us cast lots that we may know who caused this calamity to fall upon us." They cast lots and the lot fell upon Jonah. So they said to him: "What is your occupation? From where do you come? What is your country? And of what people are you?"

And he said to them: "I am a Hebrew and I fear the Lord of heaven who has made the sea and the dry land, and I fled from the Lord's presence."

And the men became very frightened because the sea grew more and more stormy, and they said to him: "What shall we do to you that the sea may become calm for us?"

And he said to them: "Take me up and throw me into the sea and the sea will become calm. I know that this great storm is upon you because of me." [4]

[But the men were reluctant to do it.] They rowed hard to bring the ship to the land, but they could not, because the sea

---

ᏋᏏ [2] HE PAID HIS FARE : So anxious was Jonah to flee the Lord that he paid for the hire of the entire ship.

ᏋᏏ [3] WE WILL NOT PERISH : Why were the ship's sailors so frightened? Because, though they were experienced seamen, they had never before seen such a storm, which raged only where their ship sailed and left other ships undisturbed.

ᏋᏏ [4] BECAUSE OF ME : The sailors did not believe at first that Jonah's disobedience could cause the storm. So they held him over the side in the

עִבְרִי אָנֹכִי, וְאֶת יְיָ אֱלֹהֵי הַשָּׁמַיִם אֲנִי יָרֵא, אֲשֶׁר עָשָׂה אֶת הַיָּם וְאֶת הַיַּבָּשָׁה.

became more and more tempestuous. [5] They cried to the Lord and said: "We beseech You, O Lord, let us not perish for this man's life, and lay not upon us [his] innocent blood. You, Yourself, have brought this about." So they picked Jonah up and threw him into the sea and the sea ceased its raging. Then the men feared the Lord exceedingly; and they offered a sacrifice to the Lord and made vows to Him.

THE GREAT FISH

NOW THE LORD had ready a great fish to swallow Jonah. And Jonah was in the belly of the fish three days and three nights. Then Jonah prayed to the Lord, his God, out of the belly of the fish:

I called out of my affliction
To the Lord, and He answered me.
Out of the belly of the netherworld
I cried

---

sea up to his waist and the storm stopped and the sea calmed. When they drew him back on deck, the storm raged as before. Again the sailors put him over the side, this time up to his neck, and the storm once more ceased and the sea grew calm. Yet no sooner did they lift him to the vessel when the storm burst forth with full fury once more. At last, before casting Jonah overboard, the sailors cried out, "We beseech Thee, O Lord, lay not upon us the innocent blood of Jonah. We are doing this to fulfill Your desire that we cast him into the sea."

[5] MORE AND MORE TEMPESTUOUS: The Book of Jonah may be seen as an allegory of man's journey through the world. Jonah's descent into the ship is symbolic of man's descent into this world, which is so full of vexation. Man, then, is in the world as in a ship which is traversing a great and stormy ocean. Man believes that when he commits a sin, he can flee from the presence of the Master who takes no notice of the world. The Almighty then rouses a furious tempest which assails the ship, and man, caught in the tempest, is struck down. Although man is prostrate, his soul does not exert itself to return to the Master to make good its omissions. Some plead in behalf of the accused, as the sailors did for Jonah, and strive to restore him to the world. But they cannot. for the "sea grew more and more stormy against them."

קָרָאתִי מִצָּרָה לִי אֶל יְיָ וַיַּעֲנֵנִי, מִבֶּטֶן שְׁאוֹל שִׁוַּעְתִּי, שָׁמַעְתָּ קוֹלִי.

And You heard my voice.
You cast me into the depth,
In the heart of the seas,
And the flood surrounded me.
All Your waves and Your billows
Passed over me.
And I said: "I am cast out
From before Your eyes"; [6]
Yet I will look again toward Your
  holy temple.
The waters compassed me around,
  even to the soul;

The deep was round about me;
The weeds were wrapped about
  my head.
I went down to the bottoms of the
  mountains;
The earth with her bars closed upon
  me for ever;
Yet have You brought up my life
  from the pit,
O, Lord my God.
And the Lord spoke to the fish [7] and
it vomited Jonah upon dry land.

---

[6] FROM BEFORE YOUR EYES: Our Sages said that three prophets were different in their views. The prophet Jeremiah defended the people of Israel and demanded honor for the Lord, saying: "We have transgressed and have rebelled, but Thou hast not pardoned" (Lamentations 3:42). Jeremiah demanded that the people honor God but also demanded compassion from the Lord for the people.

The prophet Elijah demanded only that the children of Israel honor the Lord, but did not demand compassion for the Israelites from God. Elijah said, "I have been zealous for the Lord, because the children of Israel have forsaken Thy covenant" (I Kings 19:10). Because of that Elijah was punished. The Lord took away his gift of prophecy.

But the prophet Jonah demanded honor only for Israel, and refused the Lord's summons to go to Nineveh. He feared that if he succeeded in his mission, the Lord would forgive Nineveh. But the Lord punished him for his refusal and spoke to him only once more. As it is written, "And the word of the Lord came to Jonah the second time" (3:1).

[7] THE LORD SPOKE TO THE FISH: When the Lord is said to have spoken to the fish, it means that He gave the fish the will to act in that way;

אֲפָפוּנִי מַיִם עַד נֶפֶשׁ, תְּהוֹם יְסוֹבְבֵנִי, סוּף חָבוּשׁ לְרֹאשִׁי.

THE PROPHET GOES TO NINEVEH

AND THE WORD OF THE LORD came to Jonah a second time, saying: "Go to Nineveh, that great city, and proclaim to her all that I bid you." [8] So Jonah arose and went to Nineveh as the Lord had commanded him. Now, Nineveh was a very great city, a city of three days journey [from one end to the other].

Jonah entered into the city and walked a day's journey into it, and called out:

"After forty days Nineveh shall be over-thrown."

Then Jonah went out of the city and sat down on the east side of it. There he made for himself a booth and sat in its shade, and waited to see what would become of the city.

And the people of Nineveh believed in God; [9] and they proclaimed a fast and put on sackcloth, from the greatest of them to the least of them. When the news reached the king of Nineveh, he

---

therefore, the prophet ascribes the act, the deed, directly to God. Similarly, "Events caused by man's free will, such as war, the dominion of one nation over another, the attempt of one person to hurt or insult another, are ascribed to God."

[8] ALL THAT I BID YOU: The yoke of the Lord is sometimes heavy, and Moses at first refused it and did not wish to be the Lord's messenger. "I pray Thee," he begged, "send anyone but me" (Exodus 4:13). "O, Lord, I am not a man of words… for I am slow of speech, and of a heavy tongue" (Exodus 4:10). Jeremiah also did not wish to prophesy and begged God, "O Lord, God, I cannot speak because I am so young." But, like Moses, he too obeyed. Jonah also first refused the Lord's summons to go to Nineveh and went only when the mission was thrust upon him.

[9] NINEVEH BELIEVED IN GOD: Because the people of Nineveh believed Jonah, they turned from their evil ways and repented with their whole hearts. Our Sages tell us that they even restored stolen things to their rightful owners. When the Lord saw their deeds, he accepted their repentance and did not punish them as He had planned.

וַיִּקְרָא וַיֹּאמַר : עוֹד אַרְבָּעִים יוֹם וְנִינְוֵה נֶהְפָּכֶת.

arose from his throne, put off his royal robe, covered himself with a sackcloth and sat in ashes. And he commanded it to be proclaimed throughout Nineveh: "Let neither man nor beast, cattle nor sheep, taste anything, food or drink. Let them be covered with sackcloth, both man and beast, and let them cry mightily to God. Let every one turn away from his evil ways, and from the violence that is in their hands. Who knows? God may repent and turn away from His fierce anger and we shall not perish."

And God saw their deeds, that they did turn away from their evil ways. God relented of the calamity which He said He would bring upon them, and He did it not.

JONAH REBUKED

AND THIS WAS EVIL to Jonah, very evil, and he was vexed. He prayed to the Lord and said: "O Lord, is it not this I said when I was yet upon the earth of my own country? Therefore I fled to Tarshish, because I knew that You are a gracious God and compassionate, long-suffering and abundant in mercy and ready to relent. Therefore, O Lord, I beseech You, take my life from me; for it is better for me to die than to live."

Then the Lord God prepared a gourd to be a shade over Jonah's head to save him from discomfort. And Jonah was exceedingly glad of the gourd. But God prepared a worm, and the next morning, when the sun arose, the worm gnawed the gourd till it withered. And it came to pass when the sun arose that God sent a burning east wind and the sun beat upon the head of Jonah that he fainted, and he wished himself dead. "It is better for me to die than to live."

Then God said to Jonah: "Are you sorry for the gourd?" And Jonah answered: "I am very sorry, even to death."

Then the Lord said: "You have had pity on the gourd, for which you have not labored, nor did you make it grow, which came up in a night and perished in a night. And should I not have pity on Nineveh, that great city, in which there are more than a hundred and twenty thousand children who cannot distinguish between their right hand and their left hand, and also much cattle?"

וַיִּנָּחֶם הָאֱלֹהִים עַל הָרָעָה אֲשֶׁר דִּבֶּר לַעֲשׂוֹת לָהֶם וְלֹא עָשָׂה.

19. MICAH [1–7]

THE WORD OF THE LORD [1] that came to Micah [2] the Morashtite in the days of Jotham, Ahaz and Hezekiah, kings of Judah, concerning Samaria and Jerusalem.

---

[1] THE WORD OF THE LORD: The Lord said: "Surely I spoke to the prophets, but through a vision, therefore one prophecy is not exactly like the other." As it is written, Amos saw the Lord standing—"I saw God standing beside the altar" (9:1). Micah saw God sitting on His throne (I Kings 22:19). Moses saw Him as a warrior—"The Lord is a man of war" (Exodus 15:3). Daniel saw Him as an old man—"I beheld till thrones were placed and one that was old... did sit and the hair of his head like pure wool" (Daniel 7:9). It is also written that the Lord has spoken to the prophets and multiplied parables (Hosea 12:11).

[2] MICAH: *This is an abbreviated version of Micaiah, which means "who is like unto God."*

רָאִיתִי אֶת יְיָ יוֹשֵׁב עַל כִּסְאוֹ.

THE LORD JUDGES SAMARIA

HEAR, YOU PEOPLES, all of you; give heed earth and all her fullness; and let the Lord God be my witness against you, the Lord from His holy temple.

Behold, the Lord comes forth from His place and will come down and tread upon the high places of the earth. The mountains shall melt under Him like wax under fire, and the valleys shall split asunder as [when] waters are poured down from a steep place. All this [comes] because of the transgression of Jacob and the sins of Israel. What is the transgression of Jacob? Is it not Samaria? And what is the sin of Judah? Is it not Jerusalem?

I will make Samaria a ruined field, [3] a place for planting vineyards. I will pour down stones into the valley and lay bare its foundation. All her graven images shall be shattered and all her gifts to her temples shall be burned in fire, and all her wooden and metal idols will lie desolate because she has gathered them from the hire of a harlot [4] and to a harlot's hire they shall return.

For this I will lament and wail, I will go barefoot and naked. [5] I will howl like a jackal and moan like an ostrich. For her wound is incurable! It comes to Judah, it reaches the gate of my people, even to Jerusalem.

OPPRESSION OF THE POOR

WOE TO THEM who devise iniquity during the night and plan to carry out the evil. In the morning light they execute it because the power is in their hands. They covet fields and seize them, and houses they take away. Thus they crush a man

---

✥ [3] A RUINED FIELD: No prophet or sage has ever announced the destruction of the universe, or a change in the present conditions, or a permanent change in any of its properties.

✥ [4] THE HIRE OF A HARLOT: *Idolatry and harlotry are often identified, so that sacrifices to graven images are considered "the hire of a harlot."*

✥ [5] BAREFOOT AND NAKED: *Jews did not indulge in nudity as did the Greeks. Instead, what is meant here is removing shoes and outer clothing to demonstrate mourning.*

הוֹי חֹשְׁבֵי אָוֶן וּפֹעֲלֵי רָע עַל מִשְׁכְּבוֹתָם, בְּאוֹר הַבֹּקֶר יַעֲשׂוּהָ כִּי יֶשׁ לְאֵל יָדָם.

and his household, even a man and his heritage. [6]

You became My people's enemy. You strip the garment and the mantle from those who pass by peacefully so that they appear as men returning from war. The women of My people you drive out of their pleasant homes, and from their young children you take away My splendor.

Therefore, I am devising a disaster against this family, said the Lord, from which you shall not be able to remove your neck nor will you be able to walk upright. [7] It shall be an evil time. In that day a taunting song shall be sung against you and a lament shall be raised, saying: "We are utterly ruined; the heritage of my people has changed masters. How was it removed from me? To the enemy were my fields allotted, and now we are utterly ruined." Therefore, there will be no heirs [8] that shall be measured by a measuring line or by casting lots in the congregation of Israel.

THE LEADERS DENOUNCED

AND I SAID: Hear this, you heads of the house of Jacob and rulers of the house of Israel. [9] Is it not for you to know justice? But they hate good and love evil,

---

&ย [6] A MAN AND HIS HERITAGE: Whoever causes his fellowman loss of property whether indirectly or directly, as by stealing, cannot be considered truly repentant until he has repaid the money, or restored the property.

&ย [7] TO WALK UPRIGHT: *The yoke will force them to walk bent over, burdened, like animals.*

&ย [8] NO HEIRS: The children of Israel, when they were in God's good graces, prayed for power over the *yetzer hara*, but they were warned, "Know that if you destroy the *yetzer hara*, the world will end." Nonetheless they took power over the evil propensity and imprisoned it for three days; but in those three days not a child was conceived or born in all of Israel.

&ย [9] THE HOUSE OF ISRAEL: Rav said that scholars do not have to be warned about doing evil because they cannot claim to be ignorant of the

וָאֹמַר: שִׁמְעוּ נָא רָאשֵׁי יַעֲקֹב וּקְצִינֵי בֵּית יִשְׂרָאֵל, הֲלֹא לָכֶם לָדַעַת אֶת הַמִּשְׁפָּט.

they flay the skin from them and their flesh from their bones. Then they eat the flesh of My people and break their bones; yes, they chop them in pieces, like meat which is put in a pot and flesh in a cauldron. Then, when they shall cry to the Lord, He will not answer them. He will hide His face from them because they did evil things.

THE PROPHETS DENOUNCED

THUS SAID THE LORD concerning the prophets who lead my people astray. They cry, "Peace," when their teeth have any thing to bite. [10] But when one does not put anything into their mouths, they declare war against him. Therefore, it shall be night to you, that you shall have no vision; darkness for you, that you shall not divine. The sun shall set upon these prophets and the day shall become black over them. [11] The seers shall be put to shame, the diviners confounded. They shall all cover their upper lips, for there shall be no answer from God. But I am full of power and justice and strength by the spirit of God, to declare to Jacob his transgression and to Israel his sin.

ISRAEL'S MORAL DECLINE

WOE IS ME, as in the last of the summer fruit, as in the time of grape gleaning of the vintage; there is no cluster to eat, nor an early fig that my soul desires.

> The godly man is perished from out
>   of the earth
> And there is none righteous among
>   men.
> They all lie in wait for blood;
> Each hunts his brother with a net.
> They have made ready their hands
>   to do evil diligently;

---

law as ordinary people can. Rabbi Johanan said that it was like fine linen which is ruined if it is even slightly soiled, while rough burlap can hardly even be harmed by dirt.

ᵉᑭ [10] ANY THING TO BITE: *People who paid prophets were sure to receive favorable forecasts.*

ᵉᑭ [11] SHALL BECOME BLACK OVER THEM: *The image of an eclipse is meant symbolically to be the eclipse of these prophets and diviners. It also speaks of the darkness of mind in which they work.*

אָבַד חָסִיד מִן הָאָרֶץ, וְיָשָׁר בָּאָדָם אָיִן.

The prince asks for a bribe, and the
  judge renders a decision
  for a reward.
The great man speaks openly the
  evil desire of his soul;
Thus they are woven together in
  the conspiracy to pervert justice.
The best of them is like a brier,
The most upright is worse than a
  thorn hedge.
The day that was foretold to you,
  the day of punishment, has
  come.
Now it shall be their wrack and
  ruin.
Trust not in a friend.
Put no confidence in an intimate;
From her that lies in your bosom
Guard the doors of your mouth.
The son dishonors the father,
The daughter rises up against her
  mother,
The daughter-in-law against her
  her mother-in-law,

A man's enemies are the men in his
  own house.

THE DOOM OF JERUSALEM

HEAR THIS NOW, heads of the house of
Jacob and rulers of the house of Israel,
that abhor justice and make crooked
everything which is straight, that build
Zion with blood and Jerusalem with
iniquity. Her heads judge for bribes, the
priests give decisions for hire, and the
prophets divine for money. Yet they
lean upon the Lord and say: "Is not the
Lord in our midst? How can evil befall
us?" [12] Therefore, because of you,
Zion shall be plowed as a field, and Jerusalem will become a ruin, and the mountain of the house a high place in the
forest.

GOD CONTENDS WITH ISRAEL

HEAR YOU NOW what the Lord said [to
me]: "Plead your case before the moun-

⋙ [12] HOW CAN EVIL BEFALL US: What kinds of prayers are forbidden?
Prayers which seek to undo what had been done, or to reverse the
course of nature. He who utters such prayers does so in vain. If a man
should see a fire in the distance, he may not pray, "May it not be my
house!" The fire already rages in that particular house and it may very
well be his. A man should not pray to God regarding what is already
done and past.

לָכֵן בִּגְלַלְכֶם צִיּוֹן שָׂדֶה תֵחָרֵשׁ, וִירוּשָׁלַיִם עִיִּין תִּהְיֶה, וְהַר הַבַּיִת לְבָמוֹת יָעַר.

tains and let the hills hear your voice."
O, you mountains, hear the Lord's controversy and give ear you foundations of the earth. The Lord has a controversy with His people and will contend with Israel:

"My people, what have I done to you? And with what have I wearied you? Answer Me. I brought you up out of the land of Egypt and redeemed you out of the house of bondage. O, My people, remember what Balak, king of Moab, devised, and what did Balaam, the son of Beor, answer him. [Remember what happened] from Shittim to Gilgal that you may understand the righteous acts of the Lord." [13]

With what shall I come before the Lord,
And bow myself before God most high?
Shall I come before Him with burnt-offerings,
With year-old calves?
Will the Lord be pleased with thousand of rams,
With ten thousand rivers of oil?
Shall I give [Him] my first-born for my transgression,
The fruit of my body for the sin of my soul? [14]
This is what you, O man, have been told is good, [15]
And what the Lord requires of you:

---

[13] THE RIGHTEOUS ACTS OF THE LORD: A king had wounded his son with a sharp blow and bandaged the wound, saying, "My son, as long as this bandage covers your wound, you may do anything you want, yet you will suffer no ill effects. But if you take the bandage off, a profound sore will plague you." Thus the Lord spoke of the *yetzer hara*, for the Lord had created the propensity for evil and then given the children of Israel the Torah as an antidote. So long as Israel occupies itself with Torah, the *yetzer hara* will not be able to control man nor bring him harm.

[14] THE SIN OF MY SOUL: The child who is descended from you often teaches you.

[15] WHAT MAN HAS BEEN TOLD IS GOOD: He who persuades his fellow-man to perform a good deed, it is as if he himself had performed it.

הִגִּיד לְךָ אָדָם מַה טּוֹב, וּמָה יְיָ דוֹרֵשׁ מִמְּךָ:

Only to do justice and to love
mercy [16]
And to walk humbly before the
Lord.

THE GATHERING OF EXILES

ON THAT DAY, said the Lord, I will gather the lame and the lost and the afflicted. I will preserve the cast-off as a remnant, and make those who are weary of wandering into a mighty nation. And the Lord shall reign over them in mount Zion for ever. I will surely assemble all of you, O Jacob; I will surely gather the remnant of Israel. I will put them together as sheep in the fold, as a flock in the midst of the pasture, and the cities shall become a multitude of men.

The one who clears a way will go forth before them. They will break through the gate and go forth through it. Their king shall pass on before them and the Lord at their head. And the remnant of Jacob shall be in the midst of many nations, [17] as dew from the Lord, as showers upon grass, that does not put its hope in man and does not need the aid of men.

And it shall come to pass on that day that I will cut off the horses from your midst and destroy your chariots. I will cut off the [fortified] cities of your land and I will throw down all your strongholds. I will cut off witchcraft from your land and you shall have no more soothsayers; and I will cut off graven images and your pillars out of your midst, and you shall no longer worship the work of your hand. I will uproot your Asherim from your midst and I will destroy your enemies. [18]

---

[16] TO LOVE MERCY: If you tear your hearts with repentance, it will not be necessary for you to tear your clothes in mourning for the deaths of your sons.

[17] IN THE MIDST OF MANY NATIONS: Rabbi Johanan said: "After the Temple was destroyed, prophecy was taken from the mouths of prophets and put into the mouths of the foolish and into the mouths of babes."

[18] I WILL DESTROY YOUR ENEMIES: When an idol is smashed, its priests are terrified.

כִּי אִם עֲשׂוֹת מִשְׁפָּט וְאַהֲבַת חֶסֶד וְהַצְנֵעַ לֶכֶת עִם אֱלֹהֶיךָ.

THE FUTURE GLORY

IN THE END OF DAYS it shall come to pass that the mountain of the Lord's house shall be established on top of the mountain, and it shall be exalted above all the hills. Many nations shall go and say: "Come, let us go up to the mountain of the Lord, and to the house of the God of Jacob, that He may teach us His ways and we will walk in His paths." [19] For out of Zion shall go forth the law and the word of the Lord from Jerusalem. [20]

And He shall judge between many peoples and shall decide concerning mighty nations afar off; and they shall beat their swords into plowshares and their spears into pruning hooks. Nation shall not lift up sword against nation, neither shall they learn war any more. [21] But they shall sit every man under his vine and fig-tree, and none shall make them afraid; for the mouth of the Lord of the host has spoken. All the people shall walk each one in the name of its god, and we will walk in the name of the Lord our God forever and ever.

Who is like You, O God, who forgives the iniquity and passes by the transgression of the remnant of His heritage? He does not keep His anger for ever, because He delights in mercy. He will again have compassion upon us. He will subdue our iniquities and cast all our sins into the ocean. You shall show faithfulness to Jacob, mercy to Abraham, as You have sworn to our fathers from days of old.

◄§ [19] WALK IN HIS PATHS: A Jew is commanded to perform deeds of mercy for those who are not of his brotherhood.

◄§ [20] FROM JERUSALEM: In this world, only individuals were prophets; in the world to come, all the children of Israel will be prophets.

◄§ [21] LEARN WAR ANY MORE: The Lord required that Moses make war on Sihon (Deut. 2:24), but instead Moses sent messengers of peace to Sihon. Then the Lord said, "I commanded you to make war, but you have made overtures of peace." "There is no peace for the wicked," says the Lord. How great must be the command for peace if Israel disobeyed God's word for the sake of peace—and the Lord was not angry with them.

תִּתֵּן אֱמֶת לְיַעֲקֹב, חֶסֶד לְאַבְרָהָם, אֲשֶׁר נִשְׁבַּעְתָּ לַאֲבוֹתֵינוּ מִימֵי קֶדֶם.

20. NAHUM [1-3]

THE AVENGING GOD

THE PROPHECY on Nineveh, [1] the book of vision of Nahum [2] the Elkoshite.

The Lord is a jealous God. He avenges and is full of wrath. The Lord takes vengeance on His adversaries and He bears wrath for His enemies. The Lord is long-suffering and great in power, and He will by no means clear the guilty. The whirlwind and the tempest are His way, and the clouds are the dust of His feet. He rebukes the sea and dries it up, and He dries up all the rivers. Bashan and Carmel wither and the flower of Lebanon fades away. The mountains quake

---

[1] NINEVEH: *The capital of the Assyrian empire. After its people had repented during the time when Jonah prophesied, they returned to their evil-doings.*

[2] NAHUM: *A name meaning "full of comfort." Nahum is a comforting prophet who foretells only the destruction of Nineveh, and does not rebuke Israel.*

יְיָ אֶרֶךְ אַפַּיִם וּגְדָל־כֹּחַ, וְנַקֵּה לֹא יְנַקֶּה.

before Him and the hills melt. The earth shakes at His presence, the world and all who dwell in it.

Who can stand before His wrath? And who can endure the fierceness of His anger? His fury is poured out like fire, and the rocks are shattered before Him.

The Lord is good, a stronghold in the day of trouble to those who seek refuge in Him. [3]

But with an overrunning flood, He will make a full end to Nineveh and darkness shall pursue His enemies.

NINEVEH'S DOOM

WOE TO THE BLOODY CITY, full of lies and plunder. Slaughter does not cease in her. I am against you, says the Lord, I will burn and send your chariots up in smoke and the sword shall devour your young lions. I will cut off your prey from the earth, and the voice of your messengers shall be heard no more.

The gates of the rivers are opened and the palace melts away. [4] Nineveh has been, as of old, full of defenders like a pool of water, yet they flee away. [One cries:] "Stand! Stand!" but none looks back.

The crack of the whip, the rattling of wheels, prancing of horses and jolting of chariots. The horsemen charge, the flashing sword, and the glittering spear. A multitude of slain, a heap of carcasses, and there is no end to corpses. They stumble upon their corpses.

[All this came to you] Because of the many harlotries, your greatly favored harlot, mistress of witchcraft, that sold nations through her harlotries, and peoples through her witchcraft.

I am against you, says the Lord of hosts. I will pull up your skirts to your face, [5] and I will let the nations see your

---

> ◄§ [3] WHO SEEK REFUGE IN HIM: The children of Israel lamented, asking when the day of their redemption would come, and the Lord replied: "My children, when great afflictions are upon you, you may be sure that redemption is near."

> ◄§ [4] THE PALACE MELTS AWAY: *Nineveh was surrounded by a moat.*

> ◄§ [5] YOUR SKIRTS TO YOUR FACE: *Such exposure was the punishment for adultery. All those who had suffered by Assyrian betrayal will now see how Nineveh is humiliated.*

פָּרָשׁ מַעֲלֶה וְלַהַב חֶרֶב וּבְרַק חֲנִית וְרֹב חָלָל וְכֹבֶד פָּגֶר, וְאֵין קֵצֶה לַגְּוִיָּה.

nakedness, and the kingdoms your shame. I will throw loathsome things upon you and make you vile, and I will make you as dung so that everyone that sees you will flee from you and say: "Nineveh is destroyed. Who will bemoan her? Whence shall I seek comforters for her?"

Are you better than No-amon, [6] that sat among rivers, with water all around her, whose rampart was the sea and the sea her wall [of the stronghold]? Yet she was carried away and went into captivity. Her young children were dashed to pieces at the head of every street. They cast lots for her honored men and all her great men were bound in chains. [7]

You too will be made drunk and reel, and you shall seek refuge from the enemy. All your fortresses shall be like figtrees with the first ripe fruit; if they be shaken, they fall into the eater's mouth. Behold, the warriors among you are but women. The gates of your land will be opened wide to your enemies. The fire has devoured the bars [of the gates].

Your shepherds slumber, O king of Assyria, your nobles are dead, your people are scattered upon the mountains, and there is none to gather them. There is no healing your wound; your wound is mortal. All who hear the report [of your fall] shall clap hands, for upon whom has not your wickedness passed continually? [8]

---

[6] NO-AMON: *A city in Egypt, also thought to be an impregnable fortress, but which had been breached and burned to the ground half a century before Ashurbanipal destroyed Nineveh.*

[7] BOUND IN CHAINS: The sword comes into the world because justice is delayed and perverted; and the sword also comes into the world because of those who pervert the meaning of the Law. Captivity enters the world because of idolatry, immorality and bloodshed.

[8] YOUR WICKEDNESS PASSED CONTINUALLY: If the Lord wishes the world to continue, there cannot be strict justice; if the Lord insists on strict justice, the world cannot endure.

כֹּל שֹׁמְעֵי שִׁמְעֲךָ תָּקְעוּ כַף עָלֶיךָ, כִּי עַל מִי לֹא עָבְרָה רָעָתְךָ תָּמִיד?

GOOD TIDINGS TO JUDAH

BEHOLD upon the mountain the feet of him that brings good tidings, that proclaims peace. Celebrate your feasts, Judah, fulfill your vows; for the wicked one shall never again pass through you; [9] he was utterly cut off. Though the destroyers have devastated Jacob and Israel and marred their branches, I will restore the vine of Jacob and likewise the vine of Israel.

◄§ [9] PASS THROUGH YOU: Rabbi Johanan said that a man was walking on the road one night when his lantern went out. He lit it again, but again it went out. So he said to himself, "Why should I bother with this lantern? I will wait by the roadside until the sun comes up and then I will continue my journey."

So it is with the children of Israel. They were enslaved in Egypt and Moses brought them forth. They were enslaved in Babylon and Zerubbabel led them out. They were enslaved in Persia and Mordecai led them forth. They were enslaved by Greece and the Maccabees freed them. When, once again, they were enslaved by Rome, they pleaded, "O, Lord, do not free us again through the intervention of a man. We are weary with the succession of enslavement, freedom and enslavement again. Free us Yourself, O Lord, our Redeemer."

חַגִּי יְהוּדָה חַגַּיִךְ, שַׁלְּמִי נְדָרָיִךְ, כִּי לֹא יוֹסִיף עוֹד לַעֲבָר־בָּךְ בְּלִיַּעַל, כֻּלֹּה נִכְרָת.

21. HABAKKUK [1-3]

THE PROPHET'S QUESTION

THE PROPHECY which Habakkuk [1] the prophet saw in a vision: How long, O Lord, shall I cry to You and You will not hear? I cry to You about violence and You do not help. Why do You show me iniquity? You look at mischief, and there is pillage and violence before me. Strife occurs and contention arises. Therefore the law is numbed and justice [2] never

---

[1] HABAKKUK: *The name may derive from the Hebrew word* habag, *which means "to embrace."*

[2] JUSTICE NEVER GOES FORTH: A king had a lovely drinking cup so delicately fashioned that if he poured hot water into it it would crack; and if he poured ice-cold water into it, it would also crack. Therefore he mixed hot and cold so that he could pour it safely into the cup.

So it is with the Lord, who said that had He created the world only

עַד אָנָה יְיָ שִׁוַּעְתִּי וְלֹא תִשְׁמָע, אֶזְעַק אֵלֶיךָ חָמָס וְלֹא תוֹשִׁיעַ.

goes forth. The wicked besets the righteous and perverted justice goes forth. [3]

THE SUCCESS OF THE VIOLENT

LOOK YOU among the nations and look
on in amazement, [for behold] a deed
shall be done in your days which you
will not believe were it told to you. He
has raised up the Chaldeans, that bitter
and impetuous nation, that march
through the breadth of the land to seize
dwelling places that are not theirs. They

are terrible and dreadful. They carry
their own law and justice. [4]

Their horses are swifter than leopards
and fiercer than the wolves of the desert;
their horsemen are many and come from
afar, they swoop like vultures that hasten
to devour. All of them come for violence
and gather captives like sand. They scoff
at kings and deride princes. They laugh
at all strongholds, they heap up earth
[opposite it] and take it. Then they sweep
on like wind, pass on. They make strength
their god. [5]

---

with mercy, sin would multiply beyond all limits. Had he created the
world only with justice, the world could not have endured. And so the
Lord created the world with both justice and mercy.

ᴈ [3] PERVERTED JUSTICE GOES FORTH: Do not abandon your belief in
retribution.

ᴈ [4] THEIR OWN LAW AND JUSTICE: Rabbi Judah ben Tema says: Be
strong as the leopard, swift as the eagle, fleet as the gazelle, and brave
as the lion, to do the will of the Lord who is in heaven.

ᴈ [5] THEY MAKE STRENGTH THEIR GOD: Ten strong things were created in
the world: a moutain is strong but iron can break it; iron is strong but
fire can melt it; fire is strong but water can extinguish it; water is strong
but clouds can carry it; clouds are strong but winds can scatter them;
wind is strong but the body can carry it as breath; the body is strong
but terror can break it; terror is strong but wine can drive it out; wine
is strong but sleep can overcome it; death, however, is stronger than
all.

וְקַלּוּ מִנְּמֵרִים סוּסָיו וְחַדּוּ מִזְּאֵבֵי עֶרֶב, וּפָשׁוּ פָּרָשָׁיו.

THE QUESTION REPEATED

BUT ARE YOU NOT FROM EVERLASTING,
Lord my God, my Holy One, Immortal
One? Have You ordained him for judgment; O Rock, have You established
him for chastisement? But You are too
pure of eye to look upon evil. You cannot gaze upon wrongdoing. Why, then,
do you look upon treacherous men and
keep silent, when the wicked swallows
up the man that is more righteous than
he? [6]

You make man as the fishes of the sea,
as creeping things, that have no ruler
over them. He brings them all up with
the hook. He catches them in his net and
gathers them in his seine. Therefore he
rejoices and exults, and sacrifices to his
net and burns incense to his seine. Shall
he keep emptying his net and never cease
to slay nations? [7]

I will stand upon my watch and station
myself upon the tower, and will look out
to see what He will speak to me and what
answer He will make to my complaint.

GOD'S REPLY ONCE MORE

AND THE LORD ANSWERED ME and said:
Write the vision clearly upon tablets that
one may read it readily. The vision is for
a set time; it speaks of the end and does
not lie. If it tarry, wait for it, for it will

&ent; [6] MORE RIGHTEOUS THAN HE: Everything is given on pledge, and a net
is spread for all living men: the shop is open, the shopkeeper gives
credit, the ledger lies open, the hand writes, and whosoever wishes to
borrow may come and borrow. But the collectors make their daily
round and exact payment from man, whether he wishes it or not; for
they have the necessary evidence in the form of records that have been
kept. The judgment is the judgment of truth, and everything is prepared for the feast in the world-to-come.

&ent; [7] TO SLAY NATIONS: Rabbi Meir said that when the Lord declared,
"I will be gracious to whom I will be gracious" (Exodus 33:19), God
meant it, although that person may not be deserving. When the Lord
declared, "and I will show mercy on whom I will show mercy," He
likewise meant it, although that person may not be deserving of mercy.

עוֹד חָזוֹן לַמּוֹעֵד וְיָפֵחַ לַקֵּץ וְלֹא יְכַזֵּב; אִם יִתְמַהְמָהּ חַכֵּה לוֹ כִּי בֹא יָבֹא,
לֹא יְאַחֵר.

surely come; it will not fail its set time.
[8] And the righteous shall live by His
faithfulness.

He who enlarged his desire like Sheol
and is as insatiable as death, gathered all
the nations to himself, assembled all the
peoples. Shall not all these take up a
taunting song against him, saying: "Woe
to him that enriches himself with that
which is not his own, loads himself with
many pledges; for how long?"

Will not your creditors rise up suddenly and exact interest of you, and
awake those that shall make you quake,
[9] and you shall become spoil to them?

Because you have despoiled many
nations, all the rest of the people shall
despoil you; because the blood of men
and the violence done to the land, to the
city and to all who dwell therein.

The stone cries out of the wall and the
beam out of the woodwork shall answer it.

You shall be sated with shame instead
of glory. You shall drink also and be poi-
soned. The cup of the Lord's right hand
shall be passed to you and disgrace shall
be upon your glory.

THE PROPHET'S FAITH

The Lord is in His holy temple,
Let all the earth be hushed before
   Him.
I will rejoice in the Lord,
I will exult in the God of my
   salvation.
God, the Lord, is my strength,
And He makes my feet like hinds' feet
And He makes me walk on the high
   places.

❧ [8] ITS SET TIME: It is the duty of man to say a benediction for the bad
even as he recites one for the good.

❧ [9] MAKE YOU QUAKE: The wife of Rabbi Hanninah asked her husband
to pray that he be given on earth some of the good that was reserved
for the righteous in the world to come. Rabbi Hanninah prayed and a
leg of a golden table was thrown to him. Later he dreamed that he sat
in the next world at a table with only two legs while all the others sat
at golden tables with three legs. When he told the dream to his wife,
she begged him to pray that the golden table leg be returned to the
world to come. The rabbi did, and it was. So his wife learned that you
cannot eat at two tables or have the best of both worlds.

וַיָי בְּהֵיכַל קָדְשׁוֹ, הַס מִפָּנָיו כָּל הָאָרֶץ.

22. ZEPHANIAH [1–3]

THE WORD OF THE LORD which came to Zephaniah [1] the son of Cushi, the son of Gedaliah, the son of Amariah, the son of Hezekiah, in the days of Josiah [2] the son of Amon, King of Judah.

APPROACHING DOOM

I WILL UTTERLY DESTROY all things from off the face of the earth. I will destroy man and beast. I will consume the fowls of the heavens and the fishes of the sea, the idols and their worshipers, said the Lord.

I will stretch out My hand against Judah, and against all the inhabitants of Jerusalem; I will cut off Baal [3] to the last remnant in this place, and the name

---

[1] ZEPHANIAH: *The name means "he whom God hath hidden (from evil)."*

[2] JOSIAH: *Zephaniah was a contemporary of Jeremiah and preached in the reign of the Josiah of the Great Reformation.*

[3] BAAL: *The idol worshiped by the Canaanites and Phoenicians.*

אָסֵף אָדָם וּבְהֵמָה, אָסֵף עוֹף הַשָּׁמַיִם וּדְגֵי הַיָּם וְהַמַּכְשֵׁלוֹת אֶת הָרְשָׁעִים.

of the idolatrous priests with the priests; and those who prostrate themselves upon the housetops to the host of heaven. And those who worship the Lord and swear by Malcam; [4] and those who have turned away from following the Lord, and those who have not sought the Lord nor inquired after Him.

On that day I will punish the princes and the king's sons who fill their master's house with violence and deceit, and all who dress themselves in foreign gar-ments. [5] And on the same day I will punish everyone who leaps over the threshold. [6]

On that day, says the Lord, a cry will be heard from the fish gate [7] and a wailing from the second quarter and a great crash from the hills. Wail, you in-habitants of the valley of Kidron, because all the merchant people are undone; and those who are laden with silver are cut off. [8] And it shall come to pass at that time, that I will search through Jerusalem

---

⤷ [4] MALCAM: *The idol worshiped by the Ammonites.*

⤷ [5] FOREIGN GARMENTS: *Not only will punishment be meted out to those who worship foreign idols, but to those who adopt foreign manners of dress.*

⤷ [6] LEAPS OVER THE THRESHOLD: *The thresholds were places where many of the primitive people made sacrifices when building their houses. Those who leaped over the threshold may also have been those who robbed the poor.*

⤷ [7] FROM THE FISH GATE: *The fish gate was near the north wall of the city, where the Tyrians traded in dried fish.*

⤷ [8] THOSE WHO ARE LADEN WITH SILVER ARE CUT OFF: *There are four types of men: One says, "Mine is mine and thine is thine." He is an ordinary man. A second says, "Mine is thine and thine is mine." He is an* am ha'aretz. *A third says, "Mine is thine and thine is thine." That man is a saint. But the wicked man says, "Thine is mine and mine is mine."*

וְהָיָה בָּעֵת הַהִיא אֲחַפֵּשׂ אֶת יְרוּשָׁלַיִם בַּנֵּרוֹת . . .

with lamps and I will punish the men who are settled on their lees, [9] that say in their heart: "The Lord will not do good, neither will He do evil." [10] Therefore their wealth shall become a booty and their house a desolation. They shall build houses, but shall not dwell in them; and they shall plant vineyards, but shall not drink their wine.

THE DAY OF THE LORD

SILENCE in the presence of the Lord, for the day of the Lord is at hand. The Lord has prepared a sacrifice and has sanctified the guests.

The great day of the Lord is near,
Near and speeding fast;
The sound of the day of the Lord is
    such

That the mighty man shall cry
    bitterly.
That day is a day of wrath,
A day of trouble and distress,
A day of desolation and waste,
A day of darkness and gloom,
A day of cloud and thick darkness,
A day of shofar and battle cry,
Against the fortified cities
And against the high towers.
I will bring distress upon men.
They shall walk like blind,
Because they have sinned against
    the Lord. [11]
Neither their silver nor their gold
Shall be able to save them.
In the day of the Lord's wrath,
When the fire of His jealousy shall
    devour the whole earth;
For He will make a fearful end.
Of all the inhabitants of the earth.

---

෫ [9] SETTLED ON THEIR LEES: *This is a figure of speech from winemaking; it refers to men who have become smug amd complacent so that their moral discrimination has been dulled.*

෫ [10] NEITHER WILL HE DO EVIL: With Him there is no unrighteousness, nor forgetfulness, nor respect for persons, nor taking of bribes.

෫ [11] SINNED AGAINST THE LORD: The *yetzer hara* does not walk on the sidewalks but in the middle of the road. When the evil impulse sees a man swaggering, it says: "This person belongs to me."

וּפָקַדְתִּי עַל הָאֲנָשִׁים הַקּוֹפְאִים עַל שִׁמְרֵיהֶם, הָאוֹמְרִים בִּלְבָבָם: לֹא יֵיטִיב יְיָ וְלֹא יָרֵעַ.

ASSYRIA'S DOOM

HE [the Lord], will stretch out His hand against the north and destroy Assyria. He will make Nineveh a desolation, dry as a desert. And droves of all kinds of beasts shall lie down in her midst. The pelican and the night owl will roost on the top of the broken pillars. Birds shall sing in the windows because all the cedar beams shall be laid bare. Desolation shall be on the thresholds.

This is the joyous city, that dwelt in security, that said in her heart: "I am, and there is none else beside me." How has she become a desolation, a lair for beasts. Every one that passes by her shall hiss and make a gesture with his hand.

JERUSALEM ARRAIGNED

WOE, defiant and defiled one, the oppressing city! [12] She has not accepted correction. She has listened to no voice. She has not trusted in the Lord and she has not drawn near to her God.

The princes in her midst are roaring lions, her judges are desert wolves. [13] They leave not a bone until the morning. Her prophets are reckless [14] and treacherous men. Her priests profaned that which is holy; they have done violence to the Law. [15]

I have cut off nations. I have destroyed their battlements. I have made their squares desolate. I have laid waste their cities so there is no man, so that there is

---

⋙ [12] THE OPPRESSING CITY: *The prophet now turns to indict Jerusalem for its evils.*

⋙ [13] HER JUDGES ARE DESERT WOLVES: *Power buries its possessors.*

⋙ [14] HER PROPHETS ARE RECKLESS: *The prophets were false prophets, and they did not present the Lord's true arraignment of the people's sins.*

⋙ [15] VIOLENCE TO THE LAW: *The priests did not carry out their duty to teach people the law truthfully.*

זֹאת הָעִיר הָעַלִּיזָה, הַיּוֹשֶׁבֶת לָבֶטַח, הָאוֹמְרָה בִּלְבָבָהּ: אֲנִי, וְאַפְסִי עוֹד.

no inhabitant. I said: "Surely you will
fear Me, you will take correction; [16] it
cannot be cut off from their eyes all that
I did to them but they have zealously
made all their doings corrupt.

Seek the Lord, all you humble of
    the earth
That did His bidding;
Seek righteousness, seek humility.
It may be that you shall be hidden
    on the day of the Lord's anger.

CALL TO REPENT

Gather yourselves together,
Yes, gather together
You people who yearn for God,
Before darkness descends
The day passes like chaff,
Before the fierce wrath of the Lord
    comes upon you,
Before the day of the Lord's anger
    comes upon you.

PROMISE TO THE FAITHFUL

WAIT FOR ME, said the Lord, until the day
I rise up as a witness against the nations;
for My decision is to gather up the nations, to assemble kingdoms, to pour
upon them My indignation, all My
fierce anger. In the fire of My zeal all the
earth shall be devoured. Then I will restore to the people a pure language that

∾ [16] YOU WILL TAKE CORRECTION: In Rome the Empress lost her bracelet
and Rabbi Samuel found it. A herald announced that whoever returned the bracelet within thirty days would receive a rich reward,
but if the bracelet were found on his person thereafter, he would be
beheaded. Rabbi Samuel, however, did not return the bracelet to the
Empress until after the thirty days had passed. "Did you have the
bracelet earlier?" she asked him. He nodded. "Did you hear the proc-
lamation?" Again he nodded. "Then why did you not return the
bracelet before the thirty days were past?" she asked. Then Rabbi
Samuel replied, "So that you might not say that I feared you, or coveted
the reward; but that I returned it only because I feared God."

בַּקְּשׁוּ צֶדֶק, בַּקְּשׁוּ עֲנָוָה, אוּלַי תִּסָּתְרוּ בְּיוֹם אַף יְיָ.

they may all call upon the name of the
Lord, [17] to serve Him shoulder to
shoulder.

From beyond the rivers of Ethiopia
they shall bring gifts to the gates of Zion
for Me. On that day you shall not be
ashamed of all your deeds, wherein you
have transgressed [18] against Me, for I
shall remove from you the arrogant and
haughty ones and you shall be no more
haughty on My holy mountain. I will
leave in the midst of you a humble and a
poor people, and they shall take refuge in
the name of the Lord.

The remnant of Israel shall not do
iniquity,

Nor speak lies,
Neither shall a deceitful tongue [19]
   be found in their mouth.
They shall feed and lie down,
And none shall make them afraid.

ISRAEL REDEEMED

Sing, O daughter of Zion,
Shout, O Israel;
Be glad and rejoice with all your
   heart,
Daughter of Jerusalem,
The Lord has taken away your
   opponents.
He has cast out your enemy;

---

[17] THE NAME OF THE LORD: However high the Lord be above the
world, let a man but enter a synagogue, stand behind a pillar and whisper a prayer, and the Holy One, blessed be He, hearkens to his prayer.
Can there be a God nearer than this, who is as close to His creatures as
the mouth is to the ear?

[18] WHEREIN YOU HAVE TRANSGRESSED: A man does not commit a
transgression unless a spirit of madness has entered into him.

[19] A DECEITFUL TONGUE: Rabbi Abbahu said in the name of Rabbi
Johanan: If a man seeks to praise God in an excessive way he is banished
from the world. As it is written, "Who can utter the mighty acts of
the Lord and show forth all His praise?" (Psalms 106:2).

רָנִּי בַּת צִיּוֹן, הָרִיעוּ יִשְׂרָאֵל, שִׂמְחִי וְעָלְזִי בְּכָל לֵב בַּת יְרוּשָׁלָיִם.

The King of Israel, the Lord, is in your midst.

You shall not fear evil any more. [20]

On that day it shall be said to Jerusalem:

"Fear you not,

Zion, let not your hands droop in despair.

The Lord your God is in your midst,

A Mighty One who will save.

He will rejoice over you [21] with gladness,

He will be silent in His love,

He will exult over you with singing."

I shall gather together the grief-stricken, [22] who absented themselves from the festivals,

And those who have borne the burden of reproach.

⊱ [20] FEAR EVIL ANY MORE: Antoninus asked Rabbi Judah Ha-Nasi when the *yetzer hara* begins to exert its influence on the human being; from the time of the embryo's formation, or when it emerges from the body? Rabbi Judah replied that the *yetzer hara* exercised its power from the time of the embryo's formation. Then Antoninus remarked, "In that case it should surely kick in the womb and come out of its own accord."

⊱ [21] HE WILL REJOICE OVER YOU: Scripture says that the Lord repented that He had made man, and it grieved Him at His heart (Genesis 6:6). In explaining this, the Sages asked the man who had sought explanation about it, "Have you ever had a son born to you?" "Yes," the man replied. "What did you do when he was born?" "I rejoiced and had others rejoice with me." "But didn't you know that a time would come when your son would die?" "Surely," the man said, "but in a time of joy, let there be joy, and in a time of mourning, mourning." So, too, explained the rabbis, did it happen with the Lord and His creation of man.

⊱ [22] THE GRIEF-STRICKEN: A man in Sepphoris had a son who died, and Rabbi Jose ben Halafta went to visit him. While there, the man's

יָשִׂישׂ עָלַיִךְ בְּשִׂמְחָה, יַחֲרִישׁ בְּאַהֲבָתוֹ, יָגִיל עָלַיִךְ בְּרִנָּה.

At that time, I will deal with all
   your oppressors,
I will deliver the lame,
And those that wandered away, I
   will gather.

At that time I will bring you in. [23]
And at the time that I will gather
   you,
I will make you renowned [24]
Among all the peoples of the earth.

---

relative, an infidel, saw the Rabbi smile and asked him why he did so.
Rabbi Jose said that he trusted the Lord to see that the father would
see his son again in the world-to-come. Then the infidel said, "Can
broken shards be made to cleave together again? Is it not written, 'Thou
shalt break them in pieces like a potter's vessel' " (Psalms 2:9). Then
Rabbi Jose replied, "Earthen vessels are made by water and perfected
by fire. Vessels of glass are made by fire and perfected by fire. The
former, when broken, cannot be repaired. But the latter, if broken,
can be." "How?" the infidel inquired. Rabbi Jose explained, "Because
they are made by blowing. If the glass vessel blown by a mortal man
can be repaired, how much more the being who is made by the breath
of God."

❧ [23] I WILL BRING YOU IN: *The Lord will bring Israel into its own land.*

❧ [24] I WILL MAKE YOU RENOWNED: Pieces of fine lumber were discarded
on the muddy ground and noone paid attention to them. But a skilled
cabinetmaker recognized their worth and wrought them into beautiful furniture. When the former owner saw what the cabinetmaker
had done, he said, "I thought the wood worthless, yet what beautiful
things you have made of it."

So, too, Pharaoh and other tyrants have forced Israel to live in degra-
dation and to occupy itself with menial work. But when they see the
beauty and glory of Israel emancipated, they will regret what they
have done and admire what Israel is.

כִּי אֶתֵּן אֶתְכֶם לְשֵׁם וְלִתְהִלָּה בְּכֹל עַמֵּי הָאָרֶץ.

23. HAGGAI [1, 2]

THE LORD'S REBUKE

IN THE SECOND YEAR of Darius the king,

[1] in the sixth month, in the first day of the month, came the word of the Lord through Haggai [2] the prophet to Zerubbabel, [3] the son of Shealtiel, governor

---

[1] DARIUS THE KING: *He ruled Persia from 521–486 B.C.E., so that Haggai's appeal to the people was during the fall of 520.*

[2] HAGGAI: *The name probably derives from an abbreviation for* haggigah, *which means "the festival of the Lord."*

[3] ZERUBBABEL: *He was the grandson of Jehoiachin, king of Judah, who had been taken captive to Babylon, and was now the leader of the exiled Jews who returned from Babylon to the Holy Land.*

הָיָה דְבַר יְיָ בְּיַד חַגַּי הַנָּבִיא אֶל זְרֻבָּבֶל בֶּן שְׁאַלְתִּיאֵל.

of Judah, and to Joshua [4] the son of Jehozadak, the high priest, saying: Thus spoke the Lord of the host: "This people say: The time is not yet come to rebuild the Lord's house." Is it a time for you yourselves to live in your paneled houses while this house lies waste? [5]

Thus said the Lord of hosts:
Consider how you have fared.
You have sown much and it brought little.
You eat but you cannot be sated.
You drink but you cannot get your fill.
You put on clothes but you are not warmed.
And he that earns wages has only a bag with a hole. [6]

You looked for much and it became little; and when you brought it home, I blew upon it. Why? said the Lord of host. Because My house lies waste while you yourself run each to his own house. Therefore, because of you, the heavens kept back the dew, and the earth withheld her yield. I called for a drought upon the land [7] and upon the mountains, and upon the corn and wine, upon the oil and upon everything which the earth brings forth; and upon men and cattle, and upon all the labor of hands.

Thus said the Lord of the host: Go up to the mountain and bring wood, and build the house; I will be pleased with it and I will be glorified, said the Lord.

THE PEOPLE RESPOND

THEN ZERUBBABEL, the son of Shealtiel, and Joshua, the son of Jehozadak, the

---

◦§ [4] JOSHUA: *The son of the high priest who had also been taken captive into Babylon.*

◦§ [5] THIS HOUSE LIES WASTE: Greater is the study of Torah than rebuilding the Temple.

◦§ [6] A BAG WITH A HOLE: Even in the time of His anger, the Lord remembers mercy.

◦§ [7] DROUGHT UPON THE LAND: Rabbi Abba ben Abbin said in the name of Rabbi Aha: In the time of drought when men show mercy one to the other, God will be filled with mercy for them.

זְרַעְתֶּם הַרְבֵּה וְהָבֵא מְעָט, אָכוֹל וְאֵין לְשָׂבְעָה, שָׁתוֹ וְאֵין לְשָׁכְרָה.

high priest, and all the rest of the people listened to the voice of the Lord and to the words of Haggai the prophet, as God had sent him. And the people began to fear because of the Lord. Then Haggai, the Lord's messenger, spoke to the people with a message from the Lord: [8] "I am with you," said the lord.

And the Lord roused the spirit of Zerubbabel, governor of Judah, and the spirit of Joshua, the high priest, and the spirit of all the rest of the people; and they came and began to work upon the house of the Lord of hosts. It was in the twenty-fourth day of the sixth month, [9] in the second year of Darius the king.

On the twenty-first day in the seventh month the word of the Lord came through Haggai, saying: Now speak to Zerubbabel and Joshua and to the rest of the people, saying, "Who is left among you that saw this house in its former glory? [10] How do you see it now? Does it not seem to you like nothing in your eyes?" But now be strong, O Zerubbabel, said the Lord; and be strong, Joshua, and be strong all you people of the land, because I am with you. My spirit abides among you, also My covenant which I made with you when you came out of Egypt. Fear not. [11]

Thus said the Lord of the host: "Very soon I will shake the heavens and the earth, the sea and the dry land. I will shake all nations, and the choicest of things of all nations shall come in and I will fill this house with splendor. Mine is all the silver. Mine is all the gold. The

---

[8] A MESSAGE FROM THE LORD: Whoever causes the multitude to be righteous, through him is no sin brought about; but he who causes the multitude to sin will have no means to repent.

[9] THE TWENTY-FOURTH DAY OF THE SIXTH MONTH: *Only a little more than three weeks passed between the prophet's first appeal and beginning the work of restoring the Temple.*

[10] THIS HOUSE IN ITS FORMER GLORY: *The First Temple was destroyed in 586, so that 66 years had passed since then.*

[11] FEAR NOT: A farmer had two cows, a weak one and a strong one. On which one did he put the yoke? Upon the strong. In the same way does the Lord test the righteous.

וּמִלֵּאתִי אֶת הַבַּיִת הַזֶּה כָּבוֹד, לִי הַכֶּסֶף וְלִי הַזָּהָב.

future glory of this house shall be greater than that of the former," says the Lord. "And in this place I will give peace."

THE UNCLEAN SACRIFICES

IN THE TWENTY-FOURTH DAY of the ninth month in the second year of Darius came the word of the Lord through Haggai the prophet, saying: Thus said the Lord: Ask the priests for a decision. If one carries hallowed flesh in the skirt of a garment and with that skirt touches bread or pottage or wine or oil, or any kind of food, will it become holy? And the priests answered and said: No.

Then Haggai said: If one who is unclean because he touched a dead body touches any of these things, will it become unclean? And the priests answered and said: It shall be unclean.

Then Haggai answered, saying: So is this people before Me, said the Lord. And so is all the work of their hands and all that they offer here is unclean.

Now I pray you, consider it: Before a stone was laid upon a stone in the temple of the Lord, see how you fared. When one came to a heap of twenty measures, there were but ten. When one came to the wine vat to draw out fifty press-measures, there were but twenty. But from this day forward, from the twenty-fourth day of the ninth month, the day that the foundations of the Lord's temple were laid, consider it. Is there seed in the barn? Yes. [Thus,] the vine and the fig-tree, the promegranate and the olive-tree, have not yet brought forth [any fruit], yet from this day I will bless you. [12]

FALL OF THE PAGAN KINGDOMS

AND THE WORD OF THE LORD came a second time to Haggai in the twenty-fourth day of the same month: Tell Zerubbabel, governor of Judah: I will shake the heavens and the earth; and I will overthrow the thrones of the kingdoms; and I will destroy the strength of the kingdoms of the nations. I will overthrow the chariots and those who ride in them; and the horses and their riders shall come down, each one by the sword of his brother. On that day, says the Lord of the host, I will take you, Zerubbabel, My servant, the son of Shealtiel, and I will make you as a signet. For I have chosen you, says the Lord of the host.

  ⪥ [12] I WILL BLESS YOU: Rabbi Johanan said that anyone can enter the Jerusalem of this world, but only those who are ordained can enter the Jerusalem of the world-to-come.

גָּדוֹל יִהְיֶה כְּבוֹד הַבַּיִת הַזֶּה הָאַחֲרוֹן מִן הָרִאשׁוֹן אָמַר יְיָ, וּבַמָּקוֹם הַזֶּה אֶתֵּן שָׁלוֹם.

24. ZECHARIAH [1–14]

IN THE EIGHTH MONTH in the second year of Darius [1] the word of the Lord came to Zechariah, [2] son of Berechiah, the son of Iddo the prophet, saying:

Return to Me and I will return to you, [3] said the Lord of the host. Be not like your fathers. The former prophets cried to them saying, Thus said the Lord: Turn away from your evil ways and from your evil deeds.

But they did not listen, nor did they give heed. Your fathers, where are

---

[1] DARIUS: *The second year of Darius' reign was 520 B.C.E. Zechariah's mission began, then, only two months after Haggai's.*

[2] ZECHARIAH: *He probably came from both a prophetic and priestly family.*

[3] I WILL RETURN TO YOU: *To have the presence of God, the* Shechinah, *dwelling among them, the children of Israel would have to return to law and righteousness.*

שׁוּבוּ אֵלַי וְאָשׁוּב אֲלֵיכֶם, אָמַר יְיָ צְבָאוֹת.

they? [4] And the prophets, do they live forever? [5] But My words and decrees which I commanded My servants the prophets, did they not overtake your fathers? [6] So they turned and said: As the Lord of hosts determined to do to us, according to our ways and according to our deeds, so has He done to us.

THE VISION OF HEAVENLY RIDERS

IN THE TWENTY-FOURTH DAY of the eleventh month, which is Shevat, [7] in the second year of Darius, I saw in the night a man riding upon a red horse, and he stood among the myrtle-trees in the bottom of the valley and behind him men on red, sorrel and white horses.

Then I said: "O Lord, what are they?" The man who stood among the myrtle-trees said: "They are those whom the Lord has sent to and fro through the earth." And the riders said to the angel of the Lord who stood among the myrtle-trees: "We have been going to and fro through the earth, and the whole earth is quiet and at peace." [8] Then the angel of the Lord cried out, saying: "O Lord

---

⊷ [4] WHERE ARE THEY: *The preaching of the prophets came to pass. The former generations were punished by being taken into captivity and by the destruction of Jerusalem.*

⊷ [5] DO THEY LIVE FOREVER: When a human being comes into the world his fists are clenched as if he were proclaiming, "Everything is mine to grasp." When he departs from the world, his hands are open as if to declare, "I can take nothing with me from the world."

⊷ [6] OVERTAKE YOUR FATHERS: Would that life were a shadow cast by a wall or tree instead of like the shadow cast by a bird in flight.

⊷ [7] SHEVAT: *The Babylonian name for February-March was Shevat and it was the term used by the Israelites who had so recently left Babylon. The date was 519 B.C.E.*

⊷ [8] QUIET AND AT PEACE: *Other nations are at peace; only Israel is persecuted.*

הִתְהַלַּכְנוּ בָאָרֶץ, וְהִנֵּה כָל הָאָרֶץ יוֹשֶׁבֶת וְשׁוֹקָטֶת.

of the host, how long will You have no compassion on Jerusalem and the cities of Judah with which You have been angry for seventy years?" [9]

Then the Lord answered the angel who spoke with me, with good words, comforting words, so the angel said to me: "Thus spoke the Lord of the host: I am deeply moved by Jerusalem and Zion, and I am very angry with the nations that are now quiet and at ease. I was a little angry and they used it to further disaster. [10] Therefore, said the Lord, I will return to Jerusalem with mercy. [11] My house shall be built in it and a build-

er's line shall be stretched over Jerusalem." [12]

Again proclaim: Thus said the Lord of the host, "My cities shall again overflow with prosperity; and the Lord shall once more comfort Zion and once again choose Jerusalem."

THE VISION OF FOUR HORNS

I LIFTED UP MY EYES and saw, and behold, [there were] four horns. I said to the angel that spoke to me: "What are these?" And he said to me: "These are the four horns [13] which have scattered Judah,

---

&ε [9] FOR SEVENTY YEARS: *This is a round number which covers the time during which the Temple lay in ruins, from 587 to 519 B.C.E. The time was, in fact, 67 years.*

&ε [10] TO FURTHER DISASTER: According to the nature of man, a prosecutor does not also become the defender. But God called Israel "a nation heavy with sin," and He also said of them, "And Thy people are all righteous."

&ε [11] JERUSALEM WITH MERCY: Rabbi Abin said, "It is written, 'And you shall be unto me (*lamed yod*) a peculiar treasure' (Exodus 19:5). The *lamed* is the highest letter; the *yod* the lowest. Is it not right for the smallest to cleave to the greatest!"

&ε [12] JERUSALEM: *The builder's line indicates that the city will be rebuilt.*

&ε [13] THE FOUR HORNS: *The four horns stand both for the four quarters of the*

וְנִחַם יְיָ עוֹד אֶת צִיּוֹן, וּבָחַר עוֹד בִּירוּשָׁלָיִם.

Israel and Jerusalem so that not a man could walk upright."

Then the Lord showed me four blacksmiths, [14] and I said, "What have they come to do?" And the angel spoke to me, saying: "They came to terrify, to cast down the horns of the nations which lifted up their horns against the land of Judah to destroy it." [15]

THE VISION OF THE SURVEYOR

I LIFTED UP MY EYES and saw a man with a measuring line in his hand. Then I said: "Where are you going?" And he said to me: "To measure Jerusalem, to see what her length and breadth should be." As the angel spoke to me and was departing, another angel went out to meet him, and he said to him: "Run and speak to this young man and say to him: Jerusalem will be inhabited and be a city without walls, because of the multitude of men and cattle in it. For I, said the Lord, will be a wall of fire round about her; and I will be a glory in her midst."

Thus said the Lord of the host regarding the nations who plundered you: Surely, he who touches you, touches the apple of his eye. I will wave My hand against them and they shall be despoiled by their victims.

Sing and rejoice, [16] O daughter of Zion, for I am coming to dwell in your

---

heavens and for the four kingdoms which have afflicted Israel—Babylon, Persia, Greece and Rome.

[14] FOUR BLACKSMITHS: The four blacksmiths are the artisans who will rebuild the Temple; they are the Messiah the son of David, the Messiah the son of Joseph, the prophet Elijah and the righteous priest Melchizedek.

[15] TO DESTROY IT: A man came to Raba saying, "The ruler of the city in which I live has commanded me to kill a certain man. If I refuse, he will kill me. What shall I do?" Raba replied, "Be killed and do not kill." But if someone comes intending to kill you, be first and kill him.

[16] SING AND REJOICE: *Levi* means cleaving, and all those who heard the Levites singing at once cleaved to the Lord.

כִּי הַנּוֹגֵעַ בָּכֶם נוֹגֵעַ בְּבָבַת עֵינוֹ; כִּי הִנְנִי מֵנִיף אֶת יָדִי עֲלֵיהֶם וְהָיוּ שָׁלָל לְעַבְדֵיהֶם.

midst, said the Lord. And many nations shall attach themselves to the Lord on that day and shall be My people. And the Lord shall take Judah for His own possession in the holy land and shall choose Jerusalem again. [17] Be silent, all flesh, before the Lord; for He has roused Himself from His holy dwelling place.

THE VISION OF JOSHUA'S VINDICATION

HE SHOWED ME JOSHUA, the chief priest, standing before the angel of the Lord, and Satan standing at his right hand to accuse him. And the angel of the Lord said to him: "The Lord rebukes you, O Satan. [18] Yes, the Lord that has chosen Jerusalem rebukes you. Is this man not a brand plucked out of the fire?" [19]

Now Joshua was dressed in filthy garments as he stood before the angel. And [the angel] spoke to those who stood before him, saying: "Take the filthy garments off him."

To Joshua, he said: "See, I have removed the guilt from you and will dress you in clean garments."

Then I said; "Let them put a clean turban on his head." They put a clean turban on his head and dressed him in [fresh] garments, and the angel of the Lord stood by. And the angel of the Lord forewarned Joshua, saying: "Thus said the Lord: If you walk in My ways and keep My commandments, then you shall also judge My house and have charge of My courts, and I will give you free access [20] among those who stand there."

ﬁ [17] CHOOSE JERUSALEM AGAIN: Only when you conduct yourselves like the children of God shall you be called His children.

ﬁ [18] O SATAN: *Here Satan is the celestial prosecutor of the Lord, not the adversary or tempter, as he appears in later literature.*

ﬁ [19] PLUCKED OUT OF THE FIRE: *Israel is the wick, the Torah is the oil, and the* Shechinah *is the light.*

ﬁ [20] FREE ACCESS: Rabbi Judah said, "The children of Israel will not be delivered unless they repent, and they repent only through tribulations, oppression, exile and the lack of a livelihood."

הַס כָּל בָּשָׂר מִפְּנֵי יְיָ, כִּי נֵעוֹר מִמְּעוֹן קָדְשׁוֹ.

THE VISION OF THE CANDELABRUM

THE ANGEL who spoke to me aroused me [and I was] like a man awakened from sleep. He said to me: "What do you see?" And I said: "I see a candelabrum [21] all gold with a bowl on the top of it, and seven lamps are on it. There are seven pipes to the lamps which are on top. And there are two olive-trees beside the candlestick, one on the right side of the bowl and one on the left."

I said to the angel; "What are these, my Lord?" The angel answered and said to me: "Do you not know what these are?" I said: "No, my Lord." Then he answered and said to me: "Those seven lamps are the eyes of the Lord that are roving over the whole earth." Then I said to him: "What are those two olive-trees upon the right of the candelabrum and upon the left of it?" And he said:

"Those are the anointed ones, who stand by the Lord of the whole earth."

And the angel said to me: "This is the word of the Lord to Zerubbabel: Not by arms, nor by might, but by My spirit, said the Lord of the host. [22] Who are you, O great mountain before Zerubbabel! You shall become a plain and he shall bring out the top stone with shouts of: How beautiful it is!"

The word of the Lord came to me, saying: The hands of Zerubbabel have laid the foundation of this house and his hands shall also finish it. [23] And you shall know that the Lord of the host has sent me to you. He who has despised the day of small things shall yet rejoice to see the plummet in the hands of Zerubbabel.

THE VISION OF THE FLYING SCROLL

THEN AGAIN I lifted up my eyes and saw a flying scroll. He said to me: "What

---

⋖§ [21] A CANDELABRUM: *The candelabrum symbolizes the restoration of the Jewish state.*

⋖§ [22] LORD OF THE HOST: Let others rely on the arm of flesh; Israel's weapon is prayer.

⋖§ [23] FINISH IT: Iron, the metal of weapons and warfare, cannot build an altar to the God of life and of peace.

לֹא בְחַיִל וְלֹא בְכֹחַ כִּי אִם בְּרוּחִי, אָמַר יְיָ צְבָאוֹת.

do you see?" I said: "I see a flying scroll, [24] its length twenty cubits and its width ten cubits." And he said to me: "This is the curse that goes forth over the face of the whole land. For how long have all thieves remained unpunished? For how long have all those who swear falsely gone unpunished? So I sent forth [this curse], said the Lord of the host, and it shall enter the house of the thief and the house of him who swears falsely by My name. [25] It shall make its abode in the midst of his house and destroy him and the timber and the stones."

THE VISION OF THE WOMAN

THE ANGEL who spoke to me came forward and said: "Lift up your eyes and see what this is that goes forth." I said: "What is it?" And he said: "This measure that goes forth contains the iniquity of all the land." [Then I saw] the lead cover lifted and there was a woman sitting in the measure. The angel pushed her down in the measure and closed the leaden cover over the opening, and said: "This is wickedness." [26]

Then I lifted up my eyes and looked, and there were two women [27] and they had wings like the stork, and the wind was in their wings. They lifted up the measure between the earth and the sky.

I said to the angel who talked to me: "Where are they taking the measure?" And he said to me: "To the land of Shinar [28] where they will build her a

―――――――――――――――――――――――――――――――――――――

&ᶿ [24] FLYING SCROLL: *The flying scroll has inscribed on its parchment curses against the evils of mankind. It destroys the wicked.*

&ᶿ [25] WHO SWEARS FALSELY BY MY NAME: Do no good to the evil man and no evil will befall you.

&ᶿ [26] THIS IS WICKEDNESS: *The woman symbolizes evil, and is therefore confined by the leaden cover.*

&ᶿ [27] TWO WOMEN: *The two women are symbolic of hypocrisy and pride which, with evil, settle in Babylon.*

&ᶿ [28] SHINAR: *Shinar is the ancient name for Babylon, looked on as the land of iniquity.*

וְהִנֵּה שְׁתַּיִם נָשִׁים יוֹצְאוֹת וְרוּחַ בְּכַנְפֵיהֶם, וְלָהֵנָּה כְנָפַיִם כְּכַנְפֵי הַחֲסִידָה.

house, and when it is ready, they will set her down in her own place."

have set My spirit at rest in the north country."

THE VISION OF FOUR CHARIOTS

AGAIN I lifted up my eyes and I saw four chariots come out from between the two mountains; and the mountains were mountains of brass. In the first chariot there were red horses, in the second chariot black horses, in the third chariot white horses, and in the fourth chariot spotted horses. I said to the angel that spoke with me: "What are these, my Lord?" The angel answered me, saying: "These chariots, the four winds of heaven, go forth after standing before the Lord of all the earth. The black horses go to the northland, the white horses, behind them, to the west, the spotted horses toward the south, and the red horses to the east." [They were straining to go] and he said: "Go and traverse the earth." Then he cried out to me, saying: "Look at those going to the northland. They

ZERUBBABEL AND JOSHUA CROWNED

THE WORD OF THE LORD came to me, saying: Take the gold and the silver brought by Heldai, Tobijah and Jedaiah, the exiles who have arrived from Babylon, and go on the same day to the house of Josiah, the son of Zephaniah. Take the silver and the gold and make two crowns. [29] Set one crown on the head of Zerubbabel, the son of Shealtiel, the other crown put on the head of Joshua the high priest, And you shall speak to Zerubbabel, saying: "Thus said the Lord of the host: Here is a man whose name is the Branch; [30] and he will branch forth from his place and shall rebuild the temple of the Lord, and he shall bear the glory, and he shall sit and reign upon his throne. Joshua shall be at his right hand and there shall be peaceful counsel [31] between them.

ᏮᎦ [29] MAKE TWO CROWNS: The years of the man who runs after leadership are shortened.

ᏮᎦ [30] BRANCH: *This refers to Zerubbabel for whom Haggai had already forecast a great, almost messianic, role in reviving Jewish life.*

ᏮᎦ [31] PEACEFUL COUNSEL: When two people quarrel, the one who keeps silence first is the more praiseworthy.

אֵלֶּה אַרְבַּע רוּחוֹת הַשָּׁמַיִם יוֹצְאוֹת מֵהִתְיַצֵּב עַל אֲדוֹן כָּל הָאָרֶץ.

And the crowns shall be [put] as a memorial in the temple of the Lord. And those who are far off shall come and rebuild the temple of the Lord, and you shall know that the Lord of the host has sent me to you. It shall come to pass, if you diligently hearken to the voice of the Lord God.

FASTING AND MOURNING

IT CAME TO PASS in the fourth year [32] of King Darius, in the fourth day in the ninth month of Kislev, the people of Beth-el sent Sarezer, Regemelech and his men to present offerings to the Lord and to speak to the priests of the house of the Lord, and to the prophets, saying: "Are we to mourn and fast in the fifth month as we have been doing these many years?"

And the word of the Lord of hosts came to Zechariah, saying: Speak to all the people of the land and to the priests, saying: When you fasted and mourned in the fifth and in the seventh month these seventy years, did I command you to fast? Was it for Me that you did fast? When you eat and drink, do you not eat and drink for yourselves? [33] Are not these the words which the Lord proclaimed through His former prophets, when Jerusalem was inhabited and at peace, and her town round about her, and the negev and the lowlands were inhabited? The word of the Lord of the host was: Render true judgment and show mercy and compassion every man to his brother. Oppress not the widow, nor the orphan, nor the stranger, [34] nor the poor. Let none of you devise evil in your heart against your neighbor, and love no false oath, for all these things I hate, says the Lord.

Thus said the Lord of the host: The fast of the fourth month, the fast of the fifth, of the seventh and the tenth shall become to the house of Judah a joy and a cheerful season. Therefore, love truth and peace.

ু [32] THE FOURTH YEAR: *The year 518 B.C.E.*

ু [33] DRINK FOR YOURSELVES: Food and drink may be abundant, but if there is no peace they are as if they were nothing.

ু [34] NOR THE STRANGER: The heathen is your neighbor and your brother; to do him wrong is a sin.

צוֹם הָרְבִיעִי וְצוֹם הַחֲמִישִׁי וְצוֹם הַשְּׁבִיעִי וְצוֹם הָעֲשִׂירִי יִהְיֶה לְבֵית יְהוּדָה לְשָׂשׂוֹן וּלְשִׂמְחָה וּלְמוֹעֲדִים טוֹבִים.

THE PEACEFUL PROMISE

THE WORD OF THE LORD of the host came, saying: I am greatly concerned about Zion; and I am concerned about her with great fury.

Thus said the Lord: I will return to Zion and I will dwell in the midst of Jerusalem; and Jerusalem shall be called "The City of Truth," and the mountain of the Lord of the host shall be called "The Holy Mountain."

Thus said the Lord of the host: There shall yet sit again old men and old women in the streets of Jerusalem, each man with his staff in his hand, because of his great age. The streets of the city shall be full of boys and girls playing. [35]

Thus said the Lord of the host: I will deliver My people from the east country and from the west country. I will gather them in and they shall dwell in the midst of Jerusalem; and they shall be My people and I will be their God in truth and in righteousness.

THE LORD'S PEOPLE

THUS SAID THE LORD of the host: It shall come to pass that there shall come people, inhabitants of many cities. The people of one city shall go to another, saying: "Let us go at once to seek the Lord of the host and entreat His favor." "Yes, we will also go," [they answered]. Many peoples and mighty nations shall come to seek the Lord of the host in Jerusalem and to entreat the favor of the Lord.

Thus said the Lord of the host: In those days it shall come to pass that ten men from nations of different tongues shall take hold of the skirt of him who is a Jew, saying, "We will go with you because we have heard that God is with your people."

THE KINGDOM OF THE MESSIAH

Rejoice greatly, [36] O daughter of Zion,

&ᶘ [35] BOYS AND GIRLS PLAYING: Rabbi Nathan said, "The vision is for the time appointed. It hastens to the end and does not deceive. If it delay, wait for it confidently, for it will surely come and will not delay indefinitely."

&ᶘ [36] REJOICE GREATLY: The spirit of the Lord rests not upon the sad and the forlorn, but upon those who do their duty and are glad.

וְהֶחֱזִיקוּ בִּכְנַף אִישׁ יְהוּדִי לֵאמֹר: נֵלְכָה עִמָּכֶם, כִּי שָׁמַעְנוּ אֱלֹהִים עִמָּכֶם.

Shout joyfully, O daughter of
Jerusalem.
Behold, your King comes to you,
He is just and filled with salvation,
Lowly, and riding upon an ass,
Or upon a colt, the foal of an ass.
And he will destroy the chariots of
Ephraim,
And the horses from Jerusalem.
The battle bow shall be destroyed.
And he shall proclaim peace to the
nations; [37]
And his dominion shall be from sea
to sea,
From the Euphrates to the end of
the earth.

JERUSALEM DELIVERED

Behold, a day of the Lord is com-
ing, [38]
When I will gather all nations against
Jerusalem to battle;
The city shall be taken, and the
houses plundered,
And the women violated;

And half the city shall go into exile,
But the rest of the people shall not
be cut off from the city.
Then the Lord shall go forth,
And fight against those nations,
As once He fought in the day of
battle.
In that day His feet shall stand on
the Mount of Olives,
And the Mount of Olives shall be
split in two,
Toward the east and toward the
west,
So that there shall be a great valley.
You shall flee to the valley of the
mountain;
You shall flee as you fled from be-
fore the earthquake
In the days of Uzziah, king of Judah;
And the Lord, your God, with all
the holy ones
Will come to your help.
It shall come to pass on that day
there shall be neither heat, nor
cold, nor frost;

---

[37] PROCLAIM PEACE TO THE NATIONS: Rab said, "The time of the
Messiah is not like this time. In the messianic age there will be no eating
and drinking, no begetting of children, no commerce, no jealousy, no
hatred and no strife."

[38] A DAY OF THE LORD IS COMING: In this day of God's judgment
Jerusalem will be delivered.

גִּילִי מְאֹד בַּת צִיּוֹן, הָרִיעִי בַּת יְרוּשָׁלַיִם, הִנֵּה מַלְכֵּךְ יָבוֹא לָךְ, צַדִּיק וְנוֹשָׁע
הוּא, עָנִי וְרוֹכֵב עַל חֲמוֹר.

It shall be one continuous day
Which shall be known as the Lord's,
Not day and not night;
But at evening time there will be
  light.
And it shall come to pass in that day,
The living waters shall go out from
  Jerusalem,
Half of them toward the eastern sea,
And half of them toward the west-
  ern sea,
Flowing on through summer and
  winter.
The Lord shall be King over all the
  earth,
In that day the Lord shall be One
  and His name One.

JERUSALEM THE ONE AND ONLY

IT SHALL COME TO PASS that everyone that is left of all the nations that went up against Jerusalem, shall go up from year to year to worship the King, the Lord of the host, and celebrate the feast of tabernacles. On that day shall be [inscribed] on the bells of the horses: "Holy to the Lord." The pots in the Lord's house shall be like the sacrificial bowls before the altar. Every pot in Jerusalem and in Judah shall be holy to the Lord of hosts. All those who sacrifice shall come and take them to boil flesh in them. On that day there shall be no more traffickers in the house of the Lord of the host.

וְהָיָה יְיָ לְמֶלֶךְ עַל כָּל הָאָרֶץ, בַּיּוֹם הַהוּא יִהְיֶה יְיָ אֶחָד וּשְׁמוֹ אֶחָד.

25. MALACHI [1–3]

THE PROMISE

THE PROPHECY of the word of the Lord to Israel by Malachi. [1]

I have loved you, says the Lord. Yet you ask, "In what way have You loved us?"

Says the Lord: Was not Esau Jacob's [older] brother? Yet I loved Jacob, but I rejected Esau. [2] I made his mountains a desolation and gave his heritage to the jackals of the wilderness.

Edom may say: "We are impoverished, but we will return and rebuild the desolate places." Thus says the Lord of the host: They shall build, but I will

---

[1] MALACHI: *This means "my messenger," and is probably a description of the prophet's mission, rather than his name. Tradition ascribed the book's authorship to Ezra the Scribe.*

[2] I REJECTED ESAU: The Lord gave Israel three precious gifts, all through suffering: the Torah, the land of Israel, and the world-to-come.

אָהַבְתִּי אֶתְכֶם, אָמַר יְיָ, וַאֲמַרְתֶּם: בַּמֶּה אֲהַבְתָּנוּ?

throw it down. They shall be called the reign of wickedness and a people against whom the Lord is angry for ever. Your eyes shall see it and you shall say: "The Lord is great beyond the borders of Israel." [3]

THE PRIESTS REBUKED

A son honors his father,

And a servant his master; [4]

If, then, I be a father,

Where is the honor to Me?

And if I am a master,

Where is the fear of Me?

Says the Lord of the host

To you priests who despise My name.

You ask: "How have we despised Your name?"

You bring to My table defiled bread.

You ask: "In what way have we defiled it?"

In that you say, "The table of the Lord is something to be despised."

When you offer the blind for sacrifice, [5] [you think] it is no evil.

And when you offer the lame and sick, [you think] it is no evil.

Present it to your governor;

Will he be pleased with it?

 ❧ [3] BEYOND THE BORDERS OF ISRAEL: An unbeliever said to Rabbi Gamaliel that the rabbis had said that wherever ten people assembled to pray, the spirit of the Lord was among them. "How many *Shechinahs* are there?" he asked. Rabbi Gamaliel then called the unbeliever's servant and struck him. "Why did you strike him?" the unbeliever asked. "Because the sun is in the house of an infidel." "But the sun shines everywhere in the world!" the unbeliever protested. Then Rabbi Gamaliel said, "If the sun can be everywhere, and the sun is only one of God's many servants, how much more can the spirit of the Lord shine through the whole universe."

 ❧ [4] A SERVANT HIS MASTER: A son honors his father and a servant his master, but you, Israel, are ashamed to declare that I am your Father, or that you are My servant, says the Lord.

 ❧ [5] THE BLIND FOR SACRIFICE: *One of the blemishes that made an animal unfit for sacrifice.*

בֵּן יְכַבֵּד אָב וְעֶבֶד אֲדוֹנָיו, וְאִם אָב אָנִי – אַיֵּה כְבוֹדִי, וְאִם אֲדוֹנִים אָנִי – אַיֵּה מוֹרָאִי?

Or will he receive you kindly?
O that there were one among you
    that would shut the doors
    [of the Temple],
So that you might not kindle fire on
    My altar in vain. [6]
I take no delight in you, says the
    Lord of the host,
Neither will I accept an offering
    from your hand.
Because from the rising of the sun
    to its going down,
My name is great among nations.
And in every place offerings are
    presented in My name,
Pure offerings.

WARNING TO THE PRIESTS

NOW THIS ADMONITION is for you, O priests. If you will not listen, and if you will not take it to heart, to give glory to My name, says the Lord of the host, then I will send a curse upon you. I will curse your blessings. Yes, I will curse them, because you do not take it to your heart.

The lips of the priest should keep knowledge, and the Law is what people should seek from his mouth, for he is the messenger of the Lord of hosts. [7] But you turned aside from the way; you have caused many to stumble in the Law. You have perverted the covenant of Levi, says the Lord of the host. Therefore have I also made you contemptible and degraded before all the people, according as you have not kept My way but have shown partiality in the Law. [8]

---

[6] ON MY ALTAR IN VAIN: *Offerings presented in such a spirit were without value. Better not to sacrifice altogether and to let the altar fire die.*

[7] LORD OF HOSTS: He in whom the fear of sin comes before wisdom, his wisdom shall endure. But he in whom wisdom comes before the fear of sin, his wisdom shall not endure. He whose works exceed his wisdom, his wisdom will endure. But he whose wisdom exceeds his works, his wisdom shall not endure.

[8] PARTIALITY IN THE LAW: Old men, eunuchs and childless men should not be appointed as judges, so that justice may be tempered with mercy. And Rabbi Judah added, neither should the hard-hearted be appointed.

כִּי שִׂפְתֵי כֹהֵן יִשְׁמְרוּ דַעַת וְתוֹרָה יְבַקְשׁוּ מִפִּיהוּ, כִּי מַלְאַךְ יְיָ צְבָאוֹת הוּא.

WITHHOLDING TITHES

FROM THE DAYS of your fathers, you have turned aside from My ordinances, and have not kept them. Return to Me and I will return to you, says the Lord of the host. But you say, "How shall we return?" Can a man rob God? [9] Yet you did rob Me. You say, "How have we robbed you?" In tithes and heave-offerings. Bring the whole tithe into the storehouse that there may be food in My house, and see what I will do, says the Lord of hosts. See if I will not open for you the windows of heaven and pour out a blessing for you until there will be no more want. I will rebuke the devourer [10] of your good, and he shall not destroy the produce of the land. Neither shall your vine cast its fruit before time in the field. All nations shall call you blessed, for you shall be a land of delight.

DIVORCE AND INTERMARRIAGE

Have we not one father? [11]
Has not one God created us?
Why do we deal treacherously
    every man against his brother,
Profaning the covenant of our
    fathers?

Judah has dealt treacherously; and an abomination is committed in Israel and Jerusalem, for Judah has profaned the holy seed which the Lord loves, and

---

    [9] CAN A MAN ROB GOD: He who preoccupies himself with the Law for its own sake protects the whole world and brings redemption closer.

    [10] THE DEVOURER: *The locust is the devourer and the land had just suffered a plague of locusts.*

    [11] HAVE WE NOT ONE FATHER: "All flesh shall come to worship before me," Isaiah says (66:23). It does not say, "All Israel shall come," but "All flesh shall come." Rabbi Phinehas said, "Everyone who weakens his *yetzer* in this world is worthy to see the face of the *Shechinah*." All flesh means the heathen, but not all the heathen; only those who have not enslaved Israel, will be received by the Messiah.

הֲלוֹא אָב אֶחָד לְכֻלָּנוּ, הֲלוֹא אֵל אֶחָד בְּרָאָנוּ – מַדּוּעַ נִבְגַּד אִישׁ בְּאָחִיו?

married the daughter of a strange god. [12] The Lord will cut off a son and a grandson from the tents of Israel for the man who does this and who offers offerings to the Lord of the host.

And this is the second thing you do; you who cover the altar of the Lord with tears, weeping and groaning. Because of it, I cannot accept your offering, nor receive with good will anything from your hand.

And yet you say: "For what reason?" Because the Lord Himself has borne witness between you and the wife of your youth, [13] against whom you dealt treacherously, though she is your com-

---

⋑ [12] A STRANGE GOD: Once when Rabbi Akiba was in Rome, a certain Roman sent two beautiful women to him, bathed and anointed and dressed like brides. All night they attempted to seduce him but he would not turn to them. In the morning they returned to their master and complained that they would rather die than be given to Akiba. Their master sent for Akiba and asked him why he had not done with these women as men generally do with women. They were beautiful, weren't they? They were human beings just as he was, weren't they? Had not the Lord who created Akiba also created them? And Akiba replied, "I could not help myself. I was overcome by their breath because of the forbidden meats they ate."

⋑ [13] THE WIFE OF YOUR YOUTH: A Roman woman asked a rabbi how long it took the Lord to create the universe, and was told, six days. Shen then asked what the Lord had been doing since, and the rabbi said, "The Lord has been arranging marriages." The lady replied that if that was all He was doing, she too could do it, and since she had many male and female slaves, she would pair them off. The rabbi warned her that it might seem simple, but that it was as difficult as dividing the Red Sea.

The lady then called together a thousand of her male slaves and a thousand of her female slaves and in a single night arranged marriages for all of them. The next day they all appeared before her, one with a fractured skull, another with an eye knocked out, still another with a

עַל כִּי יְיָ הֵעִיד בֵּינְךָ וּבֵין אֵשֶׁת נְעוּרֶיךָ אֲשֶׁר בָּגַדְתָּה בָּהּ ...

panion and the wife of your covenant. No one who has [a trace of] spirit has done this. What does this one seek? The seed of God. Therefore, take heed to yourself and let none deal treacherously against the wife of his youth. Said the Lord God of Israel, I hate putting away the first wife [14] and he who covers his garment with violence. [15] Take heed that you deal not treacherously.

JUDGMENT AND LAW

YOU HAVE WEARIED THE LORD with your words. In that you say: "Every one that does evil is good in the sight of the Lord, and He delights in them. Or where is the God of justice?" [16]

---

broken leg. Angrily she asked what was the matter and heard a chorus of "I don't want him" and "I don't want her".

The lady then sent for the rabbi and said, "There is no God like your God and your Torah is true, for what you told me about making marriages is quite correct."

◆§ [14] I HATE PUTTING AWAY THE FIRST WIFE: Whenever a man divorces his first wife, even the altar sheds tears in her behalf.

A bad wife is like leprosy to her husband. What is the remedy? Let him divorce her and be cured of his leprosy.

◆§ [15] COVERS HIS GARMENT WITH VIOLENCE: *This expression signified divorce because, according to ancient custom, a woman was claimed as a wife by spreading one's garment over her.*

◆§ [16] THE GOD OF JUSTICE: God said to David, "If you see that I do good to the wicked, let it not seem evil in your heart, but go on doing good. If to the evil ones who provoke Me and do not profit Me, I do good, how much more shall I do good to you who trust in Me, and occupy yourself with the Law?" Rabbi Elazar said, "From the prosperity of the wicked in this world, you can judge the reward of the righteous in the world-to-come. If the wicked are treated so, think how much more will the righteous merit."

‏ ‎. . . וְהִיא חֲבֶרְתְּךָ וְאֵשֶׁת בְּרִיתֶךָ, וְלֹא אֶחָד עָשָׂה וּשְׁאָר רוּחַ לוֹ.‏

Behold, I will send My messen-ger, [17] and he shall clear the way before Me. The Lord whom you seek will suddenly come to His temple, and the messenger of the covenant in whom you delight, behold, he comes. And he shall sit as a refiner and a purifier, and he shall purify the sons of Levi [18] and refine them as one refines gold and silver. [19] And then they shall be worthy to bring to the Lord offerings of righteousness. Then also the offering of Judah and Jeru-salem shall be pleasant to the Lord as in the days of old and as in the years gone by.

I will come near to you in judgment; and I will be a swift witness against the sorcerers, against the adulterers, and against all who swear falsely; and against those that oppress the hireling in his wages, the widow and the orphan; and against those who turn aside the stranger from his right, and fear Me not. I, the Lord, do not change, and you, the sons of Jacob, will not be destroyed.

THOSE WHO REVERE HIS NAME

YOUR WORDS have been harsh against Me, says the Lord. You say, "How have we spoken against You?" You have said: "It is useless to serve God. What gain is it to do His bidding and that we walked humbly before the Lord of the host? How the arrogant are happy and those who do wickedness have been elevated. Yes, they tempt God and es-cape." [20] Then those who feared the

---

❧ [17] MY MESSENGER: *The Hebrew word for my messenger is* malachi. *Some commentators believe the messenger refers to Elijah, who will prepare the way for the Day of Judgment.*

❧ [18] THE SONS OF LEVI: *First the priests will be purified, then the rest of the people.*

❧ [19] GOLD AND SILVER: *The people will be refined as precious metal is refined.*

❧ [20] THEY TEMPT GOD AND ESCAPE: *Every sin of a man is engraved upon his bones.*

הִנְנִי שׁוֹלֵחַ מַלְאָכִי וּפִנָּה דֶרֶךְ לְפָנָי.

Lord spoke with one another. <u>The Lord gave heed and listened, and there was written in a book of remembrance that was before Him concerning those who revered the Lord and honored His name.</u>

They shall be Mine, says the Lord of hosts, a special treasure in the day I begin to judge. And I will have compassion upon them, just as a man has compassion upon his own son who works with him. Then you shall distinguish between the righteous and the wicked, [21] between him that serves God and between him that does not serve Him.

THE LORD'S DAY

Behold the day comes,
It burns like a furnace;
And all the arrogant,
Everyone who does wickedness
Shall be stubble;
And the day that is coming,
Says the Lord of the host,
Shall set them ablaze
And will leave
Neither root nor branch of them.
But to you that revere My name,
The sun of righteousness
Shall arise with healing in its wing.
You shall go forth,
And skip like fattened calves.
You shall tread down the wicked,
For they shall be ashes under your
    feet
In the day I begin to act.
Remember the law of Moses, My
    servant, which I commanded
    to him in Horeb for all Israel,
    statutes and ordinances.
Behold, I will send you
Elijah the prophet [22]

---

    [21] THE RIGHTEOUS AND THE WICKED: If a man comes to defile himself, the door is open to him; but if he comes to purify himself, then he is helped. In the school of Rabbi Ishmael it was taught: It is as when a man sells naphtha and balm. When a buyer for naphtha comes, the shop owner says, Measure it out for yourself. But if a buyer comes for balm, the shop owner says, Wait and I shall help you measure it so that we may both be perfumed.

    [22] ELIJAH THE PROPHET: *The prophet Elijah will come as the Lord's messenger, to prepare men for the coming Day of the Lord.*

וַיַּקְשֵׁב יְיָ וַיִּשְׁמָע, וַיִּכָּתֵב סֵפֶר זִכָּרוֹן לְפָנָיו לְיִרְאֵי יְיָ וּלְחוֹשְׁבֵי שְׁמוֹ.

Before the coming	of the fathers
Of the great and terrible day of the	To the children,
Lord,	And the heart of the children
And he shall turn the heart	To their fathers. [23]

---

[23] CHILDREN TO THEIR FATHERS: *Elijah will bring harmony to family life, reconcile the conflicts between husband and wife, between parents and children, so that family life will be restored to its virtue and meaning.*

A father's love is for his children, and the children's love for their children.

HAZAK, HAZAK, V'NIT-HAZEK.

וְהֵשִׁיב לֵב אָבוֹת עַל בָּנִים וְלֵב בָּנִים עַל אֲבוֹתָם.

SOURCES

All references to the tractates of the Talmud are from the Babylonian Talmud unless otherwise indicated.

Sources referred to are in the following editions:

M'chilta d'Rabbi Ishmael, Meir Ish Shalom, editor, Vina, 5630 (1870)

Midrash Rabbah, Epstein edition, Warsaw

Midrash Shohar Tov (Psalms, Samuel & Proverbs), Jerusalem, 5720 (1960). Generally this work is thought to refer only to Psalms. Midrash Sh'muel and Midrash Mishle are sometimes used in referring to the sections dealing with Samuel and Proverbs, but all three works are properly subsumed under the general heading.

Midrash Tanhuma, Rosen edition, Warsaw

Pirke d'Rabbi Eliezer ha-Gadol, Bamberg edition, Warsaw, 5612 (1852)

P'sikta Rabbati, Meir Ish Shalom, editor, Tel Aviv (reprint edition), 5723 (1963)

Sifra, Schlosberg edition, Vienna, 5622 (1862)

Sifri, Meir Ish Shalom, editor, Vina, 5624 (1864)

Tana D've Eliyahu Rabbah and Zuta, Tzinkes edition, Warsaw, 1883

Zohar, Rom edition (3 vol.), Vilna, 5642 (1882)

CHAPTER ONE

1. Eruvin 15a; Yalkut Shimoni I, 942
6. Leviticus Rabbah 24:1.
8. Shabbat 54b, 55a.
10. Yalkut Machiri on Isaiah 5:1.
11. Hulin 92a.
12. Lamentations Rabbah 22.
16. Tan. Vayishlach 2; Yalkut I, 764.
18. Lev. R. 10:2.

CHAPTER TWO

2. Yerushalmi Avodah Zarah, ch. 1.
7. Shabbat 33a.
9. Sanhedrin 94b; see Targum on Isaiah 8:6.
11. Lev. R. 11:7; Yerushalmi Sanhedrin, ch. 10, hal, 2.
13. Maimonides, *Guide for the Perplexed*, II, pp. 129-30, 217-18 (Friedlander translation);

see Sanhedrin 89a.
14. Tan. Shemini 10.

CHAPTER THREE

6. Sanhedrin 26a.
9. Genesis Rabbah 26:3; Exodus Rabbah 15:21.
10. Yalkut II, 417.
11. Shabbat 10a.

CHAPTER FOUR

1. Yalkut Shimoni II, 443;
   P'sikta d'Rav Kahana, ch.
   16; Rashi on Song of Songs
   8:1.
2. Yalkut I, 847.
3. Shabbat 32b.
4. Maimonides, *Hilchot Yesodei
   Hatorah*, ch. 1, hal. 8, 9.
6. Gen. R. 38:4.
7. Yalkut II, 711.
9. Sotah 5a; Lev. R. 7:2.
10. Yoma 54b.

CHAPTER FIVE

4. Tan. Mishpatim 5; Tan.
   (Buber) Mishpatim, pp. 41a, b;
   Yalkut II, 888 on Psalm
   147; see also Ex. R. 30:5.
5. Tosefta Rabbah Kamma 9.
6. Bahya ibn Pakuda, *Duties of
   the Heart*, pp. 279-81 (Cook
   ed.).
7. Tana d'vé Eliyahu Rabbah,
   ch. 18,
10. Rashi; Radak; Metzudat
    David, by implication.
14. B'rachot 6b.
17. Yerushalmi K'tubot, ch. 11,
    hal. 3.
18. Eduyot, ch. 5, mishnah 7;
    Midrash Psalms on 146, 2;
    Tana d'vé Eliyahu Rabbah,
    ch. 18; Yebamot 62b, 63a.
19. N'darim 8b.

CHAPTER SIX

3. P'sikta Rabbati, ch. 26; Lev.
   R. 10:2.
7. Ex. R. 27:9.
8. Num. R. 15:16; Yalkut II,
   264.
9. Yalkut II, 725; B'rachot 61b;
   Hovot Halvavot Shaar Ha-
   prishut, ch. 2; Gaon of Vilna
   in a letter to his wife, in
   supplement to Mesilat Ye-
   sharim, Luzzato.
10. Yalkut I, 93a.
11. Yerushalmi Taanit, ch. 2,

hal. 1.
12. Tana d'vé Eliyahu Rabbah,
    ch. 30.

CHAPTER SEVEN

1. Zohar III 101a.
2. Ecclesiastes Rabbah 7.
3. Eccl. R. 8.
7. Tan. Vayera.
8. Maimonides, *Guide*, III, ch.
   34, p. 169.
10. Horayot 6.
12. Shabbat 105b.
13. Baba Kamma, 119a.
17. Abodah Zarah 3b.
20. Sukkah 49b.
21. Tan. (Buber), Vayera, p. 55;
    Taanit 4a; see also Teacher's
    Resource Book I (The
    Rabbis' Bible) pp. 31-32,
    33-34.
22. Yoma 81.
23. P'sahim 87.

CHAPTER EIGHT

1. Zohar I, 81b.
8. Taanit 8.
9. Metzudat David 36:17; see
   Mikra Meforash on the verse.
11. B'rachot 19.
12. Midrash HaGadol 144.
13. Zohar I 249b; II 148b.
16. Zohar III 53a.
17. Zohar IV 145b.
18. Gen. R. 67.
21. Baba Kamma 93a.
22. Pirké d'Rabbi Eliezer 53.
25. Kiddushin 30a.
27. Radak and Malbim on
    Jeremiah 15:16.
28. Yoma 87.
30. Makkot 24b.

CHAPTER NINE

1. Ex. R., Ki Tissa, 97, 3.
3. Avot d'Rabbi Nathan, 32,
   36a.
6. Tana d'vé Eliyahu Rabbah,
   148.
8. Tan. Noah 21.

9. Midrash Haser ve-Yater 39.
11. Sanhedrin 104.
15. M'chilta Beshallah.
16. Eruvin 13b.
19. Tikkune Zohar, 22, 95a.
20. Midrash Psalms on 119; 10,
    246b, para. 7.
21. N'darim 64.
22. Tan. Noah 3; Gittin 88a;
    Shlomo Simon, *Yiddn Zwishn
    Felker*, pp. 30-32.
23. Tana d'vé Eliyahu, p. 71.
28. Yalkut II, 326; see also Moed
    Katan 16b; Pirké d'Rabbi
    Eliezer, ch. 53; Yalkut II,
    157.
29. Eccl. R. 7:4.
30. Gen. R. 74:2.
31. Lev. R. 11:7; Lam. R. 4:15;
    Kiddushin 31b, see Rashi.

CHAPTER TEN

1. Num. R. 3:2.
4. Midrash Psalms on 106:44,
   229a, para. 9.
7. P'sikta Rabbati, ch. 30.
8. Yoma 9.
9. B'rachot 49.
11. Lam. R. pes. 34.
12. Yoma 8, 9.
13. Gen. R. 17:3.
14. Gen. R. 58:8.
19. Song of Songs Rabbah II,
    para. 2, 6, on II 2; f 14a.
20. Pirké Avot 3:2.
22. Song of Songs Rabbah I,
    para. 16, 1, on I, 16; f 13a.
23. Midrash Shohar Tov 61.
24. Sanhedrin 106.
26. Eccl. R. 1, para. 4, 1, f 2b.
27. Baba Batra 75.
32. Eruvin 13b.
33. B'rachot 34b.

CHAPTER ELEVEN

1. Maimonides, *Guide*, II,
   pp. 215, 218; see ch. 46.
4. Yalkut II, 337, 339; Yerushalmi B'rachot, ch. 9, hal. 1.
5. Hagigah 11b; see Maharsha's

comments on Hagigah 12a;
see also Hagigah 12a,b, 13a.

7. Lev. R. 2:97; see Zohar II,
   p. 166b; Rashi and Metzudat
   David 2:1.
9. Menahot 53.
11. Taanit 27.
17. Yalkut II, 329; M'chilta Bo,
    Paskha, pes. at end; Yalkut
    II, 802.
18. Zohar I, 68a, 225a.
20. Kiddushin 40a.
35. Rashi on Psalms 83:6;
    Midrash Psalms 185a.

CHAPTER TWELVE

4. Yerushalmi Taanit 11, ch. 11,
   hal. 6, 65d.
5. Ex. R. Ki Tissa 46:4.
6. Deut. R. 11:8.
7. Lam. R. introduction.
8. Sanhedrin 74.
9. Metzudat David on 11:16.
10. Gittin 57a; K'tubot 112a.
11. Yerushalmi Yoma, ch. 4,
    hal. 1; Yalkut II, 351;
    homiletics.
12. Sifre Deuteronomy 346.
16. Shevuot 36a.
22. Zohar I, 89a.
24. Yoma 76.
26. Shabbat 89.

CHAPTER THIRTEEN

1. Kiddushin 40.
2. Pirké Avot 3:9.
3. Maimonides, *Mishneh Torah*,
   ch. 5, hal. 4.
5. B'rachot 7a.
6. B'rachot 61.
7. P'sikta d'Rav Kahana 25,
   158b.
8. Yoma 85b.
9. Yoma 86b.
10. Baba Batra 35.
11. P'sikta d'Rav Kahana 158b.
12. Sanhedrin 90a.
13. Pirké d'Rabbi Nathan, ch. 24.
14. Sanhedrin 92b.
15. P'sikta Rabbati, ch. 1; see

commentary Magen David;
Tan. (Buber) Vayehi, 197b;
Vayehi 3; see K'tubot 111a.
18. Yerushalmi Baba M'tzia 2.
19. Pirké Avot 4:5.
20. Gen. R. 98:2.
23. Zohar I, 21a.
24. Tan. Toldot 5.
25. Rosh ha-Shanah 31.
26. Betzah 32.
31. Tamid 31.
32. Baba M'tzia 62a.
33. Taanit 22a.
34. Lev. R. 112:2; Yalkut II,
    944.
36. Maimonides, *Guide*, II, 203-
    204.
37. Sanhedrin 97b.

CHAPTER FOURTEEN

1. Lev. R. 15:2.
3. P'sahim 87a, b.
8. B'rachot 7a.
12. Yalkut I, 391; Tana d'vé
    Eliyahu Rabbah, ch. 13;
    Avot d'Rabbi Nathan,
    ch. 29.
13. Metzudat David.
15. See Gittin 31a; P'sikta Lam.
    R. 25; Tan. Behukosai; Tan.
    (Buber), p. 56.
17. Avot d'Rabbi Nathan, 4:5.
19. Sotah 42a.
20. Lam. R. 1:48.
22. Tan. Numbers, Yalkut II,
    986.
23. B'rachot 32a.
24. Sukkah 49b.
25. P'sikta Rabbati, ch. 44.
26. Yoma 86a.
27. Sifri Deuteronomy 342.
28. P'sahim 88a.

CHAPTER FIFTEEN

3. Taanit 15a (Mishnah), 16a
   (Mishnah and Gemara).
4. Sukkah 52a.
5. Sifri Deuteronomy 342.
6. Moed Katan 9a.
7. Num. R. end ch. 15; Deut.

R. end. ch. 6; Yad ha-
Hazaka Hilchot Melachim,
ch. 12, hal. 4 and 5.
9. Ex. R. 15:7.
10. Gen. R. 82:9.
11. Avodah Zarah 54b.

CHAPTER SIXTEEN

1. Eccl. R. 1:2; Lev. R. 10:2.
2. N'darim 38a; Targum
   Jonathan on Amos 7:14.
10. N'darim 22a, 60a; Yeru-
    shalmi Kiddushin, end;
    N'darim 10a.
12. Tan. Behar 3.
13. Zohar II, 183b; Zohar III, 6b;
    Yalkut II, 508.
14. Baba Batra 90b.
15. Moed Katan 15a.
16. Shabbat 138b, 139a.
17. Sanhedrin 98b; see Rashi.
19. Baba M'tzia 50a.
20. Baba M'tzia 58b.
21. Makkot 24a.

CHAPTER SEVENTEEN

1. Sanhedrin 39b.
3. Sanhedrin 39b; Yalkut I, 385
4. Yalkut II, 549.
5. Yalkut I, 764, 549.
6. Avodah Zarah 10b.

CHAPTER EIGHTEEN

1. M'chilta Bo, pes. at beginning.
2. N'darim 38a.
3. Gen. R. 24:4; Yalkut II,
   550.
4. Pirké d'Rabbi Eliezer ha-
   Gadol, ch. 10; see Yalkut II,
   50.
5. Zohar II, Vayakhel, 199a, b.
6. M'chilta Bo, p'sikta; Yalkut
   II, 325 and commentary
   Zayit Raanan; see also *The
   Rabbis' Bible* II, p. 185 and
   Teacher's Resource Book, ch.
   24, pp. 135-36.
7. Maimonides, *Guide*, II, last
   chapter, pp. 222-25.

8. Ex. R. 4:3.
9. Pirké d'Rabbi Kahana, ch. 25; Yalkut II, 550; see also Taanit 16a.

CHAPTER NINETEEN
3. Maimonides, *Guide*, II, ch. 29, pp. 136, 138.
6. Bahya ibn Pakuda, *Duties of the Heart*, The Gate of Repentance, ch. 9.
8. Yoma 69b.
9. Gen. R. 17:7.
12. Mishnah B'rachot 9:3.
13. Kiddushin 30b.
14. Yebamot 63.
15. Sanhedrin 99.
16. Yerushalmi Taanit, ch. 2, hal. 1.
17. Baba Batra 12b.
18. Ex. R. 9:8.
19. Gittin 61a.
20. Ex. R. 14, end.
21. Tan. (Buber), D'varim 3b.

CHAPTER TWENTY
3. Tan. (Buber) 134, introduction.
7. Pirké Avot 5:11.
8. Gen. R. 39:6.
9. Midrash Psalms on 36:10.

CHAPTER TWENTY ONE
2. Gen. R. 12:15.
3. Pirké Avot 1:7.
4. Avot d'Rabbi Nathan, ch. 41.
5. Baba Batra 10a.

6. Pirké Avot 3:30.
7. B'rachot 7a.
8. B'rachot 9:15.
9. Taanit 25a.

CHAPTER TWENTY TWO
8. Avot d'Rabbi Nathan, ch. 40.
10. Pirké Avot 4:29.
11. Gen. R. 22:6.
13. Avot d'Rabbi Nathan, ch. 39.
16. Yerushalmi, Baba M'tzia, ch. 2, para. 5.
17. B'rachot 13a.
18. Sotah 3a.
19. Midrash Psalms on 19:1, 82b.
20. Sanhedrin 91b.
21. Gen. R. 27:4.
22. Gen. R. Bereshit, 14:7.
24. Tan. (Buber) 135, introduction.

CHAPTER TWENTY THREE
6. P'sahim 87b.
7. Gen. R. 33:3.
8. Pirké Avot 5:21.
11. Gen. R. 32:3.
12. Baba Batra 75b.

CHAPTER TWENTY FOUR
5. Eccl. R. 5:14.
6. Gen. R. 17:2.
10. Ex. R. 15:29.
11. P'sikta Rabbati 19:6.
14. Sukkah 52b.

15. P'sahim 25b; Sanhedrin 72a.
16. Zohar II, 19a.
17. Kiddushin 36.
19. Tikkune Zohar, t. 21.
20. Pirké d'Rabbi Eliezer, ch. 43.
22. Yalkut I to Genesis 27:22.
23. M'chilta ba-Hodesh, ch. 11.
25. Num. R. 18:18.
27. Sanhedrin 24a.
29. B'rachot 55.
31. Kiddushin 71b.
33. Sifra Behukotai.
34. Tana d'vé Eliyahu, p. 284.
35. Sanhedrin 97b.
36. Shabbat 30b.
37. B'rachot 17a.

CHAPTER TWENTY FIVE
2. B'rachot 5a.
3. Sanhedrin 39a.
4. Zohar I, 103a.
7. Pirké Avot 3:11f.
8. Sanhedrin 36b.
9. Sanhedrin 99b.
11. P'sahim R. 2a.
12. Avot d'Rabbi Nathan, ch. 16.
13. Gen. R. 68:4.
14. Gittin 90b; Yebamot 63b.
16. Midrash Psalms on 37:3, 127a, para. 3.
20. Kallah Rabbati 3.
21. Yoma 38b, end; 39a beginning.
23. Sotah 49a.